INTERSECTING CIRCLES

the voices of hapa women in poetry and prose

Edited by
Marie Hara and Nora Okja Keller

Bamboo Ridge Press

1999

ISBN 0-910043-59-0
This is issue #76 of *Bamboo Ridge, Journal of Hawai'i Literature and Arts* (ISSN 0733-0308).
Copyright © 1999 Bamboo Ridge Press
Published by Bamboo Ridge Press
Indexed in the American Humanities Index
Bamboo Ridge Press is a member of the Council of Literary Magazines and Presses (CLMP).

Cover: "The Evolution of Light & Loneliness: Duality" by Gelareh Khoie. Oil on canvas, 24" x 24", 1999.
Copy Editors: Joy Kobayashi-Cintrón and Gail Kuroda
Student assistants: Kara Fujita, Gail Kuroda, and Alia Yap
Book design: Susanne Yuu
Typesetting and graphics: Wayne Kawamoto

Bamboo Ridge Press is a nonprofit, tax-exempt corporation formed in 1978 to foster the appreciation, understanding, and creation of literary, visual, or performing arts by, for, or about Hawaii's people. This project is supported in part by grants from the National Endowment for the Arts (NEA), the Hawai'i Community Foundation, and the State Foundation on Culture and the Arts (SFCA), celebrating over thirty years of culture and the arts in Hawai'i. The SFCA is funded by appropriations from the Hawai'i State Legislature and by grants from the NEA.

NATIONAL
ENDOWMENT
FOR ❦ THE
ARTS

Bamboo Ridge is published twice a year. Subscriptions are $35 for 4 issues, $20 for 2 issues. Institutional rate: $25 for 2 issues. For subscription information, back issues, or a catalog please contact:

Bamboo Ridge Press
P. O. Box 61781
Honolulu, HI 96839-1781
(808) 626-1481
brinfo@bambooridge.com
www.bambooridge.com

For Our Daughters

Mayu and Kasi

Tae and Sunhi

TABLE OF CONTENTS

Thru Yesterday to Grasp Her Wholeness

NEGOTIATING THE HYPHEN

Marie Murphy Hara

If someone asked me how I define the word hapa, I'd first say, with difficulty. Working on this book has given me more insight into the complex lives of women of mixed race than my lifelong search could ever provide. I have come to understand that there is no innate problem connected to being born from more than one ethnic group. The problem most often comes from how you are defined by others who question where to pigeon-hole you.

For those of monocultural or strong ideological background, a definition of identity seems simple. They always ask me to be explicit and quick about defining myself. They like quantitative words which seem to explain parentage and background, including social class. If they belong to a powerful majority mindset, they often claim not to "see" color or any ethnic difference in me at the same time that they ask for a clear cut definition. It's their way of being polite as well as reflecting a choice about toning down their power. This lets me know that for them as well as for most Americans race can still be the determing factor in how people see each other.

Some questioners believe, for example, that humanity is divided into a few finite races instead of existing together as the human race within which are culturally imposed ethnic categories.

Some mixed race people have no problem with their ethnicity, simply because it has never been made a problem by those around them. Others may have reason to react against the idea of definition which ultimately separates people into cultural or other categories for politically defined reasons.

Today my own answer regarding definition would include some history, some observations and the statement that being hapa can mean inclusion of varied kinds of identity, such as the outsider view, as well as choosing difference, for example by excluding monocultural thinking. I'd have to add that things have changed for mixed race people since the old terminology which circled the word half has been tossed away by hapa writers who struggle to redefine stereotypes, relearning how to see themselves and others.

When I think about what being hapa in Hawai'i is all about, I realize that I was born when my existence was still stigmatized, into a long historical line of hapa people whose alliances and identity had also been questioned. Hapa haoles, for example, were often marginalized figures with a questionable role, depending on social standing, admired and reviled at once. They, like me, looked closely at their faces in societal mirrors so that they could find a place in their particular culture. We were caught in an either/or-ness that marked our generations with a specific racial intolerance.

When hapas were fewer, given the surface openness of the Hawaiian setting, we could readily ask each other upon meeting, "What are you?" This challenging of ethnicity was usually not considered rude but elementary for placing someone. Only those who for various reasons needed to hide, avoided such a discussion.

Born in 1943, I belong to the wartime generation of older Asian Caucasian people from Hawai'i. My mother was a Japanese American, a nisei, who was a plantation nurse. My father, a soldier from Pennsylvania, an American of English and Dutch descent, served in the U.S. Army. Typical of those with hapa identity, I turned out to look like neither of my biological parents. Nor was I accepted by observers to belong socially to either parent's world, worlds as different as the class structure of post-colonial Hawai'i could have made them. I was also different from people who come from majority mono-racial culture in having a bi-cultural and bi-lingual orientation.

In this situation I have a lot in common with multi-ethnic people throughout this state, those who identify today as local because of their ethnic ties. Originally hapa haole meant Hawaiian and Caucasian, later it also meant Caucasian and Asian, while mixtures today vary widely. Many connect best to the designation local because these fellow Americans have decided they can't choose just Caucasian, Asian, Pacific Islander, African or Hispanic roots. They often consider themselves to be more than only one general or one very specific category. Their identity depends on many elements grouped together when a political hyphen determines which background has precedence. They recognize many different kinds of organizing, as well as contexts for ethnicity-based connections, thus enlarging the meaning of the word Other.

Through the years I have been variously labeled by observers. Everyone had an opinion about who I really am. They have mistaken me for Russian or Japanese or Hawaiian or Armenian or even Native American. I liked it best when I was directed to a meeting by a Native Canadian aboriginal woman who saw me and one of my then-infant daughters in a Vancouver auditorium. "Over here, sister," she said, pointing the way to a tribal group. I joined a large gathering of women of all ages who mirrored my face and body. That was as much belonging as I have ever felt in quick kinship to a group that claimed its members by physical features, even in convivial error.

As a young child I had alarmingly bright red hair, freckles and a much larger head and body than my classmates in Japanese school where I was seen as an embarrassing example of haole domination over the Japanese immigrant world of our plantation community. There I was plainly a bastard, and it was *shō-ga-nai* time: "We can't help it, but must endure the hardship and embarassment." My grandparents wanted me to "pass" for Japanese then and would later have tried to marry me to a Japanese male, had they continued to raise me, in order to "submerge my genes" and wash away their shame. Had I lived in Austin, Texas with my mother and my stepfather, whom she married "to give" (me, her daughter) "a name," I would have had to live a very white life. The same happened to a large number of hapa children who were adopted by white mainland families during the period after the Korean War. I have recently met a number of adoptees who were searching for their biological families, just as I was looking for my biological father, again a very hapa thing to do.

As a teenager living here in Hawai'i in the 1950s and 1960s, I was increasingly viewed as an exotic. The word Eurasian was used. In that way I was objectified into a potential seductress and someone encouraged to enter beauty contests in the so-called cosmopolitan category. In San Francisco, I was hired as a Playboy bunny actually filling a quota slot for, in their words, "an exotic type." I bought into the stereotype; it was the best role around at the time for someone like me, someone missing validation.

Only as an adult in the 1970s witnessing the Vietnam War in TV news bites and hearing about Amerasian children, the throwaway leftover war products of our purportedly glorious victory, did I begin to piece together what my life represented in the big view of America.

I had been born, according to the conventional morality of the time, illegally, by law an illegitimate, and immorally, by racist social rules a miscegenated human being. Illegal and immoral in one breath. It was enough to make me wear the mask of either a rebel or at very least an artist.

When a University of Hawai'i colleague read my fiction, she asked in all sincerity, "So what's the real problem here, being hapa or being a bastard? Which one is the theme?" I say from this place where I stand now, and I'm almost across the river, that the two situations go hand in hand for me and for those like me. I feel personally privileged to have a chance to explore these themes intellectually and to speak for countless others who could not and cannot express this particular viewpoint with any openness.

If indeed of mixed race, people who must pass for one or another identity or who have been adopted with secrecy have been denied vital information about their heritage. Others are asked in one way or another to become more acceptable in an ethnic or social community by associating with one side of themselves exclusively—"So which side do you pull? We can like you only when you are like us." The taking of sides is a dilemma they have been forced to accept in order to keep others of racial separatist leanings happy.

In studying the literary endeavors of hapa women writers, I looked with great interest at the work of Kathleen Tamagawa, whose *Holy Prayers in a Horse's Ear* (1932) personifies the martyred hapa. In her work Tamagawa represents hapas as freaks who are inevitably betrayed by both of their parents' countries. She describes herself as a person without a home and legally "a citizen of nowhere."

> The trouble with me is my ancestry. I really should not have been born, as a matter of fact half of my world declares I never was born. They say that I am the non-existent daughter of my parents, that I am not their lineal descendant.

Tamagawa describes in detail the ordeal of being considered exotic and Asian in anti-Japanese America at the same time that she is considered foreign and non-assimilable in anti-American Japan. In a way almost inconceivable in our era, Tamagawa takes on elements of self-hate and racism towards others, notably African Americans. In summing up her life, her autobiography states that her "Orientalism" was a false direction. She declares that interracial marriages are a disaster and that her life was both chaotic and a great disappointment because of her self-described unfortunate birth.

Racism, even in self-hatred, still exists for many who are of mixed race, even after a myriad of global social changes. What is important about Tamagawa's commentary is the distinction she makes about her personal feelings about her identity, that of a person who agreed with the majority cultures she found herself straddling. While those of us who no longer feel any need to hide or blend into one culture or the other look at such a hapa with some disdain, we, too, are negotiating the hyphen in order to make sense of what some consider our role as translators between diametrically opposed ethnic groups.

Standing astride the paradox of racial assumptions, we insist upon commenting as individuals, not as bridge people or as advocates of any prescribed cultural script. Passing is passé. Instead a new kinship has developed with all kinds of people who have been viewed as outsiders. Such a vision sees that mixed race does and doesn't matter at the same time, that the hyphen affects all, and that we need to mark that fact judiciously.

Only in this era of politically charged identity politics have groups of mixed race people begun to stand out, finally strengthened by numbers and secure enough in civil rights to make public comment about personal history. Today the hapa minority of mixed race identity has grown until it comprises about forty percent of the roughly one million one hundred thousand people living in Hawai'i in 1999.

Here outmarriage, an old and tested, if sometimes contested tradition, can now be considered not only acceptable and welcomed, but also for all but the most conservative and reactionary ethnic groups to be socially progressive. This turn doesn't signify any satisfactory end to racism and bigotry, but it still heralds a different universe than the one that existed before the Supreme Court struck down state laws that prohibited legal interracial marriages in *Loving vs. the state of Virginia* in 1961.

As an individual I am relieved that the old order of thinking which promoted such ideas as miscegenation and racial exclusivity as morally correct has atrophied to the point of being the subject matter for routine public joking. But the more than fifty years of positive change to this new climate has also allowed many interracial alliances to flourish and with them alternative ways of understanding the ethnic differences amongst people.

Often those who led in this area were women who themselves had formed untraditional alliances and put their mixed race children's rights above the old attitudes and behavior of the uneducated or backward or even racist members of their own original nuclear families. In a testament to the idea that women do indeed "carry culture upon their backs" via their having given birth to and raised children, strong mothers have not only embraced cultural differences but also re-evaluated concepts such as the Other. In their actions they showed their offspring models to re-see stereotypes and look at other people directly as positive and simply human.

Many of those women at the fore of such change-creating thinking developed behavioral strategies for their families, sometimes without the help of mates and relatives, by giving dignity to and building enough self-love in offspring who were different from themselves so that they, too, would have seeds of love for the rest of humanity.

This tradition of cultural welcome, not so new in the Hawaiian setting, proved the worth of the mixed race world view. Naysayers who had predicted that intermarriage would result in a wanton corruption of old values or a pollution of their own particular root stock have long been silenced as successive crops of well-nurtured mixed race children, with sad exceptions, continued to flourish.

Such love in all of its complexity proved the primitivity of scientists such as Linnaeus whose eighteenth century theories defined only four human categories. Linnaeus called these races: mongoloid, caucasoid, negroid and australoid, terms still in use by the thoughtless who continue to use these terms not as a working definition of humanity but as fact. As many questions began to crowd the very concept of multiple races, such as issues of how to define national and ethnic backgrounds, along came the era of human genome testing. Soon enough another definition of race, perhaps a variant of the old Homo sapiens designation, may emerge with additional limits, controversial questions, and above all dialogue.

We are left with a question of equal significance. How can the understanding of mixed race identity, past and present, enlarge our view of humanity and our options? Hapa identity must ultimately be self-described.

Here are some voices, the words of mixed race women in literary forms, whose experience-based interior views may open more eyes to understanding how to straddle the hyphens of identity and the holes in the path toward being whole, not half, human beings.

CIRCLING "HAPA"
Nora Okja Keller

I. Citizen of Nowhere

I was neither American, nor Irish, nor Japanese. I had no race, nationality or home.
Kathleen Tamagawa, 1932

I don't know what it means to be "hapa." I only know this one life, this one mind, this one body. And on any given day, I question my interpretations.

How can I tease out one thread of identity's tapestry and say this is how being hapa has affected my life? And if I could, how can I presume that my experience would intersect with those of other hapa women?

* * *

As far back as I can remember, my appearance—the shape of my eyes in contrast with the slope of my nose, the color of my skin in contrast with the color of my hair—has been explained as "hapa," half-Korean, half-"American."

Swallowing this label applied to me by others, I came to define myself as hapa. Reflexively, almost as soon as I meet someone, I explain: "I am hapa." I say it definitively, "I am hapa," as if that statement, self-explanatory, says it all.

But really, it doesn't.

It's superficial, an easy way out.

* * *

When I was in third grade at Hahaione Elementary School, one of my classmates asked, "What nationality are you?"

I told her "Korean" because I knew that for sure. My mother had told me. (One afternoon as we lay on her bed for a nap, I stroked her arm, and asked, "What am I?" Slightly irritated because she was already halfway to sleep, my mother had answered, "You are Korean because I am Korean.")

"But what else?" my friend persisted, unsatisfied by my one-race answer; my eyes were too round and my hair too wavy to be "pure" Asian. "Korean and what? What kind haole is your dad?"

Because my mother and father were divorced, and my father had moved to Jersey City, I couldn't be more specific than "haole;" I wasn't even sure that there were different versions of haole. So I told her to guess and said yes to everything she said.

English?

Yes.

Irish?

Yes.

French?

Yes.

German?

Yes.

I also said yes to Italian, Dutch and American Indian even though by then I'm sure she was suspicious and running out of ethnicities to guess. I was relieved when she finally exclaimed: "Oh, chop suey! I'm mixed-up, too!"

II. Through Yesterday . . . to Grasp Her Wholeness

This curiosity [about the past], this wonder for understanding, is the hallmark of the writer, God's spy.
                                                    Han Suyin, 1965

Just before she married a Korean man, a very close (white) friend of mine from Maryland, whom I love dearly, confided that her parents, whom I also love, were concerned about their future grandchildren. "Is it fair to bring mixed-race children into the world?" they whispered in the same tones with which they would discuss cancer. "Won't they be confused?"

"Nora's half-Korean," she told me she'd said. "Wouldn't it be wonderful if my children turned out like her?"

Woodenly, I thanked my friend for her defense and for her compliment, but was stunned to hear that having mixed-race children is in some circles still an issue of concern.

Of course, I was younger then, and had grown up in Hawai'i at a time when hapa was hip. In Honolulu during the seventies and eighties "Eurasian" was considered beautiful, cosmopolitan, exotic. Friends, both Asian and haole, would say, "You're so lucky to be hapa. Best of both worlds." Certain assumptions of privilege and place were made based on the way I looked, which I enjoyed while not feeling truly worthy of special treatment.

Now, with interracial marriages becoming more prevalent, the proliferation of "hapa" is once again a source of concern—this time within Asian American communities. "Outmarriage" is politically suspect by people who denounce the dilution of blood, of culture, of community. "Don't you feel like a traitor for marrying a white man?" they ask, then add, "Your kids will be even less Korean."

I worry about these questions to some degree, working them over intellectually—apart from my real life in which I hold and clothe, feed and love the light-skinned bodies of my children, untainted by theory.

And I realize that these are the same accusations my mother faced down a generation ago when she married my German-American father. (I finally called him the year I graduated from high school to ask, with some embarrassment: "What are you, anyway?") In the way that history repeats itself, I have had to learn the same lesson my mother did: these questions are bad enough when coming from your "home" community, but they are worse when they come from yourself.

* * *

Still, I do worry about how "hapa" my children will be. I wonder how they will choose to define themselves and where their hearts will live. One born with light hair and dark eyes, the other with dark hair and light eyes, my daughters look hapa. But I am concerned about how will they feel on the inside. Will they learn how to be Korean from their mother, and their mother's mother, demonstrating the theory that culture is carried matriarchally?

Perhaps by the time they discover ethnicity—and realize that they will be offered *choices* regarding theirs—there will be new terms for the various mixtures and fractions of race. In the same dictionary that defines hapa as: "1.Portion. Fragment. Part of the whole. 2.Of mixed blood, person of mixed blood," the term "hapaha" means one quarter.[1]

But I've also heard "hapa" originally came from the Hawaiian word for the English hand held half-harp and only later came to mean "part or fraction." This portable, traveling musical instrument seems an appropriate metaphor and name for the multiracial voice, for the hapa identity itself is a traveling, always shifting, alternate form of song. Only later, as intermarriage between the European and the Hawaiian peoples became more common, was hapa haole used to describe the half-Hawaiian and half-Caucasian children of these unions.

Demonstrating how far language can travel, sometimes without regard to national origin: five years ago in Santa

Barbara, I met a woman who was half-Latina and half-Japanese. "I am *hap-pa*," she announced, spelling the word for me.

When I told her that in Hawai'i, we spell hapa with one "P," she said, "What's Hawai'i got to do with it? Isn't *happa* the Japanese word for half-breed?"

Perhaps by the time my children are grown, the definition of hapa will have, (r)evolving once again, returned home.

III. My Own Heart's Cathedral

Since I believe that clinging to one's race tears one apart and that letting go makes one whole, I wish I could say that race isn't important. But it is. . . . This is a fact which I have faced and must ultimately transcend. If this transcendence were less complex, less individual, it would lose its holiness."

Ai, 1978

A friend of mine, when she first heard of our effort in this anthology to stretch the popular definition of hapa (half-Asian, half-White), asked if she could submit a poem. "Uh, you're hapa?" I asked. I asked the question delicately, suddenly aware of how I would now be using the term in an exclusionary way, as criteria for acceptance in the book, and feeling very uncomfortable about it. Previously, I had always asked the question with exuberance—"You hapa? Me too!"—as a way to form connections, build bridges, make friends.

My friend, who looks like my sister but had always referred to herself as Japanese, giggled. "I'm kinda hapa," she said. "I'm half-Japanese, half-Okinawan. And there is a difference, you know."

She explained about the conflicts between the two cultures, about how the Japanese have traditionally viewed Okinawans as an inferior race—like an unfortunate poor relation tied to the skirts of the Motherland. "I see it even in my own family," my friend said, "the conflicts between grandparents—with the sly cuts about race—that the children have to mediate."

"I guess you could be hapa," I admitted, realizing that as we move away from other-defined to self-defined, from external to internal references for coding ethnicity, it becomes more and more difficult to question another's claim to hapa-ness. See what happens when you mess around with meaning? The term "hapa" itself became as fluid and evasive as a face you just can't place.

While my friend did not end up submitting anything, Cathy Song (Chinese-Korean), and Debra Kang Dean (Korean-Okinawan) did. And we felt the definition of "hapa" stretch yet again.

Conversely, other writers traditionally and popularly labeled "hapa" resisted the definition, saying that the term had no relevance to their work. Declining to participate in the anthology, these women explained, "I refuse to be typecast as anything. I am a writer. Period."

* * *

As a student of literature and aspiring writer (I am this every day), I am involved in the lifelong project of constructing a literary genealogy. As one of my literary mothers, Han Suyin, said: "A man's life begins with his ancestors and is continued in his descendants. My father's life, and after my father my own life, begins with the Family." In her autobiographical works, Han Suyin attempted, "through her yesterday made explicit, to grasp her wholeness."[2]

In order to find my own voice, I created a family from the hapa women writing before me. I discovered Great Grand-mothers in the Eaton sisters, two Chinese-Canadian writers who wrote amidst the intense anti-Chinese sentiment of the late 1800s and early 1900s. The bodies of their work present a type of literary argument regarding the strategies each found to write in this atmosphere of racist fear and hatred.

Winifred Eaton chose to hide her biracial identity under the cloak of the Japanese-sounding pseudonym Onoto Watanna, but Edith Eaton took on attitude. Edith Eaton, who at one time proclaimed: "What troubles me is not that I am what I am, but that others are ignorant of my superiority,"[3] adopted the Chinese name Sui Sin Far and publically challenged the racism. Through a series of stories and essays, Sui Sin Far explored her ambiguous position between "Occidental and Oriental," giving rise to the voice that was "first to speak for Asian American sensibility that was neither Asian nor white American."[4]

While Sui Sin Far eventually came to the conclusion that, "Individuality is more than nationality,"[5] Kathleen Tamagawa in *Holy Prayers in a Horse's Ear (1932)* could not escape nationality—or rather her lack of a clearly specific one. In Tamagawa, I discovered the Aunt no one likes to talk with because of her unsettling tendency to repeat: "I do not approve of Eurasian marriages. I do not approve of inter-national marriages."[6] Yet Tamagawa writes her memoir at a time when, as she says, "half of my world declares I never was born. . . that I am the non-existent daughter of my parents,"[7] and in doing so asserts her existence.

Truthfully, I love her even more for writing "while her [four] children climb around her and scream at the top of their voices."[8] Her own children, Tamagawa writes, will not be "citizens of nowhere."

Sixty years later, I gain a quiet comfort from that image of domestic chaos as I sit at my computer trying to type out a coherent thought as my eldest child whines alternately for a Jolly Rancher Ice Pop and a "Sailor Moon" video and the youngest—after having spit up something that looks like cottage cheese but smells much, much worse—is in danger of rolling out of the Barbie Doll bean bag chair I momentarily forgot her in.

Finally in Ai, I found a literary half-sister who, through her writing, taught me that "there was no identity for me *out there*," and that to find my voice, I must instead "dwell in my own heart's cathedral."[9]

* * *

This anthology of contemporary hapa women is descended from these literary pioneers who verbalized their conflicts—national, familial, cultural, personal—at a time when miscegenation was considered immoral and in most cases illegal. They are our hapa mothers, who have helped to birth this new generation of hapa women writing their own stories, according to their own visions, in their own voices.

Notes:

1. Pukui, Mary Kawena. *New Pocket Hawaiian Dictionary.* University of Hawai'i Press, 1992.

2. Suyin, Han. *The Crippled Tree.* Putnam, 1965.

3. Far, Sui Sin. *Leaves from the Mental Portfolio of an Eurasian.* Independent, January 12, 1909.

4. Chin, Chan, Inada and Wong. *Aiiieeeee! An Anthology of Asian American Literature.* Howard University Press, 1974.

5. Far, Sui Sin. *Leaves from the Mental Portfolio of an Eurasian.* Independent, January 12, 1909.

6. Tamagawa, Kathleen. *Holy Prayers in a Horse's Ear.* Ray Long and Richard R. Smith Inc, 1932.

7. Ibid.

8. Ibid.

9. Ai. *On Being 1/2 Japanese, 1/8 Choctaw, 1/4 Black, and 1/16 Irish. Ms. Magazine,* May, 1978 p. 58.

CITIZEN
OF NOWHERE

Me, Mother and Sister
Sabrena Taylor, 1989

WHAT ARE YOU?

Anne Xuan Clark

I sit and look into the mirror. When I was little, I used to open my eyes as wide as possible to erase the traces of my mother's ancestry. I wound up with an expression of surprise and my eyebrows began to ache. I would turn my face from side to side, looking at it from a variety of angles, sucking in my cheeks to look like the women from all the fashion magazines.

You look kinda Oriental.

In 1969, my family moved to the United States and I was born shortly thereafter. My Irish Catholic grandparents were not thrilled that my father brought a pregnant wife and two children back from Southeast Asia. My grandmother had always hoped he would marry the girl who lived next door. Sure she was Italian, but at least she was Catholic.

We lived with my grandparents on and off for two years. When my grandparents left the house, my mother would cook fish and rice. Before they returned, she would dump the remaining food into the toilet and air the house out. Their sensitive American noses could always detect the alien odors. They would scold her for cooking her food, scold her for breastfeeding me, scold her for being the Vietnamese mother they wished their son had never married. My parents were divorced before I was two years old.

My brothers slowly forgot how to speak and understand the first language that rolled off their tongues. My mom didn't teach me how to speak Vietnamese, she wanted me to be "a real American." When I was seven, I took Vietnamese lessons for a few months. The sound of my mother's language seemed harsh to my oh-so-American ears. I had developed an understanding that to be Vietnamese was to be the enemy, the foreigner. In my history classes I was always reminded of the 50,000 young American men that had died in the war. They never told me about the two million Vietnamese people that were killed.

When I lived with my mom in California, we ate our food with chopsticks. I never invited my friends over because I was embarrassed by her. If I didn't tell them, maybe they would think I was white, maybe I could pass. When I was 14, I moved to New York to live with my father. We ate with forks and knives. (Years later, I realized I held my silverware in the wrong hands, no one had ever taught me the correct way.) I made new friends and invited them over frequently, proud of my white family. Whenever I introduced my friends to my dad, I felt them looking at him, then back at me again, as if they couldn't understand how he could be my father.

You live in the best of both worlds.

My third week of college, I fell in love with yet another white man. He only dated women of color; I thought it was just a coincidence. My white roommate pointed this fact out to me. Before we came to college together, we had been in the same drug rehab center. When I first began to acknowledge and embrace my Vietnamese heritage, she told me I was clinging onto something false. That it took more than eating spicy food and using chopsticks to prove my authenticity. Did she forget her nickname for me in rehab was, "You fucking egg roll?"

He called me "Moonface." One day we were having another argument over racism and white privilege. The man I had loved for over two years looked at me and said, "If you wore your makeup a certain way, you could look white." But if I looked white, he probably wouldn't be sharing a bed with me.

When I wanted to be white, I lightened and permed my hair. Last year, I dyed my hair black. Did I really think it would make me look more Asian? Was I overcompensating for my whiteness?

You can be the bridge between two cultures.

My mother lives in Orange County, California along with 150,000 other Vietnamese people. The streets are lined with Vietnamese dentists, doctors, travel agencies, grocery stores. When I'm walking amidst a sea of shiny black heads, I hear the banter of people speaking a language I don't understand and I see people staring at me. I often grow uncomfortable around my supposed "community." When they look at me, what do they see? The product of two cultures, intertwined into one unique individual. Or am I just another reminder of the war? Do they feel betrayed that my mother slept with the enemy?

My old boss is a veteran of the American war in Vietnam. He called me "Babysan" and couldn't understand why I found this offensive. He found the term very endearing. He told me it was a "Thai term of affection." His ex-wife was Asian. That makes his children mixed like me. Is he going to call them "his little babysans?"

I don't talk to my father much anymore. He thinks I'm going through a phase: Why can't I just keep blending into his liberal notion of the American melting pot and stop being so militant and angry? He doesn't understand that though he is my father, I am my mother's daughter. My dad was working for a Chinese man. I asked him how he found the job. He said to me, "You know I have that Oriental connection."

My father doesn't acknowledge his racism. How can he be racist if he was married to an Asian woman? When I tried to tell him about the pain I feel over being biracial, he said he never thinks of me as Asian or white. That he doesn't see color, we're all members of the human race. Instead of listening to me and accepting my identity, he told me stories of the "racism he experienced in Vietnam because he was white." Never mind that his people were killing my mother's people by the millions. He was experiencing the devastation of racism.

Mixed children are so beautiful.

My mother and her friend were discussing plastic surgery. She mentioned that I was opposed to Asian women altering their eyes and noses. Her friend grew angry at my pseudo-politically correct position. It forced me to rethink the privilege I possess as a woman of mixed ethnicity. When Asian women go to plastic surgeons to alter their features, they bring in photos of women who look like me. Eyes with a hint of Asiatic exotica, a nose with a bit of a bridge. I can open my eyes until my eyebrows fall off, but in the end, I will never need surgery to "look more white," to be more palatable to white society. Don't you know, the mixed look is in? We fulfill their quotas without being "too ethnic."

I stare into the mirror and see the same face I've been looking into for twenty-three years. Some people look at me and yell, "Vietcong!" while others think I look Italian. Does it really matter what other people think I am? I wish I could state that I am Asian American and a woman of color without that small voice creeping in and questioning my authenticity. When will I be able to walk into a room filled with people of color and feel confident that no one will say, "What are you doing here? You don't belong here." I know in my head that no one can determine who or what I am, but when will I believe that in my heart?

TRACKS

Mei-mei Berssenbrugge

One day you trip and jar yourself
and look around—all your friends
take out their false teeth and offer them
yellow as old elephant bones

You touch your jaw
you can't tell
what animal shape you are—
your spine curls
eyes grow shy
ears lengthen toward a muttering
you can't understand

There's a confusion of tracks
your nostrils catch
something recent
in the middle of an empty space
in the evening wind

Snout hooves a shining pelt
you set out in the blue air
remembering a horse you loved
as a child pressing its nose
against your plaid shirt

Try to remember now
what is a child?

MINH
Lo Ri Ly Griffin

The silver car smelled like worn tires. That was the first thing the child noticed when the door shut behind him, leaving him alone. The door had sealed the boy from the unfamiliar cold and from the two men standing out on the sidewalk. It was the Big Man who had led him into this harsh weather and to the Stranger, a thin, pasty-skinned man with bright red hair. Now they were standing there talking. Talking about him.

The child sat alone, waiting. Watching.

I mustn't be afraid, he said to himself.

"You're only afraid of the unknown," Sister Anne had told him. But Sister Anne was not there to hold his hand. To turn on the lights, sending the devil spirits scrambling under the cots and bureaus. Instead, the red-haired spirit stood there with the Big Man, talking. Laughing. The Big Man was nudging crushed ice against the building, smearing it into the rocky surface. His cheeks and the tip of his nose had turned pink from the crisp breeze. His lips were white. A dark blue cap was pulled snug over his head, protecting his ears from the cold. He had a funny shaped head, the boy thought. Much like the yellow striped melons Mama had once bought at the market. Or were they squash? He could not remember. The Big Man held his heavy coat close to his large body. The tassel on his cap fluttered in the breeze.

The men continued to huddle alongside the building, their heads angled together against the wind. The child did not like this red-haired stranger. This Devil Spirit. He was too loud. Too bold. He wore no extra clothing for protection from the cold, except for the gray-speckled scarf tied loosely under his chin. His cheeks did not turn red from the wind, but instead remained white as the crushed ice on the ground. Tossing his head back, the Stranger laughed. Wispy clouds lifted from his mouth, contrasting with the thunder of his laughter and the sharpness of the bitter air. The boy buried his chin deeper into the fur neck of the coat—the coat given to him when he first arrived at the airport.

The coat smelled old, he thought. Like the ancient woman who sold tea at the market, like the moss that grew on the dying jasmine bush near the church grounds, or like the mourning tomb in the graveyard. The boy shivered.

The Stranger approached the car and leaned into the window, grinning at him. The child pressed his body hard against the cushions of the back seat and held his breath. The man's fire-red hair blew wildly in the wind and lapped against the window. His breath fogged the glass concealing his pale face. Pointing at the boy, he spoke over his shoulder to the Big Man who chuckled in response. The child squeezed his eyes closed, praying the man would disappear.

The boy was afraid. He wanted to be back, safe in the warmth of the church. Safe in the village with the people he knew so well. He should not have left the Sister. He should have disobeyed Mother Superior's wishes and not boarded the plane. But she would not have been pleased. He could hear the soft clicking of her tongue as she shook her head. The look in her eye would have told him just how angry she was. Like when he chased Aunt Thuy's laying hen around the yard and she would not give up an egg for a whole week. Or when he and Rip slipped away from Mass to watch the last of the Americans ride through the city. He could still see the fire in her eyes. Like the fire of the man's hair. The Stranger was a Devil Spirit, that was for certain. If Rip were here, he would agree.

Slowly, tentatively, the boy reopened his eyes. The two men were once again standing together, talking and laughing.

The Big Man still held onto the folder that he had had since the child first met him hours before. It was this folder that knew so much about the boy's life and his present situation. Any question the Big Man could ask would be answered by the folder.

"What is your name?" the woman had asked him in his native language. The Big Man had sat at his desk waiting for the boy's reply. The boy looked at the woman who looked so familiar, yet so foreign.

"I am afraid," he wanted to say but it was that fear that forced his silence. It was then the Big Man had opened the folder for the first time.

"Le Minh?" the man asked the woman, struggling somewhat with his pronunciation. He did not seem aware that the boy could understand these words.

Placing his hand to his breast, Minh nodded in confirmation. The woman smiled at him then turned to the Big Man and nodded too. The Big Man exhaled, looking both bored and agitated. He asked the woman another question. Minh waited for the woman to speak.

"How old are you, Minh?" the woman asked. Again, the boy stayed silent. Again, the folder knew the answer. He heard the Big Man speak once more.

"Seven?" she asked the boy. He nodded. The Big Man marked the paper in front of him. The two adults smiled awkwardly to one another. The child fidgeted in his chair. It had been a long day since he had boarded the airplane, leaving the Sisters behind. But time was swallowed during his confinement in the plane. It was another day. Another world. He yawned quietly.

The man continued to consult the folder and to address the small woman. She stood alone between the Big Man's desk and the chair Minh sat in, speaking only to ask Minh questions and to answer the man. The child watched this woman before him. She looked much like the women in the village. Her hair was black and pressed in large curls. Her hair was much thicker than Minh's, whose hair was fine and light in color.

Looking at the woman, he remembered his Mama's thick coarse hair shining in the sun. He used to pray each night that he would wake up with her hair on his head. Instead, each morning his thin brown hair remained and each morning this hair would be tangled in knots. Mama would comb through the tangles, ripping out clumps of ugly brown hair. One morning, Mama shaved his head telling him it would grow back thicker and black. But his old hair returned and Mama could only pull a cap over his head, making him promise never to remove it except in church.

One evening when he was left to play on the beach while Mama gathered coconuts, he pulled the cap from his head, throwing it into the water. He watched it sink into the slow outgoing tide and disappear into the waves of the ocean. When she returned, his Mama was much too tired and burdened with her load to notice his loss. She would have scolded him, but the next morning she became ill. He closed his eyes, visualizing his Mama well again, standing in the fields, her hat against her back and the warm breeze in her hair. His thoughts were interrupted by another question.

He had grown weary of the Big Man, of the woman, and of the room. It was an ugly room, Minh thought. The walls were pale, painted the color of rocks that lined the river bed. The room was cold and filled with hard, metal furnishings. Only the Big Man's chair looked soft and it seemed to swallow his large form. Minh wondered if the Big Man could get up from the chair. He would need help from someone very strong. Perhaps the man could not stand. He had not left his chair since Minh and the woman arrived from the airport. He did not have to. Peddling his feet on the floor, the Big Man could maneuver his chair across the shiny green tile. He had ridden his chair across the room to the cabinet to get Minh's folder. Perhaps he was born in the chair. The Big Man Who Lived in a Chair. Minh concealed a smile. They would not understand.

As the questions dragged on, Minh became aware of his bladder, full, calling for relief. He began to squirm noiselessly. Looking at the woman then at the Big Man, Minh crossed his legs, opened his mouth but the Big Man spoke instead. The boy began to swing his foot, up and down, faster and faster, still too afraid to speak or to raise his hand to be excused. But to be excused where, he did not know. The man continued to read through his folder, slowly removing the sheets of paper only to return them to the stack. The woman remained still; Minh fidgeted in his seat. Without looking up, the man spoke to the woman, waving his hand as though brushing dust from the air. The folder was closed.

The woman told Minh it was time to eat. It was then that he realized he had not eaten since the meal on the airplane. Hunger gnawed at his stomach, adding to his discomfort. Yes, he would eat with the woman.

Taking Minh's hand in hers, the woman led him down a long hallway and away from the Big Man. The sounds of the woman's heels clicking against the marble floor reminded Minh of Sister Margaret. He could still see her gliding down the church aisle, candle in hand. When Minh first saw Sister Margaret, he truly believed she was floating like an angel until echoes of her solid heels striking the floor filled the vestibule. Minh gripped the woman's hand tighter. She pressed his fingers gently and smiled down at him. Embarrassed, Minh pulled his hand away from the woman's. Trying to avoid the dark brown eyes above him, Minh looked straight ahead as he continued down the passageway. Minh was saddened by the image of the Sister and these memories of home. But he had to be good. He had to be strong. He had to pee. He clenched his hands firmly, concentrating on his present predicament.

Walking down the hallway, Minh became aware that his whole body was as one big knotted fist. Closing his eyes, Minh was no longer with the woman, but alone, tumbling down a wild river as heavy raindrops splashed into the water around him, slapping his face and falling into his open mouth. A drop of warm liquid escaped into his underpants. He tightened his fist. Minh opened his eyes to find himself back in the hallway standing before a tall green metal door.

"I'll wait for you here," the woman said softly.

Pushing the large door open, Minh left the woman behind, urgently making his way past the long line of white, upright water basins toward the closest stall. He had been led to a similar room in the Tokyo airport before boarding for the final leg of his trip to America. He stood staring into the white bowl, watching the water whirl violently into the hole. When the water quieted, he pushed the silver handle down again and leaned closer to see where the water was going. He grabbed the handle one more time but then remembered the woman waiting in the hallway.

After washing his hands he found the door to be much lighter. Everything felt lighter. He pulled the door open to find the woman leaning against the far wall. She smiled at him.

She could have been a village woman from back home except for the strange clothes she wore, Minh thought. Her shirt was pink and was covered with red and white swirls. The blue pants she wore were heavy and draped over her feet. When she walked, the cuffs of her slacks flipped into the air and revealed her shoes. She looked funny dressed as an American. She was no American. She didn't look like one as Minh and the Big Man did. The boy raised his chin confidently.

"I am an American," he said slowly and precisely in English. These were the only words he knew to speak in the language of the Big Man. The Sisters had taught him this simple phrase between his French and mathematics studies. The woman stopped and knelt beside the child.

She asked him a question in the Big Man's tongue. Minh looked puzzled. The woman laughed softly.

The woman spoke again in their native language. Touching her breast she said: "I am an American, too."

The boy shook his head. "No, you are not!" he cried. No, he thought. It could not be true. The woman could not be an American. She was not special like him. No matter how she tried to pretend dressing up like an American, speaking their language, she was just like all the others in the village. All the others who teased him and called him dirty names. The woman looked frightened and tried to reach for him but he backed away.

"American bastard!" the older children had called him.

"No, I am not!" he had yelled back. With tears streaming down his face, Minh would run to Sister Margaret who would stand him up and cite passages from the Bible. Minh learned not to cry. He learned to be proud of his Papa. He learned to be proud he was an American. Because of his Papa, Minh knew he was something the others could never be. Something this woman could never be.

She was lying, he thought. She had to be. He was special. Very special. The woman slowly stood and tried again to take his hand but he snapped it away and hid it behind his back. Without a word, the woman continued down the hallway. Minh followed obediently, his eyes lowered.

Minh found this cafeteria to be much larger than the one at the mission. The floor was white, the bins silver. Everything sparkled from strong scented cleansers that made his eyes itch.

The woman guided him along the rows of food that were already served up in separate little dishes. Humming to herself, the woman selected dishes for both herself and Minh. Minh stared intently at the foreign food. There were so many colors and smells. So much to choose from. Beyond the rows of vegetables Minh noticed something. Something unusual. He wished the woman would pick this dish of fluffy, pink clouds.

He tried to guess the flavor. Lobster? Minh wrinkled his nose. No, he decided, this food was as sweet as heaven. He stared at the dishes of pink fluff until they all seemed to blend together, the bright color absorbing the ceramic bowls. The clouds floated about his head, swirling. He wanted to reach for them, to taste them.

"Come," the woman said and Minh looked up to find himself alone among his pink clouds. The woman was standing at the far end of the counter. Minh looked again at the bin then turned away, hurrying after the woman. When he caught up to her, he noticed that the woman had a tray full of plates and dishes.

And two bowls of his special pink clouds.

Minh grinned. Catching the woman's eye, he promptly looked down again. He was not ready to stop being mad. Not yet.

The cafeteria was empty except for three men sitting near the exit. Minh and the woman sat at the small round table at the opposite end of the room.

"Thank you," Minh whispered.

"You're very welcome," she replied.

Minh lifted the silver spoon from the table, feeling it cool and smooth against his skin. Hesitating at first, he swiftly buried the spoon deep into the pink dish. Minh carried a spoonful of clouds to his mouth. The sweet taste seemed to fill his head as his tongue absorbed the flavor. It was fruity, he decided. With each bite, Minh would let the cloud sit on his tongue until it was liquid. Then he would swallow hard. The warm sweetness would pour past his tongue, past his throat, and to his waiting stomach.

When the bowl was empty, he hid his disappointment. He did not wish to appear unappreciative. Minh began eating from another dish. The food was bland. He washed it down with milk, strange tasting milk.

When Minh cleared his plate, he looked up. The woman was still picking lightly at the noodles on her plate. He had eaten more than he ever had before. The woman offered the child her untouched bowl of fruity clouds. Minh did not hesitate.

After eating the final spoonful he suddenly felt ashamed. He should have remembered what the Sisters had taught him about gluttony and about excess and declined the woman's offering. Now Minh had denied her the joy he had selfishly hoarded. He had already eaten plenty. He did not need more food. Minh hung his head.

"Do you want more?" the woman asked, sensing his disappointment.

Minh shook his head. The woman began returning the empty dishes to the tray.

"In America, you can eat all you want."

This did not make Minh feel better. He had accepted the woman's kindness even though he was unkind to her and even when his stomach was already bulging. This would disappoint the Sisters very much.

He gingerly followed the woman out of the cafeteria and back down the hallway toward the Big Man's office.

"They will be taking you to your new home soon, Minh."

"To Papa," he said, nodding.

The woman did not speak.

"To Papa, right?" Minh asked, pleading for the woman to respond. Finally, she shook her head. The sadness in her face frightened him. He remembered the same look in the eyes of their neighbors when his Mama was sick. Minh stopped.

"Where is my Papa? Why hasn't he come for me? The Sisters said he would be waiting for me." Minh had been patient long enough. Every moment he had expected his Papa to come and to claim him from the Big Man's office. Yet he did not come. "Trust these people," Mother Superior had told him. "They will take care of you." And Minh had trusted them but now Minh was really scared.

"Your Papa is sick," the woman said. "He's in a place where doctors—very good men—can help him."

But Papa couldn't be sick, he thought. Papa is a big strong American and Americans don't get sick.

"You will be taken to live with your Papa's mama and papa. They want you to live with them . . . until your Papa is well."

"No . . . no," he muttered, turning away from the woman. Mama wouldn't be able to find him, not if he wasn't with Papa . . . he had to be with Papa.

"When your Papa gets well, they will take you to see him."

Minh nodded. "I must see Papa."

"And you will," she said. "I promise."

As they began to walk again toward the Big Man's office, he stood close to the woman, allowing her hand to brush his shoulder. Looking up at her now, the lights from the long ceiling made her hair shine. She was beautiful, he thought. She was as beautiful as Mama used to be.

"Are you from America?" Minh asked.

The low clicking of her heavy heels stopped. She looked down at him, reached for his hands and placed them in her own. He did not protest.

"Are you from America?" he asked again, louder.

"No," she said. "I come from a village very near where you were born. I came to live here—to be with my husband."

"By airplane?"

The woman nodded her head. Releasing Minh's hands, she bent her arms at the elbows and held her hands up and waved them at the wrists. "I flew."

"Did you have to come here to this place?"

The woman chuckled softly. "Only little boys with no mamas or papas to meet them at the airport must come here first."

"Because Papa's sick and Mama's in heaven?"

The woman nodded.

He smiled then, knowing that he would soon see his Papa. Then Mama would come. She had told him so as she lay on the cot. Her eyes were empty, no longer sparkling with prayer and song. She had left him then, but not before promising him she would return; to be with him and Papa forever.

"My arms like wings I will fly," she had told him. "Nothing will keep me away." That was why Minh did not cry.

She would come back. She would not lie.

In the car, his head remained low as the two men spoke in their foreign tongue. The Big Man had given Minh's folder to the Devil Spirit. Shaking the Stranger's free hand, the Big Man then turned to the window and waved a final good-bye to Minh. The child forced a smile. The Devil Spirit took his position in the driver's seat, tossing Minh's folder into the seat beside him. He spoke to Minh in the dialect used by the people of the North.

"Is it too cold for you?"

The American spoke the language well. The man turned a switch and music blasted through the air. Minh jumped. The Devil Spirit laughed.

Minh had not said good-bye to the woman yet. He hoped that if he didn't, she would not leave. But the Big Man had sent her away shortly after they returned from lunch. The Big

Man had stood then, balancing his weight on his feeble, bird-like legs. He put on his heavy coat while the woman helped Minh on with his.

Then she was gone.

He looked out the car window hoping to see her. She could be an American.

She would not lie. She would return for him.

The Stranger began to inch the car forward when Minh saw the woman exiting the building, a purple coat surrounding her body. But she was going the wrong way. "I am here!" Minh wanted to yell, laying his hands against the cool window. The car continued to roll. Ice crushed beneath the weight of the vehicle as it rolled faster. Faster. Before the Devil Spirit could escape into traffic, Minh had the door opened. Yelling, the Stranger stopped the car as Minh jumped out onto the street and began running down the sidewalk after the woman.

"Don't leave me, Mama!" he cried, running up the sidewalk. "Come back!"

The woman turned and went to her knees. She caught the child in her outstretched arms—her wings of flight.

"Mama," the child cried again. Wrapping her arms around him, she steadied his body.

"Mama," Minh repeated over and over. Tears were running, for the first time since his mother's illness, down his light brown face. He was scared, he wanted to tell her, really scared and he didn't want her to leave him again. The Devil Spirit ran toward the two. Nearing, he slowed and approached cautiously. The woman gently petted Minh's head, smoothing his hair.

"Mama," he whispered into her chest, not wanting to let her go, afraid she would never find him again. And the woman lifted his small, quivering body and slowly followed the Stranger back to the car.

HOW DO YOU TALK TO A STRANGER

Kathleen McColley

How did this ritual of dialing a number
  talking to someone a million miles away
  who speaks empty darts come about?
A woman's sweet Sunday company voice
  tells me the weather's been a bit cold
  in the mid 50s
The Johnsons came over for dinner
  and we cooked a pot roast
  and Mrs. Johnson brought apple pie . . .
The all-American family news report
  and then the usual question soon enough—
  Do you have any good news to tell me?

How does one tell a stranger
  the dark reality of a closet
    bolted shut so tightly
    not even a psychiatric couch
  can unlock its secrets

How do you describe the feeling
  of writing a useless check week after week
    for someone to listen to exploding pain
    when the only person with the key
  may as well be on the moon
How does one tell
  a foreigner who doesn't speak your language

about the 2 a.m. walk through a park
out onto a high 50-foot bridge
stretching precariously over a freeway
How do you describe the feeling of night air
rushing freely through the dark
embracing the wish to fly like a bird
to forget selfish pain—
false plunge to safety

How do you go back in time to describe the cracks . . .

How do you go back
to the days you fought for attention
when straight A's failed
when teachers' words were too boastful
the second place music trophies not good enough
How do you explain what it felt like
to have a graduation party without presents
because guests were requested not to bring them
their presence was honor enough
along with cheap sentimental cards

How do you explain a regret
of blossoming heart-pounding love
cut short because his religion wasn't yours
and strict orthodox thoughts prevailed
twisting something so pure into guilt
How do you explain the gradual change of philosophy
that brought about the questioning
and rejection of a frigid religion
that stifled personal expression nailed to convention
trying to escape drowning in superficiality
How do you justify a costly education

bringing to life an unpredictable new world
  branding you a traitor
  to someone who lives in a different camp
in an alien land

What is the news today?
  How do meaningless myopic words convey
    so many faraway feelings stabbed with ache
    I love you too becomes a barrier
    a liturgy repeated in response

How do you talk to a stranger
  in name a relation
    indeed a person
      called mother

HIS MOTHER, THE WHORE

Jessica Hagedorn

There are those who say my poor whore of a mother sold me to Uncle for fifty pesos. *Zenaida*: desperate, half-crazy, unable to feed me and herself those last few months. They say she was still young and still beautiful, they shake their heads solemnly at the terrible waste. I'm not sure they're telling the whole truth; maybe she was more ordinary than they remember, an ordinary whore with a ravaged face. They describe how she jumped in the river, a watery grave black with human shit, every dead thing and piece of garbage imaginable: the rotting carcasses of wild dogs and cats, enormous rats with heads blown off by bullets, broken tree branches and the tangled bouquets of wilted banana leaves, palm fronds, and *kalachuchi* flowers. When they pulled out my mother's blue corpse, they say her long black hair was entwined in this mass of slimy foliage and decay, a gruesome veil of refuse dragging on the mud beneath her.

This is what they tell me, this is what I've chosen to believe. They say Zenaida's ghost still haunts that section of the river, a mournful apparition in the moonlight. Boy-Boy claims he's seen her more than once, but I don't believe him.

Zenaida. She was a legendary whore, my mother. Disgraced and abandoned, just like in the movies. Driven to take her own life. My father was not the first man to promise her anything, that much I know for sure. Uncle identified her bloated body, arranged for her pauper's burial. That's why I owe him. No one knew her last name, what province she came from, if she had any other family besides me. They say I was five or six years old, that I was mute for months after her death. I was so dark, small, and thin, they called me "*Gagamba*"—little spider. I went home with Uncle and never shed a tear. I don't want to remember anything else about my sad whore of a mother. I've heard enough. That's why I never ask Uncle. That's why he never brings her up.

He started me doing odd jobs on the street. I sold cigarettes, boiled peanuts, Chiclets, *sampaguita* garlands, *The Metro Manila Daily*, and movie magazines. Legitimate little things that never got me anywhere; I had to compete with all the other kids on the street, running up to cars and buses, pestering tourists, hawking our wares. I hated every minute of it. Then there were times when Uncle pretended he was crippled and blind. I would lead him up to the air-conditioned Toyotas and Mercedes-Benzes where rich people and foreigners sat with their doors locked, trying hard to ignore my outstretched hand at their windows. But Uncle had no patience and little time for begging. "That's for lazy people," he would say.

When I was seven, Uncle taught me to steal. I was wiry, fast, and fearless. A natural talent, according to him. More daring than Boy-Boy, who was two years older than me and cried all the time. I was one of the best pickpockets in Manila; just ask anyone around here. Ask Uncle. I enjoyed stealing, the heady rush that hit me as I disappeared into a crowd, stolen goods burning in my hand. A ring, a watch, a chain around someone's neck. The money sometimes still warm from someone's back pocket. A heady rush of triumph like dope, a pleasure so private, delicious, and powerful. I never once got caught—that's how good I was.

I would do anything for Uncle in those days. We all would—grateful orphans who earned our keep, eager to please and turn our loot over to Uncle. I was the youngest and the smartest, Uncle's favorite.

What they say about me and Uncle isn't true. Just ask Boy and Carding, or Chito at that dress shop in Mabini where he works. The only thing about Uncle is he made things possible. He taught me everything I know.

One of Uncle's whores fucked me when I was ten. I don't remember her name—only her sour smell. A smell that clung to me for days. She looked weary, her movements slow and lumbering, like an ox's. Her broad, ox-face and dark, bloody lipstick repulsed me. I turned my face away, wouldn't let her kiss me.

Sitting at the only table in the middle of the one-room shack, Uncle watched us fuck on the mat a few feet away from him. He was smoking opium, leaning down to scratch behind Taruk's ear while the dog slept. I remember feeling ugly because all my hair had been shaved off by Uncle after he discovered lice. But the ox-woman didn't seem to care, or notice.

Uncle watched us hump and writhe as if it was the most ordinary thing in the world, his expression benign and serene. The woman never spoke, grunting occasionally and shifting my body on top of her with rough hands. With my bald head, I felt ludicrous and smaller than ever, poised on top of the ox-woman's hefty body. I rode her as I would a horse or *carabao*. In the dusty light, her flesh quivered, covered by a film of sweat. I shut my eyes, imagining her giving in to my earnest, awkward thrusts. She may or may not have actually moaned, but I heard what I wanted to hear. Then I forgot about my bald head, my small, skinny body. The pleasure I suddenly felt was extreme and overwhelming. I came quickly. To my surprise, I was eager to fuck the ox-woman again.

Maybe she did it as a favor to Uncle; maybe he had to pay her. I don't know. After the second time fucking her, I fell into a deep sleep. When I woke up, she was long gone. Uncle and his dog were nowhere to be found. All that was left was her smell.

I've had my share of women since, but they don't really interest me. Don't ask me why. To tell you the truth, not much interests me at all. I learned early that men go for me; I like that about them. I don't have to work at being sexy. Ha-ha. Maybe it's my Negro blood.

Uncle says I prefer men because I know them best. I take advantage of the situation, run men around, make them give me money. For me, men are easy. I'm open to anything, though. If I met a rich woman, for example . . . If I met a rich woman, a rich woman who was willing to support me . . . TO LOVE ME NO MATTER WHAT . . . You'd better believe I'd get it up for her too . . . Be her pretty baby. I know how to do that. Make them love me even when I break their hearts, steal, or spend all their money. Sometimes, you'd be amazed.

Maybe I'm lying. Uncle says I was born a liar, that I can't help myself. Lies pour out of my mouth even when I'm sleeping. The truth is, maybe I really like men but just won't admit it. Shit. What's the difference? At least Uncle's proud of me. I know it, though he'd never say so.

Hell. Sometimes I feel the days go by too fast. I get worried. I won't be young forever, and then what? I don't want to end up a shower dancer like Boy-Boy, working nights in some shithole rubbing soap all over my body just so a bunch of fat old men can drool, turning twenty tricks after that, giving away my hard-eaned profits to the goddam cops or clubowner! *I'm nobody's slave.* Look at Carding—already finished at nineteen. He'll do anything for money. They've got him by the balls.

Much as I respect him, I don't want to end up like Uncle. With all his brains and experience, he's still small-time. Just an old junkie who rules Tondo, with nothing to show for it. It's not enough for me. Not anymore.

I know I deserve something better. Right now I'm biding my time. I take good care of myself, I'm in control, my life is simple. I do okay spinning my records and turning a few tricks. I'm dressed, fed, and high. I can take it or leave it, break hearts wherever I go. Life can be so sweet, sometimes.

THE TELEVISION MAN

Michelle Cruz Skinner

Hesus pounded on the stubborn, rusty nail. He managed to lodge it about a quarter inch deeper into the wood before sitting back to rest. Nene glanced up from the comic book she was reading and shook her head. Hesus wiped the sweat from his face with his faded, red handkerchief, then shoved the handkerchief back into the pocket of his old jeans and resumed pounding.

The work was going slowly, much slower than Hesus had expected. He worried that he might not have the cross ready by tomorrow.

In between the short rests he took, the chickens could be heard clucking agitatedly at him in the little corner where they had taken refuge from the two intruders. Even Nene clucked at him in irritation. She had allowed him to work on the cross in the cool, dark chicken coop under her family's house. But his constant noise was annoying her and the chickens, which consequently weren't laying any eggs. Hesus crouched over his cross, oblivious to the ill-feeling that hung almost tangibly in the thick, wet air.

Sweat glistened on his arms, shoulders and back and on the wood that lay before him. The sweat trickled in tiny rivulets down to the small of his back, forming a slick sheen there. Beads of sweat burst from his forehead to drop onto the wood of the cross.

The hammer Hesus used was old and rusty as were the nails. Only the wood was new. Rather than scavenging for some

scrap lumber as Nene had urged him to, Hesus had spent nearly all of the meager earnings from his occasional jobs for some
rich, reddish-brown narra wood from the lumberyard in town.
Not only had the wood been expensive, but the cost of hauling it
to her home in a jeepney had also been high.

"You crazy!" Nene had said when she discovered how
much he had spent. But he had stubbornly defended his pur-
chases. "There will be so many people here for the celebration. I
have to be seen. That's the only way I'll find my father."

"Maybe he doesn't want to be found," Nene had suggested gently. And when he chose to ignore her: "He doesn't
even know you're alive!" Hesus refused to listen to her and
insisted on making the cross; Nene had refused to help and had
left him awkwardly balancing the long beams in front of her
house and wondering where he should go.

Hesus couldn't work on the cross at his home because he
didn't want his mother to know what he was doing. He couldn't
claim or feign devoutness as his reason for making the cross. His
mother knew he would never be driven to such an extreme by
his devoutness. She would immediately guess his reasons if she
knew about the cross and would forbid him to complete it.

So, Hesus dragged the large beams out to the edge of the
rice fields near Nene's home and worked there. Under the
intense sun and the eyes of the broken-backed farmers in the rice
paddies, Hesus began sanding all the rough spots out of the
wood.

Every day that week Nene had walked by the nearly
bare patch of ground where a couple of goats were grazing and
where Hesus worked on his cross. Every day, twice a day, she
brought food to her parents in the field. Every time she had
passed Hesus she had made a show of ignoring him. But, on the
fourth day, Nene noticed the raw, pink blisters on his hands and
the bright, shiny sunburn on his back and took pity on him. She

had led him to her home and let him work in the cool shade of the chicken coop under her house.

"Your boyfriend is crazy," her father had observed when he came home and found Hesus working under the house.

"Yes," Nene had agreed.

"Go send him home now so we can have some peace and quiet. Besides, he disturbs the chickens."

Hesus worked under the house for two more days. On this, the sixth day, he had to finish the cross. He drove the last few nails in under the beady, accusing eyes of the chickens. He sat against one of the slender beams that kept the house tenuously rooted to the earth and wiped the sweat from his forehead. Nene looked over the top of her comic book at him.

"Are you finished?"

"Not yet. I want to oil it. Do you have any oil?"

"You didn't buy any?" Nene asked sarcastically.

"No." Hesus seemed not to notice her mocking tone. Nene gave an exaggerated sigh and climbed up the rickety, bamboo stairs into her house. She returned with a small bottle of baby oil and a large can of Baguio Cooking Oil. She dropped them in front of Hesus hoping they would make at least a dull thud. There was hardly any noise. She returned to her corner and started angrily reading one of her many gossip magazines.

"You could help."

"I think it's crazy," Nene shot back without looking up from her magazine.

Hesus poured the thick, golden cooking oil, which smelled vaguely of chicken fat and old meals, into his cupped hand. Oil slid through his fingers onto the wood and the dirt floor. He smeared oil on all the surfaces of the cross, kneading and caressing the wood until it glowed with a reddish-brown light.

Nene laid her magazine down. "It is beautiful," she finally admitted. "And just in time too. The crucifixion is tomorrow."

Hesus smiled contentedly. Nene walked over and sat beside him. She laid a hand on his back and felt the blisters and heat of his sunburn. "You're so pale, you burn easily."

"My father's skin," Hesus said. Nene peeled large pieces of the loose, nearly-transparent skin off his back. It was pale. Pale and so dry it fell apart in her hand. The skin of his father.

Hesus's father was an American who had come through the barrio years ago. "The television man" they had called him whenever they talked about him. No one knew his name except (so they assumed) Hesus's mother or, if they had once known it, they had long ago forgotten it. Nene, like the other townspeople, often wondered which, if any, of the many men she saw on the television in Mayor Balimbing's coffee shop was Hesus's father. She took it for granted that Hesus wondered too although he never did so aloud.

Hesus's father was one of the men in the first television crew to visit the town. So the story went, they drove into town on a hot, rainy day, unusual and unwelcome weather for April. It was the day before the annual fiesta and the townspeople worried it would not clear up enough for them to celebrate the next day.

But the television men, along with an elegantly dressed Filipino man who turned out to be from the Bureau of Tourism, ran about in the rain and muck and mud shouting back and forth to each other and conferring with the astounded and very confused mayor. That evening the rain stopped and everyone slept fitfully in the still and heavy darkness. In the morning a few last-minute changes were made to the procession route and the television men sent back to America the first live footage of a bloody religious celebration that featured penitents flogging themselves and reenacting the crucifixion of Jesus.

The town was never the same after that. The people were the same people who had lived there for generations but the town changed. Every year in anticipation of the third week in March, in the streets along the new procession route, potholes were filled and houses repaired and painted. A small but profitable religious souvenir industry cropped up.

Hesus was born on the morning of December 24, a day before the original Hesus, but his mother gave him the name anyway. Instead of being an outcast, he was welcomed as the son of the unknown television man who had made the town famous.

Now, sixteen years later, Hesus was trying to find his father. Over the past week, most of the town had seen Hesus working or heard about what he was doing. They guessed that he was trying to bring his father back but, having no proof, were reluctant to approach his mother with their information.

"Even if you get on television, how will your father know it is you?" Nene asked as she rubbed oil into Hesus's back.

"I look like him. My mother tells me so." Hesus stared at the open blisters on his hands. Nene gently took one of his hands and began applying oil to it. "And I know my family name."

Nene's hand remained suspended a few inches over his. "It's been our secret. My name is Smith." Nene wanted to cry but instead took his hand up again and lay kisses on his blisters.

"Ay, Hesus," she whispered. She kissed him with oil-stained lips. "You are the child of everyone."

The chickens started laying eggs again the next morning. Nene carefully laid all but two of the eggs in her wicker basket. They always let a few of the eggs hatch in order to replace the chickens that died or were eaten by the family. She hesitated a moment then put two more of the eggs back in their nests.

Hesus was waiting for her outside the chicken coop. "You're early," she said.

"I didn't want to be late," Hesus replied.

"You may have a long wait."

"I don't mind." He smiled. "I've been waiting a long time already."

"Your cross is inside." Nene nodded towards the door of the chicken coop. "Will you be able to carry it into town by yourself?"

"If I have to. But I'll see if I can catch a ride on a jeepney." Hesus absently picked at a blister on his hand. "Will you be there?" He spoke quietly, but Nene heard the pleading in his voice.

"Of course," Nene replied calmly. Hesus relaxed and dropped his hands back to his side. "My mother is waiting for me." Nene raised the basket of eggs to make her point. "I have to help with breakfast."

"I'll see you at the procession then."

"Yes."

Nene climbed up the rickety ladder into her home. She heard Hesus huffing and the chickens clucking under the house as she fried the rice and eggs for breakfast. Her family heard the noise too, but they knew what it was and so ignored it. Nene watched him trudge slowly from the house and along the road into town carrying the cross on his back. She watched him so intently she nearly burned the eggs.

When Nene's family got to town, a small crowd was already gathered along the procession route even though it was still an hour till the procession started. The streets were beginning to fill with the usual fiesta trash: bright red and yellow paper tissue, crushed plastic cups, popsicle sticks, corn cobs, barbecue sticks, and occasional religious trinkets (mostly crucifixes) dropped by tourists.

Nene had left her family by one of the many large tour buses parked in front of Mayor Balimbing's coffee shop. Buses always stopped there. It was the largest, cleanest coffee shop in town and Mayor Balimbing had an exclusive and lucrative agreement with the bus company. At this time of year his coffee shop was a popular gathering spot not just for tourists, but for town residents who came to see the strangers invading their town.

The tourists were beginning to flow out and along the main street, mingling with the townspeople. Nene weaved through a group of smartly dressed, dark-haired, pale-skinned men and women speaking Japanese. They were mostly young and pale as the rice Nene's parents nurtured, bent over in the fields all day.

Nene continued to wander through the crowd, picking her way carefully among the trash and the people. She looked intently at the faces she passed, searching for some of her girl-friends whom she hadn't seen since the summer began.

Few of the faces she passed were familiar. It was an uneasy feeling, she thought, to walk through your own town and feel like a stranger. She passed a group of Americans, pink and blistered like Hesus from the sun, speaking their familiar and intimidating language. Their voices tapped at her head like those of the teachers in the school where Nene and the other students were required to learn English. Nene spoke English well but had the same uneasy feeling toward it that she had toward being a stranger in her own town.

Nene inched further up the street, stopping briefly to greet Aling Rosa through the one window of her sari-sari store. Aling Rosa complained about the rude tourists but smiled happily as she did so. Of course the tourists were rude, but they bought everything she had. Nene continued down the street.

She tripped on some cords plugged into a large, dull gray generator squatting in the gutter among discarded wrappers and broken bottles. A large, hairy, pink hand grabbed her by the arm and stopped her fall.

"Watch it girl," the large man behind the hand said, as he hauled her up. "You could lose us some valuable footage."

Nene was overwhelmed by his presence. "Excuse me," she replied meekly. He ignored her. Still with a firm grip on her arm he turned to yell behind him.

"Ey Joe!" He paused. "Velasco!" A very dark, slightly plump Filipino man came stumbling out of the crowd.

"Ya boss?"

"Get some of the boys to watch the generator will you?" The large man gestured at Nene with his free hand. "This girl nearly took out power to some of our equipment. We'd be in a hell of a fix if that happened while we were transmitting to Manila."

Joe nodded. "OK boss. Will do." And he disappeared into the crowd again. Through the few gaps in the crowd, Nene now saw the cameras the other unidentifiable equipment positioned just on the other side of the barricades. The large man noticed that he was still gripping her arm and hastily dropped it as if it were a dead animal.

Nene rubbed at the fat, red marks his fingers had left just below the line of her shirt sleeve. "Hope I didn't hurt you," he mumbled. Nene shook her head. Joe returned with two "boys." They were two young men who looked overeager and excited about the work they were doing with the television crew. The large man, "boss" they all called him, posted one on either side of the generator.

"Girl, could you do me a favor?" The boss didn't wait for her answer. "Go over to one of the stores nearby and buy us some sodas." He turned to Joe. "How many do we need?"

"Six, . . . no seven."

"Make it ten." He fumbled in his pocket. "Here's twenty pesos." Nene plucked the wadded-up bill from his palm.

"We'll be over there." He pointed toward the cameras and swatted her on the behind to get her going.

Nene jumped in embarrassment. She walked hurriedly down the street, trying to get as far from him as possible and hoping that no one she knew had noticed his crude behavior. At Aling Rosa's sari-sari store she bought five Cokes and five Sprites. Aling Rosa placed the bottles of soda in an empty, wooden crate so Nene could carry them all.

Nene first offered sodas to the two "boys" guarding the generator. They shyly accepted. Then she had to make her way through the crowd that always gathered around the television crew hoping to be part of the glamorous world they represented. Nene had always found television glamorous too, but now she felt trapped by the large television man before her.

Nene offered him a soda and tried to return his change. He waved her away in irritation and indicated that she should keep the change. After distributing all the drinks she could, she stood forlornly in the midst of the cables and equipment and men with the leftover sodas. The edges of the wooden crate were digging into her fingers.

"Wait here," the boss, the television man, said. "I may need you later."

Nene nodded and shifted the crate in her hands. She hoped the procession would be over quickly so she could leave. From down the street, she heard the wailing of the penitents approaching. As they drew nearer, she could hear the sharp hiss and slap of the whips as the men flailed them against their flesh.

Their wails crashed against the crowd and dissipated among the faces. The smell of sweat and dirt and blood preceded them. Nene saw the whips flash through the air and slash through the men's already mortified flesh. She felt the heat from their bodies as they passed by her.

Blood sprayed from the whips and from the men's bare and torn backs. A drop landed on the corner of Nene's lips. It was bitter and tasted of leather and sweat.

The penitents passed, leaving their blood on the streets. They were followed by seven men carrying seven crosses. Nene saw Hesus. He was in front of the group. He must have fought for that position.

When they reached the television cameras, the men stopped and laid their crosses on the ground. A small group of men at the end of the procession rushed up to the crosses with hammers and nails. Nene watched as a young man with a faint mustache above his lip and long, slim fingers drove a nail through Hesus's right hand.

The young man looked frightened and his hands seemed unsteady. Hesus closed his eyes and bit his bottom lip. His lip started bleeding, but he continued to bite down on it. Finally, the young man raised the cross and Hesus hung before the crowd.

Blood trickled from his lip and his tongue hung limply from his mouth. The sweat shone on his limbs which appeared to be relaxed. Even his fingers drooped. All that moved were his eyes which twitched frantically back and forth scanning the crowd but seeing nothing.

Slowly, the other crosses around him were raised. They swayed before the crowd, their human burdens hanging like trophies. Somewhere behind Nene someone retched. It stank. Everything around her stank. The air was too thick with blood and bile.

Hesus's cross was lowered to the ground. The television cameras crowded around him focusing on his frantic eyes, his mouth flecked with blood and saliva. He mumbled softly. Nene thought she heard "Smith." They pried the nails out and blood poured from the holes. Hesus fainted.

The television man supervised the cameramen as they focused on the holes and the blood. Nene felt blood on her right hand and dropped the wooden crate. A long, jagged piece of wood on the edge of the crate had cut her palm and left a splinter in it. She pulled the splinter out and pressed her hand against her jeans to stop the bleeding.

Nene looked back at Hesus and saw that his hands were covered in blood. A thin sheen of red liquid floated in his palms and poured onto the damp, littered street. He shouldn't be bleeding so much. It should have slowed down by now, Nene realized. The young man who had nailed Hesus to the cross realized it too and watched in horror as the blood continued to flow profusely.

The young man removed his shirt and pressed down hard on one of Hesus's hands. The shirt was soon stained and heavy with blood. Another man came to help him. Soon a small group of men was clustered around Hesus. They spoke hurriedly and frantically to each other but didn't seem to be listening. They seemed to speak more for reassurance than out of necessity.

Each one took his turn placing his head against Hesus's chest. Nene took in their worried looks and Hesus's limp body draining onto the street. He's dead, she thought.

A woman began to cry and pray. "Lamb of God . . . " Nene was knocked to the ground by a woman who fainted. Nene sat in the road among the dirt and paper wrappers and discarded bits of food. She reached for the wooden crate and pulled herself to it. With her hands gripping the crate tightly, Nene vomited into it.

Her breath came in heaves. She had to force herself to breathe in. The wound on her hand reopened and she could feel the blood oozing out onto the crate. She started screaming.

On and on the screams shook her. Nene realized in horror that she couldn't stop. "Hesus! Hesus! Hesus!" She saw feet running around her and heard other voices getting louder and more hysterical. The familiar large, pink hand of the television man appeared, grabbed her by the arm, and dragged her to her feet. He pulled her through the crowd, colliding with tourists, vendors, and stray cats and dogs. Nene stumbled along after him. The noise converged around them. Individual screams and cries were lost in the large, pulsing sound that was the crowd. Nene took several deep, painful breaths as she ran and was finally able to stop screaming. But now she could smell and taste the stench in her mouth.

It seemed that they had been running blindly for so long that Nene was surprised to find they were only at the small hotel behind Mayor Balimbing's coffee shop. The television man dragged her through the cramped, anemically lit lobby, and down a short corridor to the end of the hall. He stopped in front of a door and searched in his pockets for his keys. Nene whimpered.

He held the door open and scowled at her as she entered. "Well, you certainly added drama to our coverage. You and your boyfriend." The television man sighed. "I assume that was him on the cross." He flicked a couple of light switches until he found one that worked. A pale, yellow light trembled above a lopsided couch, a dented coffee table, and a low bed with a large depression in the center.

The room was surprisingly neat. The bed was made. There was no trash lying about. Everything appeared to be in its place. It was the television man's room and Nene, the stranger, felt uneasy.

"I doubt they'll be able to use the audio on that. The commentary was damn near drowned out by your screaming and the rest of the noise." He flicked the bathroom light on. "What a way to get on television." Nene heard him running some water in the sink. "Hesus. God." He came out and looked at Nene who was trembling by the coffee table. "Listen, I'm sorry about what happened. I mean, it's terrible that your boyfriend . . . " He paused uneasily. His fingers fidgeted with the same towel he held. "Um, why don't you wash up? Here's a towel and there's some soap in there." He indicated the bathroom. Nene took the towel.

The water was still running in the sink, although it was only a little more than a trickle. Nene tried the shower, but it wasn't working so she stoppered up the sink and soaked her head in the water until she had to come up for air. The soap stung her eyes and the mouthwash she found in the medicine cabinet stung her mouth and throat. Nene was glad for the pain, like the sharp burning of a raw wound. Her hand still throbbed.

When she emerged from the bathroom the television man was fumbling with the dial of his small transistor radio. There was too much static though and he turned it off impatiently. "Feel better?" he asked. Nene nodded.

"Listen . . . where do you live?" He shifted uneasily on the sofa. "I mean, I can't let you stay here . . . Your parents must be looking for you." He fiddled with the tuner on the dead radio. "I could call a jeepney for you and have the driver take you home."

Nene sat on the edge of the bed and started crying. The man became flustered. "Don't cry . . . please."

He sat beside her and lay a thick arm around her shoulders. Nene continued to shudder and cry uncontrollably. Hesitantly, he began to stroke her hair. She dropped her head on to his chest and continued crying. "Shhh . . . Oh God," the television man sighed as he stroked her hair.

Nene wrapped her thin arms around him and kissed his chest as she cried. He recoiled at first, but didn't push her away. Instead he wrapped his arms around her and held her as they slid down into the depression in the center of the bed.

Nene imagined she was in the chicken coop under her house with Hesus. The damp ground was under them and the fuzzy outlines of the dirty white chickens surrounded them.

AT THE CORNER

Kathy Dee Kaleokealoha Kaloloahilani Banggo

of 4th and Cherry, she stops and says, *You understand me*
with something like conviction or insanity, but anyway,
she's passionate and scary all at once, *the way my feet*
are overgrown, about the year I ate avocados but didn't
shave my armpits, how some women make love while
others just fuck but I, of course, do both, Saffron, you
understand me.

My mother named me a color I can never really be, being
a few shades darker in tone. Because of this I tell her,
yes, yes, I do understand. My father spoke with a Filipino
accent, Tagalog or Ilocano or what I don't know, and my
mother made offerings to the gods. I was ashamed of them
both and so lay on my back with blonde men. I never once
kissed my father.

She takes my hand, gap-toothed, washed-out blonde, silicon
breasted and dark under all that transluscent skin. Some days
when she tastes of tequila and salt water, I know I could never
love her. I think of tables left uncleared, my mother worried
and waving goodbye from the front stoop, her laundry hung out
to dry in the sun and wind blowing up and down our valley.

Later we will ride the 106 Express past the train yards and the
playing fields, through Columbia City to Renton, where we live.
Jimi Hendrix is buried there. There's a factory famous for durable

cardboard boxes. Otherwise, people say there's not much
to stop for. Southbound, you hear it all. Chinese. Vietnamese.
Spanish. In that order. Even Tagalog and Ilocano, I think. Of
course, I don't understand any of it. One time, this guy who said
he was from Ethiopia starts singing, *Deez, deez, deez is Afrika.*
Deez is Afrika adorned. Children, come gather round.
Children, tell me who you are.

HYBRID

Susan Miho Nunes

She was ninety-five years old, Naomi said. I believed her. Mrs. Furuisato was the oldest person I had ever known, older than my grandparents, older than Mr. Okinaga the vegetable vendor, older than the ragman who shuffled through town like something out of a bad dream. In all the years we lived on the hill she never changed. Naomi teaches school in Honolulu now. I hear she is married and has two children. Her grandmother is long dead, of course. And yet—and this is true—I cannot separate the old woman from the place. I do not want to go back and see the house and garden and know she will not be there.

Nostalgia tends to select. I have never forgotten how she looked that first time, before I met Naomi, who would become my best friend throughout childhood, before the frail, bent figure had grown a part of the place, a fixture both fascinating and terrifying, like the hothouse with its sweaty flasks, or the cooking shed with its strange smells. We had only days before moved into the house on the hill, and because my parents were busy, I was left to wander about on my own, quite forgotten. A row of hibiscus bushes separated our yard from theirs, and I was sitting in this hedge near the cooking shed when the old woman walked past.

It was her feet I saw first, withered things the color of dried shrimp and criss-crossed with silver veins. Chalky toenails curled into the flesh. She was wearing grass slippers. Her dress drifted by, soft and white. Moments later, there were scratchy noises in the shed, like the sounds of birds nesting under the eaves. Drawn from my hiding place, I crept on hands and knees across the narrow path where she had just walked, edged along the side of the hut, and peered around the corner.

The room was small, windowless, with three walls and a dirt floor. A few rickety shelves along the far wall held an assortment of clay pots, bottles, tin cans, and several handblown flasks of the type one finds in laboratories. Several fat burlap bags stood in the corner; one had broken open leaving a mound of brown, fibrous material on the floor. Near the open front was a small circle of stones covered with a wire grating and next to it a low table holding a wooden rice pot, a blackened water kettle, and a plate of dried fish crossed with long chopsticks. The room smelled of old things and charcoal burning.

I don't know how long I stood there before I sensed her presence behind me. That impression, in the moments before I fled, has never left me. To this day, as I relate this, I remain in awe of that woman, as if part of myself were still a paralyzed child. I can hear her laugh. Mrs. Furuisato is the stuff of my dreams, my imagination. She is the ghost I cannot escape. I see the parts of my past in light of the way she appeared that day, a tiny, wrinkled shell of a woman with a toothless mouth parted in a smile, as if I were the object of a curious but amusing tale, her hands clutching the white dress that hung from the hump on her back as if there were nothing underneath. And her low laughter.

She called her granddaughter "Nao-mi," sliding the first two syllables together and giving equal weight to each part the way the Japanese language requires. The "a" is pronounced "ah," as when a doctor says, "Say ahhh." Naomi is in fact a curious name, Western when written in English, but Japanese when written with kanji. Mrs. Furuisato often called Naomi "Nao-chan." When she called from a distance, she sounded something like this: "Naochaaaaaan!"

One day when Naomi and I were on the roof of the chicken coop near the last terrace, we heard her calling. When Naomi didn't answer, I said casually, "Your grandma wants you." The reminder wasn't necessary; Naomi had already determined the nature of the call. She shoved the slingshot in her pocket—we had been trying to knock down a nest of yellow jackets—and asked, "Wannah come?"

"What does she want?"

A ghost of a smile flickered across her face. "Come see."

We headed up the hill and Mrs. Furuisato was standing by the shed holding something in her apron. When she saw us, she went inside.

She emptied the contents of her apron onto a newspaper. They were wrinkled little knobs the size of someone's thumb.

"Sweet potatoes," said Naomi. "She saves the end parts for me."

The old woman squatted before the fire and made a hole in the ashes with her chopsticks. Under the ashes, the coals glowed for a moment then faded into pinpoints of orange. She put the potato ends into the hole and covered them with hot ashes.

"Pretty soon, now," Naomi said. She helped her grandmother to the low stool and then we sat on the floor close to the fire. No one said anything, but occasionally Mrs. Furuisato murmured, "Na-o-mi," and chuckled at some private joke.

I don't remember what we did while we waited, but after a while Mrs. Furuisato bent over the fire and thrust her chopsticks into the ashes. One by one she searched out the knobs and put them on a sheet of newspaper. When she finished, she handed the paper to Naomi.

We retraced our steps down the hill, Naomi holding the newspaper in front of her with both hands. I looked back and Mrs. Furuisato was by the shed watching us. We sat on the roof of the chicken coop and ate the potato ends. They were sweet, but what I remember most is the lingering aftertaste of ashes.

"Do you love her?" I once asked Naomi. In my experience, grandmothers did not show their gums when they smiled. They were closer to you than your own parents, easy to love. You could tell them anything, and they didn't scold.

Naomi looked baffled.

"You never kiss her," I offered, "or talk to her."

"I talk to her all the time."

I believed Naomi. I set my observations aside. I reasoned that since everyone loved their grandmothers, Naomi had to love hers. I did not question this logic; it was just so. In time I came to accept Mrs. Furuisato's presence. Still, somewhere in the background was the power of the first impression, the face more skull than flesh, and always about her the aura of old wood and charcoal burning.

Naomi's father raised orchids. It was both business and passion. I now understand there are almost a thousand genera of orchidaceae, nearly twenty thousand species, and an even greater number of hybrids, bred for their vigor and strength, their ease of care. Mr. Furuisato specialized in epiphytic orchids, the kind that grow on living matter and obtain nourishment from the soil and moisture from the air. He had lined the terraced hillside with rows of tree fern on which he fixed the mature plants. The flowers and foliage burst from swollen, upright stems or shot out of the axils of leaves. Sprays of orchids arched into space, filling the air with their scent. Naomi had to remind me not to run along the cinder paths or we'd damage the blooms.

My favorite place was a screened-in greenhouse built in a sheltered corner of the yard against a wall of giant tree fern. To get there you followed a winding cinder path lined on either side with huge azalea bushes. Baskets of maiden hair framed the entrance. Inside, all was transformed. The sunlight—alive with dust motes—filtered through the slats and spilled gently onto the shady floor. The air was moist and warm, the colors dark and intense. The space smelled of tree moss, cattleyas, and an unidentifiable something else.

This was the nursery. Orchid seedlings, hundreds of them, grew in labeled flasks arranged along a high shelf. The seedlings were vulnerable to disease, so they incubated in their water medium, sealed from the world, until they were strong enough to survive outside. I don't know how long it took them to mature and flower, but I believe it was a very long time.

Naomi and I often played there. Sometimes I went alone, enduring that otherness until the humidity forced me outside. When I left, it was always as if waking from a dream, aware again of the cinders beneath my bare feet.

I was there alone the day Naomi and her grandmother found me. "I didn't touch anything," I said.

Mrs. Furuisato brushed by, and I caught the smell of old wood and charcoal burning. She reached among the clay pots and pulled one of them to her apron. It was a venerable plant crowned with three purple blooms. Silver roots traced a complex web around the pot.

She said something in Japanese to me.

"I didn't touch it," I said. The cinders hurt my feet.

Naomi said, "It's real old." She stepped around me to join her grandmother. "My father says it's more old than him." She took the plant from her grandmother, examined the aerial roots, and placed the pot back on the shelf. "All the others, they come from this plant."

The old woman looked fondly at Naomi and spoke again. I caught the English word "purebred."

She was trying to describe, I now realize, what made the plant special. But something in the meeting of the word and the experience alienated me. I felt alone. Different. Not like them. For a long time I stared at the old woman's aged face, at the toothless mouth, the purple flesh, at the hands that gripped her granddaughter's shoulder, just as the roots clasped the clay pot.

That is all I remember of that day. I don't know what we did after that. It might have been any number of things, all lost. But I do know that it was in the weeks after that experience in the greenhouse that I decided to destroy the plant, to crush each flower, snap the fleshy stems and grind them into the cinder floor, pull from the pot the moss that held the plant and sustained it, and to rub away all traces of the white roots.

They never told my parents. Never complained. Naomi and I continued to play together until we reached intermediate school and different interests pulled us apart. She was my first and dearest and only Japanese friend. But she is as alien to me as that part of myself which is like her. As alien as her grandmother. Old Mrs. Furuisato.

SECOND NATURE

Diana Chang

How do I feel
Fine wrist to small feet?
I cough Chinese.

To me, it occurs that Cezanne
Is not a Sung painter.

(My condition is no less gratuitous than this remark.)

The old China muses through me.
I am foreign to the new.
I sleep upon dead years.

Sometimes I dream in Chinese.
I dream my father's dreams.

I wake, grown up
And someone else.

I am the thin edge I sit on.
I begin to gray—white and black and in between.
My hair is America.

New England moonlights in me.

I attend what is Chinese
In everyone.

We are in the air.

I shuttle passportless within myself,
My eyes slant around both hemispheres,
Gaze through walls

And long still to be
Accustomed,
At home here,

Strange to say.

CONFEDERATE SKIES

Kara Fujita

medium rare
quiet baby

unrespitetive thief
of the impossible

in-imaginative of
the capabilities
of institutions

asylums of legacy
tenured in hospitals
suffocatingly familiar,
confined in walls
of terry-cloth white destinies

nubby knolls
the copyright mark
and tradestamp
of God's
ironshod
brandished
into my belly

blinded by the uniqueness

of being me.

I smear against
the wet ink
and
the new pages
colored in rebellion
I am transferred
under fingered pressure

positioned
in places
hollowed out milk-chalk
my dregs of powdered soot

accepted by the

Majority
as they smile
in comfort
that I fit between
remittent
remnant bindings

a few words left
over from the
last page of their
history
books

page to page
in a Dr. Seuss
chapter

My life of neither here
nor there.

My father
was not your
shogun
shotgun
in the palace
walls
throned by samurai
and their bushido leniencies

My mouth is not quiet
I am a man beneath
the red dye
of your
salt infusion offerings
mumbling to the sea
that I am a child of
the sun

I landed from the setting moon.

Carmelized denizens
from far off
fragile
languid seams

My mother was
not translucent
in her passage
from Cimmerian
fields

Doubled green
in their envy to claim
another verdant
camber

She was sifted from
England's sweetness
then poured into
Ireland's flour
prosperous she
was spooned
by handfuls
into America's
distant hour

I am not a cowboy
And I don't faint
beneath a strong
southern sun

I was born within
that furnace
cracked and fused
within the whip
and now I wander
aimlessly
and search your
tainted lips

I am a child
of weathered old
suitcases
and laundry left

to bare
I am the finished
product
of withered sips
and waisted hips
and neither here nor
there

Raw and Dangerous
Promising and Skewered
Our blood flows from
my lips
And stains your parchment power
Casting away your fragile yellow
I burn a painful white
Screaming -
"I am your enemy
I am your dream
I am your only
daughter
I am a freak
I long to speak
I tyrade you
my golden colors
streamlining them
like spider monkeys
boundless across the sky
starred
gutted
burning
STRETCHING
to the remains of
your perished galaxies."

SESSIONS

Adrienne Tien

ONE

I am frozen with anger, not fatigue. My head is woozy from the drug they forced down my throat last night, but there is one thought, a part of me that's annoyingly lucid, worried about the stitches on my lip, afraid they'll leave a scar. That's one reason I'm not talking, I don't want a torrent of words to pull the small suture apart. If I start talking, I could get really mad, I might start yelling. The best thing is to sit here immobile, acting like I can't hear a thing. I certainly can't look at Sam though he keeps glancing at me. He hasn't slept at all. There's a bluish tint to the skin under his eyes, his face bloodless, his hair even more unkempt than usual. I notice his hand coming nervously and frequently to rub over his face as if he were trying to draw off a rubber mask. I almost feel sorry for him, but how could he do this to me? True, I was sobbing and incoherent last night, but today is another day. The car has stopped at some tall wrought iron gates. Sam gets out and speaks to the guard. We drive through. Where did he get this car from? This driver? This place? I read the name on a tasteful sign of brick and concrete, "Woodlawn Psychiatric Center." The wind blows and evergreen bushes flop against the sign like long feather dusters.

During the drive Sam has been explaining. "Barbara, I wish you'd look at me. Barbara, you know I wouldn't bring you to this place if I had a choice, but you don't have any family or a close enough friend who can help right now . . . I'd stay with you night and day but I can't. The play is opening tomorrow. I'm worried—that's all . . . I don't want to leave you alone. You need someone . . . " Here it comes now—he's been trying to get me to see someone ever since our tiff over Dina Van Hess. " . . . someone professional . . . just so you can have a rest . . . Barbara, please say something." Sam reaches out and cautiously touches my knee.

My throat tightens, I look away, further away, out the window, so that he doesn't exist, so that I can't hear his pleading voice. I'm angry, damn angry. Maybe at him, but not just at him. And yes, I need a rest but what makes Sam think I need company day and night? Have I ever given any indication of being suicidal—never! Okay, dump me off and be gone, but don't expect me to forgive you for this.

A woman with cropped hair and silver studs in her ears greets us just inside the door. She and Sam speak briefly. I narrow my eyes at her as she turns and introduces herself, not too friendly but not cold either. I nod, some remnant of manners that even the foulest of moods can't eradicate. Sam stands there leaning forward as if to kiss me goodbye, but I move away, giving him one look, one blank empty look.

As soon as the woman has left me alone in my room, I'm overcome by a desire to laugh. But I can't laugh because of the stitches. Now it seems even more absurd! Suddenly, I'm happy! Happy to be here because now I don't have to hold back anything. Maybe I wasn't crazy before, but now I can be—I can let it all hang out. I can be rude and nasty and inconsiderate. All the things I have never been. Why thank you Sam, what a relief. I feel a smile pushing against the stitches, I control it and sit down on the bed. In my very own room again. I'm used to that, accustomed from childhood to spending a lot of time by myself. My parents wanted more children, but my mother had several miscarriages after I was born, and so I have only one older brother. There are cousins on my mother's side, but they are strangers.

My mother gave up everything from her past for her marriage to my father, "the Chinese." In the small Nebraska town where she grew up, she won all the math prizes—an unseemly distinction for a girl, but her parents were proud of her. A full scholarship took her to college. Several years later in her second year of graduate school, she met my father and went home the next summer to tell her parents about him. If she had been more tactful, would it have mattered? She mentioned him for the first time and then in the next breath announced that they were planning to get married. Her parents were shocked and she was shocked by their reaction. If she married this man, there would be no hometown wedding, there would be no homecoming at all! It might even be against the law. How could they hold their heads up in town with a daughter married to a man of a different race. True, it was a respectable race with a long history, but was the man even a Christian? Why must she marry *this* man when there were so many other attractive, eligible men around? What about that nice guy John Wollenstone who also studied mathematics, the one she had been seeing for a time, why not him or somebody like him! "If you marry this Chinaman, you will no longer be our daughter."

Her parents were right. In the forties, miscegenation laws were still on the books. My parents found another state and got married there by a judge.

TWO

Late in the evening, a few hours after I was born, my brother overheard the nurses talking about me. What they said applied to him as well, but when he teased me, he overlooked this obvious fact. From the moment I appeared in his world, I became the target of all the feelings and thoughts he had that were too painful for him to acknowledge. It took me two decades to realize this and when I did, I was like a hostage set free. I forgive him for wielding his superior age and intelligence over me. I don't doubt that his struggle to define and make a place for himself in this world may have been harder than mine. After all, I'm proud of who I am and he is not.

Anyway, not twenty-four hours into the world, two nurses in starched white uniforms with hair done up in twists in the back, their white winged caps held down with golden bobby pins, saw fit to judge my destiny. My father was still sitting in a chair by my mother's bed, but my five year-old brother John had slipped out of the room. He stood at the nursery window, standing on tip-toe trying to see the bundled babies in their glass bassinets. A baseball cap hid his clear, almond-shaped eyes.

He distinctly heard the nurses as they came out. "I can't help but feel sorry for them," said Nurse Marianne.

"They often turn out quite beautifully," said the other. Her name tag read "Joan." "At least they have that—I don't think it's so bad."

Nurse Marianne went on, "But it's unfair, how can the parents really make up for the fact that they've created a child that just isn't anything. These mixed up kids end up with mixed up brains."

"That's what they said about you!" My brother tells me, wanting to hurt me, because he's been hurt by others, the rhymes of other kids, by being called China Boy, Viet Cong and Jap, Ching-Chong-Chinaman, or the one that seemed to have been made up just for us. "My mother's Japanese, my father's Chinese, and I'm a mixed-up kid." The accompanying hand gestures pull the eyes see-saw-like in two different directions. I still remember the strange fear and panic that leapt into my heart when I heard that one from a neighbor girl. I felt suffocated as the feelings inside collided with the loud laughter I projected out.

My brother taunts me with his story again and again, but I don't want to hurt anybody, I'm seated at the dining table, doing a watercolor, painting flowers, and at this time, in these moments, I have complete concentration and fulfillment. Race means nothing to me. I'm very happy with my parents, I've been showered with love, I'm very happy with myself, I'm very happy with life. I'm four and a half and can already write my name, Barbara Bennett Chen.

I was born in 1950.

THREE

The stitches have been removed, I can see that the cut was tiny and that there will be no significant mark left after several months have passed. I don't know who is keeping watch over things here, but I hadn't been back in my room for more than five minutes when I was informed that my sessions with a psychologist would begin that afternoon.

My psychologist, Ezra Chapman, was seated in a swivel chair next to a small table. There was a desk in the corner of the room, another chair and an analyst's divan. A small window let in a bit of daylight, but most of the illumination in the room came from a lamp on the table. There, a small black clock silently made the rounds. Ezra looked to be about fifty, but I knew instinctively that he had not been in the profession for very long. He wore glasses and had a full gray beard that matched his hair. I noticed that his suit jacket was rather worn. As I observed this, I immediately felt less intimidated—the worn patches at the sleeves and elbows of his tweed coat, signaling that he was an ordinary person. The way in which he answered my sudden confrontation reinforced my feeling that he was new at the game.

"I think it would be better for me to see a woman." I said.

"If you insist, you could probably be switched to one of the women on staff."

"Don't you think I'd be better off seeing a woman—that another woman could better understand me?"

He answered, "My feeling is that a good therapist has both male and female within him or her and it really shouldn't make a difference."

He wanted me for a patient. He was interested in me; that is one advantage of being mixed race, people are curious. I thought him congenial enough and after I got back to my room, I decided to give him a try.

FOUR

When they were admitting me to the emergency room where Sam took me, a nurse filling out the forms said, "I'll put down here that you're White." I remember that now because it startled me. I have never classified myself that way. Yet I am as much White as Chinese and I would have felt gratified and unprotesting had she said "I'll put you down as Asian." Why is that? Do I have a choice? Is it fact or personality that makes me *other*? I have never forgotten third grade social studies class when we did a lesson on Red China. As we learned about the horrible brainwashing Communist Chinese, my face flushed red as the map in our textbook. I felt that to everyone in the class, I was a representative sample of this evil, barely human people. It never occured to me to think, "what does this have to do with me—I'm white."

I mentioned already about my mediocrity in school. It's true, I cannot begin to tell you the difference between applied and theoretical mathematics. But you can't live in two worlds like I have and not have a broader view. I have benefited from a thorough education and my upbringing in an intellectual house-

hold. I haven't told Ezra this yet, but I can't help but occasionally think that he's not as smart as me. So how can he help me?
Does he have any idea what he's dealing with? I am not your run-
of-the-mill American girl! I never tried to be. Do I look like that
girl on the cover of that magazine, that woman on TV comparing laundry detergents? Do I resemble any of the top news-
women, Barbara Walters, Jane Pauley, Judy Woodruff, Leslie
Stahl, Diane Sawyer . . . But oh, you say triumphant, there's
Connie Chung . . . oh all right.

The question is—how can Ezra understand me?

FIVE

I'm meeting Ezra in the late afternoon. This time of day
scares me. The sun slants down and slowly withdraws, like some
sinister magician pulling away his cape, orange silk one
moment, black the next. I feel I'm sinking. I feel that as soon as
dark hits, my thoughts will fly out like careening bats. I see this
silly almost cartoon image of a fifteenth century ship, going
down in a sea of evenly peaked waves. I'm afraid of my room
and of my need to speak to someone. I try as hard as I can not to
cry in front of Ezra but I keep doing it. Now I don't speak,
because I can't breathe freely enough to send the air out of my
throat. I'm choked up. Ezra hands me a tissue from a small plastic pack that he casually removes from his soft, cracked leather
briefcase.

"You've told me some facts," he says very carefully, "But
I'm wondering about your feelings."

Feelings, I don't want to talk about feelings, not too
much anyway. What about reasons for things, analysis, plans.
Feelings are too easy, anybody can talk about feelings, what's the
point? Feelings have done nothing but get me into trouble. It's
because I followed my feelings that I even dreamed of being an

actress. If I could only have taken a practical route like my brother, an established doctor now, with a wife and a child, a house and a car, if only I could have had no feelings at all. I wouldn't be here. And that's what Sam kept wanting from me, to hear my feelings. So he said, but when I told him about my strongest feeling, when he found out about that, he didn't want to know. He didn't want to know about my feeling—that's why I've been trying to kill it on my own. I know it isn't right, I know it's crazy! It's even against everything I believe. I am against racism. But eventually, I must and will tell Ezra everything because if I don't, what hope do I have of getting better, of starting over completely? The future must be fresh and new. I must be someone else. Can I get a nose job, blond ambition, turn brown eyes to blue?

SIX

My first apartment in New York was a sublet from Sheila. I met her when I was working in Boston and living in a small suburban town. My company had a summer policy of giving us Friday afternoon off and I was taking an aerobics class. The class was held in a studio at a shopping plaza. One day as I was leaving the class, I found myself walking in back of Sheila. Her long hair, pulled up into a tight ponytail, swung back and forth with her sashaying walk. Her workout attire, a shiny black sleeveless leotard and fluorescent green tights had been exchanged for tight jeans and a skimpy top. She wore plenty of makeup and had big gold hoops in her ears. She stopped so abruptly in front of her parked car that I almost bumped into her. She turned to me as if I were her best friend.

"Will you look at that! I mean, goddamn it! I got a flat tire, fuckin' flat tire! Friday night, I wanta relax and now I gotta flat tire."

"That's too bad," I said stupidly.

"Shit!" She said, lighting a cigarette, giving it a pissed off look like she didn't know how it came to be stuck between her fingers. "Do you know where there's a garage around here?"

"Do you have a spare?" I said. "I can change it."

I wasn't in a hurry and I was curious about her because I'd heard her tell someone she'd been an actress in New York.

While I changed her tire, she stood on the sidewalk telling me a steady stream of woes and throwing in every now and then about how if she hadn't been living in New York for so long, she'd know how to change the tire herself. She invited me for a drink.

We ordered Margaritas and when she was on her third, she said, "Hope you don't mind me asking, but what are you?"

"I'm part Chinese and part Caucasian."

"Caulk Asian, huh," she blew out some smoke. "Great combo. I've got German on one side and on the other some Spanish and Irish and a little bit of Italian."

She was also a little drunk and I couldn't help myself, "Any Cherokee?"

"Probably." She said, pulling on her cigarette.

I told her about my work as a fact checker for a travel publication and that my company had an office in New York. "I'm putting in a request to be transferred there." I was slightly drunk too, "I've always wanted to be an actress."

"Go for it! I'm sicka that life. I'm checkin' out this area. See if it's any good for starting my own business—my own aerobics studio. I can see my name in plastic now, 'Sheila's Sweat Stop.'"

I joined her cackle with a laugh.

She went on, "Really, I just can't take New York anymore. I've already suffered through four low budget movies that never saw the light of day, forget the theatres. Sick of it! I mighta done better, but I fuckin' wasted my best years in New York when I shoulda gone to L.A. All because of this guy I was dating. I'm thirty-eight and I have nothing to show for it. Oh, I know I look younger but believe me, I feel forty. I wanta settle down now in a nice town like this, start my business, find a decent guy, a doctor, lawyer, dentist, even an accountant, and have my own steady life. I'm not sayin' I didn't do okay—not like some people who never make a cent or get anything. At the least, I always got the nurses' parts. But now they're starting to get more realistic— giving the roles to ethnic types—yeah, like you. Yeah, go for it."

"I guess it's probably too late for me, too," I said.

"How old are you?"

"Twenty-eight."

"You're like me. You don't look your age. Give it a try. I can help you."

So, that's how I got my place for almost nothing and when she married the man who fit her plans, she signed the lease over to me.

"I don't know why I'm telling you all this," I say to Ezra.

He says, "You don't need a reason."

"Maybe I'm just any old patient of yours, ordinary, stupid."

"What if you are?" He says.

"Am I?"

"What if you are just like everyone else?" He repeats.

"Well, I'm not," I say, "I know I'm not."

I left thinking I sounded cocky. Well, I could be just any old patient but if I thought of myself that way then I wouldn't be here. I'm a twirling penny, neither heads nor tails, spinning endlessly with the possibility of being either. The fact is I am different, I'm very aware of being different, of not belonging anywhere. Sometimes of course, not *all* the time. That's the trouble with pouring out my thoughts like this—what I say isn't always true, all the time. And I sound crazier and more confused than I actually am—this is just the down side, the bad side, the side that landed me here. *Stop apologizing, stop qualifying, stop rationalizing, stop excusing* . . . I can hear Ezra telling me to stop, to let go and just feel.

SEVEN

The next time I see Ezra, I give him the silent treatment. We sit there for fifteen minutes. Finally he says, "I probably won't say this again, but don't forget we are here for you—not for me. Isn't there anything you'd like to talk about?"

"Okay," I say, "I feel it's futile for me to come see you and tell all these things about my life because, well . . . I don't think you can ever fully understand me."

"Why not?"

"Because you're a man . . . and because you're a white man."

There I've said that word which I'm so unaccustomed to using. *White man.* It gives me a certain feeling of superiority that I can slap a label on him and separate him from being synonymous with all Man. MANKIND.

"True, these are limitations, but then do you think you must be exactly like someone else in order to understand them?"

"I know the right answer is 'of course not.'"

"What's your answer?"

"I don't think we understand people when they're different from us."

"Are these differences you talk about racial? Is that what makes us different from each other? Don't you think that a black man might have more in common with a particular white man than say six other black men?"

"Yes, it's possible."

"The point here anyway is not that I understand you, but that you understand yourself."

Oh really, is that so? I'm not going to stop with this one. I say, "If I talk about race, you won't understand."

I wait for him to say something but he doesn't.

I say, "I'm sick of never talking about who I am, who I am has to do with being mixed race. You can't understand it, nobody can. I've seen them all—everyone eventually falls back on their group—the superiority of their own group. Well, what if you don't belong to any club! Can't belong—because you belong to both!"

Do I imagine it or is Ezra really troubled? I see a tight frown pinching his brow. I've turned over a stone in his mind that he never even knew was there—things are crawling out.

There is a long silence in which I can feel Ezra considering various answers. Finally, he says, "I believe that I can help you and that by telling me things which, perhaps, I may not understand, by articulating them, you may realize things yourself."

I keep silent, not in defiance, but from a mental dizziness. The walls of the room are going soft. For a moment, I feel tiny like a figure in a dollhouse, but now my head seems to be ballooning out.

"Last time you were telling me about the boyfriend you had before you met Sam . . . Benjamin?" Ezra's voice reaches towards me. "Isn't he also . . . uh . . . part-Chinese?"

My mind seizes on his question and everything goes steady again. He shifts in his chair then leans forward slightly. "I'd like to know more about your feelings towards him." He brings his hands together and attempts to give me a neutral look.

Ezra is trying, I think, and I go on with my story.

WANNA BE WHITE GIRL

Karla Brundage

I was a white girl once
who dreamed of riding a Harley Davidson
and drinking vodka straight
while leaning over a pool table
tattoo on my ankle
that said property of . . .

I was a white girl
who had white friends
and white boyfriends
who loved me and
drank with me
locked me in closets
told racial jokes and
then apologized

We drank gin and tonic
and roamed the streets
looking for trouble
because it never did seem to come to us.

I was white
yes
I was white
and I wore torn blue jeans and tie dye
I listened to the Rolling Stones

and Lynyrd Skynyrd
I lived the words and knew the pain they held.

When I was white I dreamed of being
Old Homes Day Queen
at the county fair
where music was real
and women wore cowboy boots
I had my Stetson and my
Buck knife

I danced the two step
and played Bingo on Saturday nights

when I was white I loved a man
named Cincinnatuss who drove a Harley
flew colors, and lived in West Virginia
we drank every type of liquor all
mixed up into one
we danced to country music
and fell out the door when it was time to go
when we fought
it was violent
but I loved him like I have never loved

I rode in fast cars listening to the WHO
asking "who are you?"

but I was white
I was
I was in on the secrets
the truths the lies
the only problem was

that people kept mistaking me for being
Hawaiian or Chinese
Palestinian
or Black

So I looked in the mirror and saw
my skin is brown
my hair is brown
my eyes are brown
and I wondered
where did god go wrong
because being a white girl
trapped in a Black body
is no small mistake
and the stress was beginning to take its toll.

you see even though steve miller sang
Brown Eyed Girl
I knew there was more to it than that
because didn't nobody really
seem to want to marry me
and not many people really took
me seriously
and for some reason
I just didn't seem to fit,
older I got—
no matter how much I drank.

So, I killed her
I killed that white girl that I once was
I stopped her life
cut it short with one clean swipe
no more led zeppelin

no more white boyfriends
no more dreams of making my brown eyes blue

But I was a white girl once
you wouldn't know it by looking
that once dreamed of drinking vodka
straight while laying back on a pool table
tattoo on my ankle that said
property of . . .

HAPA HAOLE GIRL

Kathleen Tyau

Annabel is hapa haole—half Chinese, half Irish. It's the Irish, the haole blood, that makes her hapa. Her hair is thick and long, the color of koa wood, dark brown with streaks of red. Her eyelashes curl like waves, and her eyelids fold back into tiny venetian blinds even without the help of Scotch tape. Her skin looks like a vanilla ice cream cone licked smooth. When she dances Tahitian at school, her skirt rides on her hips like a boat in a storm. I watch the boys as they watch her with their eyes like balloons and their mouths wide open catching flies.

"Oh, Annabel, you dance so good," the girls say when she's finished dancing and the boys are still hanging around. But later the girls crouch to see if anybody's listening from the toilet stalls, and then the talk turns stink.

"Did you see her mother? The one with the red hair and the tight skirt."

"That's her mother? Wow, she sure has a fat okole."

"How you think Annabel got the hips to hold up her hula skirt? Not from her father."

"Lucky thing she looks like her mother. You should see her sisters. Real paké, just like their father. No hips, no chi-chis, no eyes."

But Annabel isn't that lucky. She got her mother's looks, but that's all she's going to get. Her mother is her father's mistress, not his wife. Annabel has three half sisters, who look like their parents, both Chinese. Annabel's mother will never be a Pang. She won't get to live in the house at Diamond Head, and she won't inherit the family restaurant in Kaimuki. All she has is Annabel, who I am so jealous of I could scream.

"Am I a love child?" I ask my mother. If I can't be illegitimate, I want to be a love child.

She drops the chicken she's cutting. "Who told you that?"

"Nobody. Did you and daddy have to get married?"

"Of course not," she says.

"Did you ever have a haole boyfriend?"

"What? Mahealani, who told you that?"

"Never mind. I have to go wash my hands."

What's she going to say when I tell her about Tommy?

Tommy is pure haole, the American kind, all mixed up. His father is a naval officer at Pearl Harbor. Tommy's hair is so blond it's almost white in the sun. He stands straight and tall with his chin tucked in. The fur on his arms tickles when he comes near me. He likes to stand real close to people. One time he stood so close to the teacher, he stepped on her toes. She said, "Thomas McMurray, get off my toes!" "Yes, ma'am," he said, and saluted. The kids all laughed, and Tommy turned red like only a haole can get. I don't mind when he stands next to me, because he's tall, not like the local boys, who come up to my ears.

I try to picture what our children would look like. Would they have kinky brown hair and smooth pale arms, or straight blond hair and furry brown skin? I can't really see them in my mind, but I know hapa haole kids come out looking real cute. Maybe they will look like Annabel.

Tommy asks me to go to a dance at the base. Mostly haoles, service kids, will be there, but some of my friends have been invited too. My best friend, Ruthie Ito, for one. She's going with Stew Williams. Tommy catches me by surprise, and I feel guilty, as if he knows about my daydreams. He comes up to me after school and stares at me for a long minute before he speaks. His eyes are like blue marbles I want to win.

"I have to ask my mother." That's all I can say. I want him to smile so I can think of more, but he just nods, clicks his heels like a soldier, and walks away.

"Are you going?" Ruthie asks me.

"Maybe," I say. "I'm so sick of dancing with shrimps."

"Don't blame me," my mother says. "You know your father won't let you go out with a service kid."

"But his father is an officer," I say. "He's almost a general." I want her to say it's because Tommy is haole, so I can fight back. I want her to see how prejudiced they are. Prejudiced. Ignorant. Old-fashioned. But she doesn't argue. She tells me to put the rice on the table and call in the kids.

I run to my room and slam the door, but after I cry, I don't feel so bad. I think about being close to Tommy. I think about the way he smells like warm bread and the way his hair tickles my skin. But I don't want to go out with him that bad. He's just part of a recipe I'm cooking. I want to be hapa haole, like Annabel. I want her hips, her hair, her eyes. I want to be Annabel, but not her mother.

B-LEAGUE PLAYOFF

Holly Yamada

November 1969

K sat frozen on the hood of her father's Chevy, afraid to look at them. She had watched them come reeling out the door and stumble towards her; but then she had to look away. She felt the flattened beer can bounce off her knee. *They were throwing things.* She couldn't look at them. The filthy packed snow ricocheted off the windshield and splattered on her shoulder. "Squaw meat." Squaw *meat?* She couldn't look at them; but still she had seen their faces. *I'll stop wearing my hair in braids.*

Then she thought maybe it was funny. Drunk boys. Stupid boys. She thought about going inside to the dance. Her friend Lilly stood in the doorway, facing inside, knee-dipping to the live sounds of Earl and Earl. Boom chuck. Boom chuck.

Lilly didn't look ready to leave yet and K felt conspicuous just sitting there. She traced her finger around a small chili stain on her white Levis. She tried to think of it as blood in the snow but the stain wasn't red enough. Then she decided that it was rust and her leg was rotting metal. Her body—steel, rusting. She slid off the car and motioned to Lilly still knee-dipping in the doorway.

"Isn't it great," said Lilly. "I mean the whole town comes out for these things, even if they weren't invited to the wedding. Even if they don't like the bride and groom. Isn't this hilarious?"

The wedding dance was everything Lilly promised it would be. Lots of drunk friendly folk, mostly farmers—all full of sloppy piss and vinegar, ready to rabble-rouse the night away, not paying too much mind to the bride and groom who were dancing so slow that it was much more like hugging and leaning, no matter if the song was for foot stomping.

They had driven in a straight flat line across the South Dakota plain, nearly an hour out of Rapid Falls, to Lilly's old hometown of 900 people just for the occasion. Lilly's nephew, who was ten years older than she was, was getting hitched, and Lilly told her it'd be a good time and endless food for all.

"Yeah, so, when do you think we should get going?" K didn't want to sound overly anxious so she nodded her head to the music.

"I wanna get me a dance with a sweet old cowboy first. One more for the road," said Lilly, talking straight out through her nose.

"Yeah, okay. Maybe I'll just sit right out here. I'll be okay," she said, her eyes on the three stupid boys, their voices fading. They were tossing empties at each other now.

Lilly wasn't listening and went inside.

When they got back into town, they decided to shoot the loop a couple of times before going home. They swung by the Spur and saw Quigley's Ford pickup. Quigley and Chester stood up in the back of the truck bed and waved frantically. K pulled into The Spur parking lot and rolled down the window.

"Howdy, China girl."

"Hi Chester, so what's up?" she said, inching off the brake.

"She's not Chinese, Chester," said Lilly. "So you look like official Spur rejects—86ed again?" She shouted this over the top of the idling Chevy, standing from inside the car, her head and torso out the window.

"Nah, we didn't get kicked out," said Chester. "We haven't even tried to go in yet."

K fingered her braids and stopped at a stray hair, tucking it, unsuccessfully, into the proper row. Lilly would want to stay. Another night in The Spur parking lot. Maybe getting kicked out, maybe not. K looked hard at her friend and wished she could be more like her. They spent these countless nights sitting around in Quigley's truck, or getting 86ed from the only three-two beer bar in town, or driving endlessly around Oglala Avenue and up and down Highway 2, but Lilly made it seem as though they were on an adventure or a mission. She liked to shake up the regular Spur patrons—Spurheads she called them—mostly truckers, underage foosball fiends, and the other tenacious minors who could stand for hours in the icy South Dakota air, hopping form car to truck to car, and finally feeling the cold, trying again to go inside The Spur; sometimes victorious, sometimes not. Lilly always said they got kicked out for being so outrageous, never mind that none of them would be the legal 18-year-old drinking age for at least a year.

Nobody would miss the Chevy. Her father was in Minneapolis for the weekend and her mother knocked out early these days, but she used her midnight car curfew as an excuse to go home.

"So ditch the car at your house; Quigley and Chester can follow you. Besides, this might be the night we get the Quig to talk." Lilly winked, perfectly scrunching half her face, so that with each side of her profile she looked like two different people.

"God, Lilly."

Going back to The Spur in Quigley's truck suddenly seemed like a good idea. She could talk to Lilly alone on the way to her house. Tell her that they threw things at her. Tell her that she didn't care because they were stupid and drunk, and besides, it was funny how stupid they were.

"Those boys..." K said, taking the long way home.

"What, Quig and Chet?"

"No, at the dance. The ones outside. There were three of them."

"Burl and Tommy. Burl's my cousin's stepbrother." Why was everyone somehow related in that town? The life of her own small family never touched, even in passing, some second cousin, some nephew, some cousin's stepbrother. She wondered if Lilly was as unattached to her boundless family members as she appeared.

"Yeah so, he hates Indians, I guess."

"I wouldn't worry about it. He hates everybody."

"But it was weird. They thought I was Indian. I mean, I couldn't say 'no I'm not' because I'd be like saying it's a bad thing to be or something. Anyway, I felt proud. Isn't that dumb? And I felt good because they were so stupid."

Lilly thought it was great. She was eager to take credit for masterminding this serendipitous deception. But K wasn't sure if this was what she wanted to hear from her. She took precarious comfort in Lilly's approval. Lilly assured her that deception was a most powerful skill, and besides, wasn't it such fun? Perhaps it was. Yes, she would try to think of it like that. Fun. Trickery. So, she wouldn't tell Lilly about the fear. Not that she thought they would actually hurt her, but the paralysis from *not knowing how to think of this* filled her with a numbing sense of suspended panic. Still, this was not the first time. But they had never thrown things.

When she pulled in the driveway she was pleased to see only the porch light on. Her mother would be sleeping and it made sneaking out the back door easier.

The cold came crashing in. "Why can't you just roll down the window when you gotta spit, Chester?" K knew why, but when Chester opened the door she felt herself being sucked out, bulleting forever across the South Dakota plain (so beautiful in its uncompromising stinginess, brutal in its monotony) ripping up the skies and never banging into hills or trees or buildings; and at sunset folks would sit on their porches and point to the streaks in the sky. And on Rosebud they would say she was Never One of Us and they'd call her Her Too Many Wings. And one day there would be a postage stamp and a commemorative coin.

"I don't wanna dribble on Quigley's door."

"He's polite. Aren't you, Chester?" Lilly patted his knee.

It would not be until the last night of the 1970 B league basketball playoffs that she would indeed be sucked out of Quigley's pickup and find she had too few wings and land on the gravelly side of the road in her own vomit, the nervous retch stock-piled in her stomach—a delayed reaction to a playoff only she and two others would witness.

And Quigley, his Ford being a benevolent appendage, always had a sixth sense about when to slow down so his passengers might have a windless moment to light cigarettes and, on special occasions, cherry cigars; and he had a feel for windows and doors and spitting and throwing up, so he would have already slowed to first when she opened the door to let it out and went out with it; and he would have already stopped and backed up by the time she started to cry.

March 1970

Hick traffic all night long. The Bs were in town for the big event of the season. Such a welcome invasion that Quigley had a new shirt and everyone helped clean the Ford.

It was the one time out of the year the town of Rapid Falls could feel smugly worldly, for with the flood of small towners, this isolated place of fifty-some thousand seemed a metropolitan playground.

K ironed her newly bleached bell bottoms then sat softly next to her father on the lumpy sofa. She squinted, blurring his silent profile, then focused on the face that appeared on the black and white Motorola. This face, so angry. The grumbling of Pine Ridge. He wears a headband and he is facing the unseen reporter; the words, so angry. This face and the one next to her— he could Never Be One of Them. Her father tucked a pillow under his head. And then the commercial about assimilating . . . what? Nutrients to build strong bodies 12 ways. Assimilating. Wondrous bread.

Her father, looking collegiate in his baggy cords and letter sweater with no letters, was starting to snore, a familiar routine in front of the TV during the news. Her mother came in from the hallway and gently pinched his nose till he sputtered some and opened his eyes. "He stops breathing sometimes," she said. "This is very dangerous."

"I need a ride to Quigley's, Mom. Everybody's meeting there before the game."

It was decided her father would drop her off at Quigley's. Her mother pinched his nose once more for he had loudly stopped breathing again.

There was a yellow Volkswagen and the face inside made her heart tighten. Was that the one? Well of course he would be in town: wasn't everybody? "Dad, I'm not sure this is the way we should take to Quigley's." She risked a look in the rearview mirror. *It was turning around. It was following her.*

Her father said nothing and gave her an unreadable glance, but she knew it meant he knew where he was going and how he was going to get there. She wanted to turn around. The back of her head was burning. She took off her stocking cap and her scalp felt squirmy.

They were passing her father now. She tried to look and not be seen at the same time. Wadding her cap in her fist, she slid down and leaned forward, trying to focus through the smeary driver's side window. So now *they* were following the yellow Volkswagen, but soon it sped up, leaving them behind, and leaving her wondering how she could be so moronic.

But there it was, everywhere, all night. One more time before they reached Quigley's. In the parking lot at the game. One lane over when they were all packed in the pickup driving down Oglala Avenue. At The Spur. And even, as she came around the silo and to the west side of the tool shed, there it was. Still, she couldn't be sure about the face.

She was glad she had already peed before she saw it sitting there, abandoned—temporarily, she guessed, for the passenger door was open and tinny car-radio music hit the dead air. But by then it almost annoyed her, for she had finally peed and could finally relax and allow the waves of fatigue to wash over her. But now she felt the tightening in her heart. Still she thought, well, why not? Let's get this over with. Scalp me.

Well, it was too late to be sorry she hadn't gone right home after the game. But why didn't she just stay closer to the truck with the others? Always wandering off to pee. Well, it was too late. Come out then. Show me his face.

The old Beckner place still smelled like a farm even though the main house had burned down the summer before. The fire had taken everything except the foundation, the hand-crank pump, the silo, and the tool shed. The smell. So strong, even in the snow. How is it that the cow chips survived? She picked up one in her mitten and skipped it. Well come on then. Where is your face?

The fatigue again. How long did they drive up and down and around Oglala Avenue and finally in a straight flat line down Highway 2, listening to Quigley's broken 8-track Buffalo

Springfield tape? And in the middle of "Broken Arrow," when it starts to warble, and leaks from the other tracks start seeping through, Chester pulls out the tape and Lilly keeps singing in her best nasal-twang-quasi-falsetto, Neil Young voice, and nobody seems to notice the difference because she sure can sound a lot like him. These nights always seemed to culminate in a disjunction at the Beckner's place: everyone separating from the captive Ford, checking out the unmarred snow and then marring it, and then coming back together to lounge around the pickup before getting back inside for the tight squeeze home.

The snow crunches behind her. She looks not over her shoulder but down at the boots and then the face. Yes, it is him. The voice behind him saying, "Damn, Burl, I'm freezing my ass off. Let's get on home." This other, from behind, notices her now. "Lord, what's some girl doing out here? You must be freezing." Not an unkind voice.

Burl is slow and says, "Well, you need a ride somewhere or something?"

She is stunned at that moment. Maybe her mouth opens a little. There is no fatigue: her thinking only he *doesn't even remember.* Well why should he? It was a small and careless thing. Still she cannot speak.

"Shit, what's wrong with you, Pocahontas? Hey, maybe you're Chink or Cong or something? No speakee English?" Burl is moving toward her now and she is inching closer to what remains of the corral fence, three leaning posts, the wood shredded and sagging in the middle.

"Come on Burl, leave her alone." The kind voice.

"Is that it? You're Cong or something? Hey, maybe you know kung fu and you could chop me in two, huh?"

"Burl. Let's travel, come on." But the kind voice is in the car now.

"Yeah maybe I could."

This stops him. He studies her. Her face gives him nothing; she is as dead and cold as the air between them.

"Yeah, well maybe you could." He takes a swipe at her head and misses but her cap falls off when she jerks back.

She is trying to think of a movie or perhaps a TV show where they fight by leaping in the air and kicking, and where they use their hands, not wadded up in a fist but straight and flat with bare edges. But she can only think of fist fights and shootouts at the O.K. Corral. Well it was true, she had only seen one, maybe two scenes, where their straight flat hands were weapons. But Burl's sudden lunge makes her remember and invent something that stupefies them both, and sends him in retreat to the yellow Volkswagen.

She slams the edge of her mittened hand in a straight flat line into the decrepit fence beside her, splitting the top frayed rail, which, from the weight of the splinters and powdery sawdust, disintegrates the feeble second rung too. She is startled to hear the wordless sound that comes out of her; a sound meaning only that a heartfelt war whoop could never be a bluff.

GREEN TEA GIRL IN ORANGE PEKOE COUNTRY

Velina Hasu Houston

The water is lucid liquid humidity
pouring over fine green tea leaves
bathing, steeping in the porcelain as
one-year-old eyes observe the ritual.
There is okonomiyaki on the table,
a peeled peach and steamed rice,
o-tsukemono and immigrant dreams.
The ivory white Japanese mother
stares across these dreams in awe
at her cinnamon Amerasian child.

Ready for the cup, ready for the soul,
green tea as discipline for culture.
Into the teaspoon preventive medicine,
into the maiden child's mouth.
Down deep into the gut where life begins.
And so she lives, Japanese, deeply,
her shoes at the door, her soul at bay,
her summer kimono trailing the parquet,
pink chopsticks next to unused forks.

The house serene as Shikoku before war
is a sanctuary of tea and time,
the stronghold for a rage to live
that shall mark the Amerasian life.
She grows with every sip of gyokuro,

Gaman shite kudasai, gaman shite kudasai.
Yes, she shall persevere but counsel us
how fares Oriental grace in an Occidental world.

Outside the hold there is no green tea.
The peaches, small, easily fester.
Shoes track streets like cleaners
dragging rot back into American homes.
The tea is black and bitter, sweet
only with the complement of sugar.
It stains the teeth and hands.
The cups reek orange pekoe tea.
What will become of me, what of me.

The orange pekoe country blares outside.
Out of place, bittersweet, the Amerasian dares.
Green tea girl in a land of milk and honey,
tea in bags without fine leaves to read.
She learns to drink the blacker brew
with nothing to sweeten the bitter truth.
She learns a different gaman to survive
in a land where the soul is in the fist.

But is it her land; they call it their land.
One moment she is a Jap without a home,
another moment a nigger, homeless yet.
The rage to live flows in her like a river
and life becomes a time and a politic
and land is only earthly confusion.
But the cup of green tea awaits her still
and she sips, caressing the cup,
and it sinks deeply into the gut,
feeding the fortitude, gaman, gaman.

DOWNTOWN
HONO., T.H.
Marie Murphy Hara

There was a man who worked downtown who could have made it different for us. I saw him twice, once from far away, once close up. I wished with all my heart that he was really my father. And I was scared of him. He was not the kind of haole, a big old white guy, that you could talk to.

Of course I would see him this time. Whenever I went downtown, for whatever the reason, I would follow a route past several tall buildings. Two had columns. One was old brick, important for the government, you could tell.

Is this the right building? Which window would be his office? Where does he stay when he goes outside?

I remember where as a child I had seen him. The Tax Office. He strolled through the lobby wearing a gray jacket over a dull business-like aloha shirt. Greying hair. My mother was frozen. Waiting.

So hard to figure when the adult tells a secret. Maybe a lie, too.

She stood close to the blind candy vendor as if she were already in a conversation. I knew something was wrong but not what to look for. I hoped she wouldn't take one foot out of her slipper and rest it on the other one. Nothing happened, only her face.

Did they look at each other? Didn't I have to wait and wait? Where did she disappear after she bought me the crack seed?

So long ago and yet the feeling of that waiting, of that nothing happening until they were finished, that still, clear in remembering.

I remember just before I went to the new school, during the summer, when I had seen him. Downtown, at lunchtime. In the middle of all the people in the world in that crowded dining space. He was eating something at the old Kress coffee shop. He did not see me peeping. Would he have even known who I was? There must have been at least another time, way back, which I forgot to make sure to underline. No words spoken.

In those days our recreation was the Saturday morning trip downtown. We stood patiently at the bus stop. Mama and I caught the number four, Nuʻuanu Puʻunui bus which took us directly to Fort Street where we would all be let off into a moving crowd. The packed bus held familiar faces, regulars who knew us, "Huu-iii, how you nowadays? Long time no see, yeah?" Sometimes the driver let her in free. Sometimes he laughed and said, "Eh, *manuwahi*," no charge, pointing at me with a wink. She didn't like it, though.

In the long back seat, the nursing mothers' babies' bright dark eyes peeked out from under clothing. Some heads stayed like lumps under blankets, hidden. If Mama had to work that morning, I knew how to get there by myself. First I had to go to the big library to kill time and then I had to meet her downtown exactly at noon when she would get off duty.

Always looking forward to the big time bustle of Fort Street, the stores, the red candy popcorn I knew I would buy, Mama's girl friends spotting us and giving me dimes or gum, the Lil' Lulu comic book I would beg for, the regular skinny hot dog at the counter or the extra special hamburger Patti-Melt with the bright yellow peach half on the side to match the cheese that we sat down on steel stools to consume in order to celebrate a special event, the bundles of food for later and the little treats—some soap or tooth powder or paper napkins—to take home, I waited through long weekdays for that time out. Saturday.

If she had extra money, she said, "Okay, we feeling flush," and we could take in a late matinee at the King Theater, worth getting excited over. The shopping trip meant we would add a new thing or two to the plainness of the wooden frame rooms we lived in, something nice for the eye to see, something to hold for a while, something shiny, bought downtown.

Although it fed my eyes each Saturday, the old Fort Street felt dustier, more like the small town's main drag that it was. Still, crowds travelled up and down the two-lane street in vehicles or by foot. It felt like the center of things. You wouldn't call it either a fancy or a depressed shopping area. People clustered everywhere anyway, because it was a heart of activity. Lines of cars and buses pulled in or out all at once, while the gaudy storefronts advertised all kinds of goods in bright blue, red or orange lettering on painted paper window signs.

At Christmastime the store owners went all out with fancy displays. Liberty House worked hard to outdo its big rival, McInerny's, with moveable dolls and mechanical lights. Families turned out at night to walk the strip of storefronts and have ice cream afterwards. We watched them go. They didn't have to worry about parking their cars or passing the crack addicts in pee filled corners. But it was the ordinary Saturday which was a good enough lure, the magnet to go downtown, for Mama and me.

The signs that said Seconds, Remnants, Closeouts, Bargain Bin, Lay-A-Way, Reduced, Going Out of Business, Buy-One-Get-One-Free, Super Buy, Save Now, Plenty Cheap, called my mother's attention fastest. We would storm in past the doorway to see for ouselves if anything was "good kine, fo' real." Mama showed me how she watched her money, made me witness as she firmly said to the slickest, pretend friendly saleswoman, "Nah, 'as too deah." Then she turned her back and ooshed me out in front of her.

Mama pointed out the expensive stores, "Ova dea, get bettah kine," but we went where the sign said "Worth $ More, Buy Today." Mama showed me her empty hand, ready for holding cash. "Bumbye, no mo' rent money for da landlord." I came to think of Kress Store as the place we could finally buy stuff after all the looking-for exercise. After all, we were doing our shopping, which was hard work, like everything else we did together. It was like speaking good English which was my job. She listened. I had to practice. So it made sense and maybe something good would come of it.

Kress's had everything I ever wanted. All of it. It was arranged in dazzling rows, on aisles, in piles, by scattered but proficient floor ladies, each hung at her neck with a ribbon dangling a key to the nearest cash register. Having more of everything, which was cheaper and more interesting in displays where you could handle anything you wanted, than anywhere else, Kress's bustled with goods that everybody needed, dock strike on or dock strike over.

I desired the *Evening in Paris* perfume in a dark blue bottle or the cologne in a green circle flask with a tiny cap of red for its cover, if I couldn't have the big *Paris*. Or the tiny handled glass jiggers of bubble bath powder, the flacon of lavender bubbling bath oil that looked like a Genie's bottle that I rushed to touch lightly each time with a wish,

-if I had two extra cents, I could get a Japanese stick candy in a swirl of red, green and yellow on a white ball of glistening, no-distinct flavor, unwrapped spun sugar-

rows of cards with glitter on fading colors, silken corsages of deep purple violets, shocking pink roses, flat white gardenias, 10 toilet paper rolls for the price of eight, 12 unwrapped soaps in a plastic sleeve, cunning paper and metal office supplies of every kind, bright jewelry in that new plastic, gold metal pendants and bracelets that were engravable yet turned green,

-our neighbor, the bosomy Portuguese lady in her white uniform who kept a bowl of sweet gardenias on top of the decorated pastries counter, held out a snowflake cookie, but I headed away, not hearing, her sugary intimacy, "Huu-iii, Sweetie! No make high maka muck, you!"-

the very latest slippery aluminum trucks and planes, wind-up animals, sleek metallic cars, glossy plastic cups, games and games, sunglasses in every shape and shade of pastel plastic, stacked piles of cans of Spam, Vienna Sausage and Libby's Corned Beef that were heaped into islands taller than people walking past,

-wishing that the guys who hung around and played games with girls would call out to me,

"Hey goodlooking, ova hea! Looka-me. Ho, no look den, shark bait!" So I could sidestep them and act like I was ignoring it-

barrettes, hairpins, hairnets for when you would go to work at the pineapple cannery or for when your mother saw a picture of Elizabeth Taylor in the Sunday paper and said,

-"I gon' make one chig-non from yo' ponytail. Eh, hold still. Bumbye I gon' pull mo' tight. And yo' eyes gonna come iriko," even if you wouldn't become a movie star unless you could be who you wanted to be, which was Audrey Hepburn-

ribbons in profusion, sheet music, instruments, musical gadgets, curios of ceramic or wood studded with shells that spelled Hawai'i but were Made in Japan which made them cheap, lace hankies or doilies or runners that were impressive in size or all the stamped pillowcases and tablecloths and bibs you could ever want to choose from, ball-point colored paint pens so that you wouldn't have to embroider all those blue stamped goods, black velvet paintings which were too expensive, some being Jesus pictures,

-and we needed a photograph of Mama and me which meant wishing for a camera but I also wanted a record player, then a regular house, then a car that we could stand in front of, and then, what? She always said, "Jes take me as I am, you undastand?"-

a gorgeous assortment of flocked holiday items for whatever the next holiday would be, including Columbus Day, yarns and crochet threads amongst the heaps of yardage, an alluring stamp and coin corner where the old three-cent purple

King Kamehameha issue, selling for 60 cents, held out his arm from years long gone to catch my eye, though not my purse,

-emergency money: three dimes knotted in the corner of one of her hankies, the one I liked to smell, embroidered by the girl in the TB ward with four four-leaf clovers which reversed the bad luck of four, but you could never find even one in real life-

endless rows of lace displayed in a romantic wall of fine details above piles of remnants consistently surrounded by old ladies who fingered pieces of velvet, leopard-patterned corduroy and bright splashes of color with their discriminating touch

-I saw the picture again and again: how it was when Mama screamed, "Jiii-shin!" and we could hear the walls groan and things rattling as we ran away from the house shaking in the earthquake, glad to be out, alive-

while the key maker who also stood guard over the hardware section watched the array of locks and metal objects, each in its tiny glass compartment, with secretive, keen eyes.

I always avoided that stuff. Heading back to the area past the paper flowers, socks of every description and pom pom attachments, I went for my favorite rhinestone everything counter.

Shoulder bag over my shoulder, I tossed the strap over my head, too, just in case someone should try to take it away. I felt inside to be sure the small *lauhala* coin purse was secure within the zippered pocket. Pigtails on either side of my chubby cheeks, *chawan* cut bangs already in my eyes, my face was *Kokeshi* doll smooth as I eyed all the endless products. I wore a *Paké* shirt with frogs not buttons and bright pedal pushers. Mine were Poi Pounders, Da Bes' Kine, that we bought full price. I moved forward through the throng of thrifty toilet paper buyers prepared to stockpile for the sure to be coming dock strike.

Saturday morning early as I fingered sparkly rings for size, a retarded boy squirmed around me and pinched my *okole* hard. I was shocked by this guy, a kid my age.

"The nerve!" When I turned on him, he grinned with pleasure and pretended he would do it again, motioning a pinch with his sausage fingers.

His face was wide open and excited by my response. He had come right up behind me with no sound. His tongue waggled in his mouth while he made a *ckckck* sound. But his eyes were surprised at my fury.

I hated him, how dare he, with his mouth gaping, his over-eagerness, touch me. Any part. I got ready to shove him down.

A clerk looked over us from her counter. Cued in by the sudden motions of us squared off face to face, she gave him a fierce stink eye and warning.

"Eh, haole boy, you like I call yo' Papa, ah?"

He tried to get closer to hide behind me as I stepped aside. He wanted to touch me again.

I waited. He began to look nervous and about to cry.

Springing forward at him, I pointed a finger at his baby face and said what I had heard my mother say, "I'm calling the cops on you!"

He held his hands up like the movies. "Not me. Not me!"

He walked in a backwards cringe away from the rhinestones, down the escalator, away from the lady saying, "Beat it! Mongolian idiot." She muttered that he was the son of a famous senator from the mainland who had family in Honolulu.

"'As the one they cannot hide. Good fo' nothing. Scare everybody, him."

Outside in the sunlight reading my comic, I felt sad for him and angry at myself, my entire body still hot at his invasion. What did he know, ran through my mind. All haoles were alike, I knew that.

Why did he pick on me? Do I look like him? But he's got his dad.

I wanted to go back to my business, the bright, gaudily-lit store with all its goods heaped in its enormous cavern of space filling upwards and continuing downwards and snaking underground into another world. But I couldn't go on the escalator if he was down there.

Forget him.

Once satiated by the sparkling tiaras, earrings, cigarette holders and sophisticated necklaces that I knew I would surely own some day later on, I took a quick survey of the bra counter to see what else the future might have in store for me, shook off the sight of zipper-locked girdles, and found my place in the line which led first to the shave ice and then the popcorn machine, both of which offered only one choice: the deep red flavor.

On special Saturdays on the way out I had both reds, capped off with a sweet-flavored cone sushi from the snack bar, a decision I hid from Mama, because one, she didn't approve of over-sugared rice and two, each one sold for 15 cents there instead of two for a quarter, what they cost at the saimin stand near us, where Kay-san, who was the cook and the waitress, took care of us when we went to dine out.

With the sound of the bright Kress music following me as I made my way through the jing- jing-jing of the cash registers, I stopped cold at the sight of a man's back.

He was a customer eating lunch, but I knew I had recognized the guy: sure enough, when he turned. My father, eating alone at one of the dining tables in the crowded lunchroom. No one else mattered. When I realized who he was, my body registered the knowledge first, as Mama's would have. It was a cautious feeling, a stepping on eyeballs queasiness—who's watching me peeping—a fervent hope that I could learn something about him, this one that held what kind of secret? I had to see for myself. He had been a storybook figure for me for so long. Maybe it was a dream I made out of wanting it.

So who did he think he was, anyway?

Would he look at me and recognize his daughter? Would he rush over to talk, to urge me to sit down and eat with him, to ask me questions, to hug me and wish me good luck, to give me and Mama the money we needed?

No.

I just watched him eat. I could taste the yellowness of the mustard, but how? I wasn't hungry. I licked my lip. He up and left, looking at his watch. I saw his empty plate and after a while I walked in the direction he took. But in a few minutes of following, heat? no, shame grew on my burning face. I hurried the opposite way to catch my bus.

When I wandered through the streets, I liked best seeing all kinds of people, their faces in motion with their unspoken thoughts, rushing along to the fancier department stores or the Chinatown markets. I liked it when Mama said she would be late. Then I could explore downtown Honolulu, the center of commerce, when it was still the Territory of Hawai'i, and things were different then.

My favorite shops were the small florists where they regularly changed the drama display for holidays and seasons, even for the Community Chest: "Make Someone Happy" Heart with a graph of how much money they raised. Even the warm and delicate aromas coming from the Young Hotel's bakery and the gush and tinkle of piano music from Thayer's couldn't beat the sight of women oohing and aahing over the latest fashions.

There was a New York Dress Shoppe whose big competitor was Goodwear Fashions. Every dancing dream of lace as well as seriously low-cut numbers and cheap but up-to-the-minute outfits could be found here. I climbed the wooden stairs to the top floor of the Ritz Department Store which was truly a warehouse of garments. Bridal gowns, dresses of every color and shape and size with miles of yardage in each skirt met my focused attention. I wanted to go to a *soirée,* whatever that was, because the sign "For your next *soirée*" spoke to me. Sequins, rhinestones, beads, lace, feathers, made texture upon detail for the fanciness I craved. Whole sets of rainbow-colored wedding attire got capped off by fancy cocktail party hats and bridal crowns with overflowing veils, like whipped cream on shimmering jello.

I sometimes took two helpings and went from the Ritz to Margo's which was a boutique for custom-made gowns. You could tell quality waited there to be bought as Mama pointed out when we passed it from our bus window. Costly gowns in tulle, net, satin, taffeta and vari-colored silks told me there was nothing I could possibly buy with my dollar and a half in those racks, but the allure of all the shining stuff, brightly lit like a jewelry store window kept me coming back to look.

Venturing out of safety into ritual visits at Liberty House, I had to avoid the stern Portuguese saleswomen who ran the departments and wore stiffly starched linen outfits in pastels which hid their ferocious style. I got nervous when one pointedly asked me, "Where's your mother? Where's your father?" in proper English. That one also whispered, "Eh, you no' fooling nobody. Beat it." But she knew I ignored them when I was nosing around.

By the time I headed up to the Fair Department Store for a different kind of shopping, I felt heavy with all the weight of the latest fashion in city style. But I held on to my last two quarters against the day when I might be shopping with a five-dollar bill.

I got used to traveling alone. I was quick to take a fast look. I could disappear before someone important asked me, "Can I help you?" with cold eyes, meaning "Get lost. Outa here, you don't belong." But not before I saw for myself how money changed hands quickly when people got excited by the stuff they decided they wanted.

I watched haole women with hats and gloves on, how they were called "Miss Abby" and "Mrs. Hightower," while the "Yes, Ma'am," and "No, Ma'am," came out loud enough so every person around could hear the respect. So my appetite grew, and the choices for what I might want grew in order that I could think something might possibly be within my reach, that could be justified by paying for it someday, maybe later.

The music was "How Much is that Doggy in the Window?" which they played a lot at Kress's. Changing Doggy to Daddy or humming along, the words *Had A Dad, had a dad, had-dadad* amused me, but not in a funny way.

I had known, of course, one of these times I would see him downtown. Sure enough, he had appeared again for me, because I had wished it so. At the dining room, watching him eat, I felt nervous because what I thought would happen had. I questioned myself.

He's really the same guy?

He had ordered a ham sandwich on white bread with a pinky look to the thin slices of meat. After he bit in, the corner of his mouth was left with a smear of yellow mustard. A folded newspaper lay on the table next to his plate. Seeming not to be really hungry, he ate the pickle and the olive and the potato chips anyway. He ate slowly and wiped his mouth carefully. He read and ate mostly. He smoothed his tie down. He took pains not to get his white sleeves dirty.

Yes, he's the one.

I clutched the tubular metal railing that separated the dining area from the section for sewing materials where I stood off to the right back of him. I did not want to tremble. I did not want to feel all the things around me start shaking before I could move. Nothing messy, nothing falling, nothing breaking. No earthquake, not if I could help it.

I kept my eyes down so that he would not feel me staring. I kept my body locked against the side of a partition which held rows of sewing items, hung on efficient little hooks. If anyone had seen me standing, I would be taken for a customer intent on checking out sewing machine accessories. I prayed I would not be seen by anyone I knew. I wondered if he alone could see me, if he would only look up. A second.

I watched him drink from a cup of coffee, slowly, methodically. He stirred it just so. He used sugar and cream. He looked like any old haole, how they all look pretty much the same. Sort of baldy. He was losing his hair and his pinkish face stretched up and backwards giving him a bigger surface for his mouth and nose and eyes than most people because of the bigness of his face.

Or-di-nary.

My assessment was calm. Nothing about him stood out. I didn't think he and I looked alike. I would look in the mirror later to be sure.

He did not smile at the Filipino waiter who poured more coffee for him. The waiter and he did not look at each other at all.

He looked so clean in his whiteness. The top of his head gleamed from the overhead lighting. He looked like a straight shooter, a man who never broke laws or got drunk. He looked like nobody I knew.

Then he up and left, grabbing his jacket as if he might have forgotten it otherwise. On a hot day. All that was left was the empty plate which he left behind on the little table with its white cloth.

Did he leave a tip?

From my angle I had a hard time seeing, but I didn't think so at first. I followed for a bit when he left. I was back on the busy streets. I had all the time in the world to do whatever I wanted. I had my childhood. I walked around humming.

Away from the Fort Street center, I found myself in Iida's which was really a warehouse where the immense clutter of fine goods called to me. Everything Japanese was there, row after row of ceramic, glass, metal, stone, wood and the new kind of plastic tools stretched out into the dark raftered storeroom with its bare, hanging bulbs. Fastened by hooks from the cross-beamed ceiling, banners and other calligraphy, decorative art with energetic black ink characters, dangled into view. Clumps of larger standing things, such as stone lanterns, took up dusty corners. The mess was uncontainable. Here I thought a lot about the condition of being Japanese.

Take rice for example. Japanese people like sticky rice. They stick together like the rice, too.

All kinds of goods, from rice pots and bowls and measures, colanders, serving utensils, to storage bins and cleaners were devoted to the way in which you were supposed to make rice perfect. Then came the sushi makers and molds, plus decorative vegetable cutters and special knives. It took a lot of work just to get rice ready to eat.

If I moved away from the things for rice, I entered a world of garden tools in a bigger jumble where things felt Japanese, even smelling slightly of incense, maybe mosquito punk. I followed my way into the maze.

The old Japanese man who watched me sometimes from the side of a wall hung around there. He had no expression but the way he casually appeared and left felt okay to me. All the things piled so carefully spoke of a way to do activities correctly. Objects, pieces of crockery, a certain bamboo broom, a kind of hand or foot gear or head covering, a decoration for seasons I never knew and inventions for small things like cleaning ears or sizing rocks to line your dry stream bed made me see more possibilities that would bring up questions again.

Colors here were subdued and then neon shockers. The new thick kind of plastic showed up in patches of bright pink rice bowls and throwaway vases in glowing muddy yellow for grave flowers. They had plastic flowers, too, but those looked different.

They looked Japanesey and somehow spare, unless they were cherry blossoms which bunched up like magic.

The nice lady, the one who was old but noticed people with a short nod of her head said, "O-hio gozaemasu," to me, and I was always surprised. I nodded back. She must have belonged to the old man who watched.

I left slowly, because I had my eye on a glass case where tiny metal frogs were stored—*kaeru*, to come back, was the message. I reviewed the frog gathering and spotted the one-legged bronze crane when I said goodbye to the forest of miniatures there.

At the Fair Department Store next door, the clientele was mostly Japanese women as far as I could see. It was the equivalent of lively Yat Loy at the other end of town. The Fair boasted whole floors of bargain price clothing and yard goods and a new section of modern style *mu'u mu'u* made in the new factories. A loudspeaker system periodically advertised specials. "Two for the Price of One: On Sale, Today Only!" A squawky voice. Female and nervous. The *ton-ton-ton of* jumbly quick xylophone notes ended with a slide, then a flourish.

On the main floor women gathered around an island of cloth heaped high to sort and toss or clutch tightly to save. The frenzy came on when two of them reached for the same garment at once. The loudspeaker voice punctuated the heat of the battle, "Red Hot, Buy Now, Pay for One and Get Two, Cannot Beat, Go for Broke!" Out of sight, on the fringe of the action, even though I wanted to watch, I kept my guard up.

The Fair was where they talked about me. Aloud or in whispers.

The nisei and Japanese national salesladies didn't like it when I bought nothing. They sneered when I said, "Just looking," in answer to their stilted high-pitched, "May I helpu you find something?" Pretending to ignore me, they just talked louder in Japanese, then English so I would get it. "Laabu keedu," they intoned, talking about *"abura-mushi"* cockroach women who pop out babies and repeating their hiss of "Shame-shame, yes, shamu, shame, *hai!*"

My face grew hot. Curious, stolid, used to it, I stood still. Quiet. And I listened cautiously, moved hangers on the rack of blouses in front of me, waiting until they seemed to finish. I looked up in their direction trying to sense the moment they did something else so I could escape their vision.

One, wearing a fake plumeria in her hair, awkward in her over-large *mu'u mu'u*, flashed angry eyes at me, then turned her back. She had been waiting, daring me to look at her directly. The other moved away to greet a customer. I stood frozen at the rack of clothes and pushed hangers away. Eventually, I walked out.

When I felt something damp on my chest, I realized hot tears had fallen to wet the front of my blouse. But I didn't remember crying. When I cried, I bawled, so I must not have cried. Soberly I thought about how all along people must have been discussing me and Mama like that. It was clear then that was how it was.

No wonder O-Baban lied about it.

I felt the bead of anger in my throat and swallowed what became resignation as I walked away.

I did not want to see this man I thought was my father. I did not especially want to watch him eat.

But it was I who stood there and tasted the ham in his mouth, the white bread that had been spread with bright mustard. I noticed the way he held his cup with one hand and the newspaper with the other. He would not see me. He knew what he was doing. He would not hear me. He had it all down, a confident man.

That was when I realized I was frozen. All the things to notice became more important than anything else. It happened to me sometimes in school. I was stopped in the middle of everything, because it was so hard to keep concentrating on what was going on while my body disconnected and blended into what was around me. Though people were aware that I stood there, there was something so quiet inside of me that they walked right past and did whatever they had been doing.

Lost in thought wasn't the exact way to describe the frozen feeling, no, it was more like growing into the things around me, a protective coloring. I chose not to show up then. To myself I thought just that I was stuck. Again. I became part of the collected stacks of material in bolts beside me, part of the jungle of details of stuff, all colors, all textures, piled up for sale. Nothing shaky, everything in place. Safer for me then.

Staying there, watching, my eyes did not cause him to turn or feel that someone was staring at him.

Got it. Understood. Wa-katta.

No reason for him to see me.

I was stuck for a few breaths after he absently left a quarter for the tip. He wore a tan jacket with a navy blue striped tie although the day was muggy. In finally getting back into motion, I produced no more evidence of my having been there than in my leaving. I took no risk, made no noise, no jerky motion. No emotion leaked out. I left nothing.

From a distance I trailed him very slowly down the street, until he disappeared. I knew he was returning to his familiar building, that the elevator would swallow him, and I would not see his physical presence for a long time, if ever again. I noted his quick evaporation from the street, a fast left turn and gone.

Of course it was meant for me to see him again that time at Kress's and through the years I did, once or maybe twice, again.

I remember when I went to visit him and he refused to talk to me.

I remember much later clearer. That was when I wished him dead and made plans to sew a skintight red party dress to wear to his funeral.

Of course it's not at all like before. Downtown is like all downtowns, nothing special, just solid business areas, some grim and aging, with a few beautification projects to ensure pedestrian traffic. I used to get hungry to walk through the old places, but I got over it. I could do without the malls and the endlessly uniform landscaping, without all the matching planter boxes that are meant to discourage the old and the poor from sitting around like a messy row of mynah birds. We don't like to see that kind of stuff where it's supposed to be a real city, as in Honolulu, Paradise of the Pacific.

Of course it was different the way it turned out. Like a wind bringing big changes in the weather after it, like the way a downtown changes so that certain things remain just enough like before to fool you, while so many important details disappear, that's how it felt for me.

I could recognize him if I had to. I knew full well what he looked like once. I doubt that he could ever say that about me. He did not want to see me or remember the past as it once was. So we do not ever meet or share the same space and time now.

What is strange to me is that there is no Kress Store any more. They tore it down, dug a giant hole into the ground, thought they erased all the shadows and echoes of people once held in motion there on Fort Street. They lifted off the seediness, threw away the gritty surface and left a hole showing layers of the missing business, the multiple strata like a canyon of memory. They said they beautified it by calling it Territorial Post Modern. This beginning to build something totally different over all that was once downtown Honolulu so that the last remnants of the 1950s colors and signs, shapes and place marks would soon be forever gone turned out an interesting detail. Another lie. Fillers for their new map.

But none of it can change anything now.

STITCHES

Debra Kang Dean

What can I say? I've even forgotten how
to busy my hands with scraps of needle-
work, dumb hands unwilling to commit to
what the heart won't. Instead, I sit idle
staring out windows. Nothing fits the contours
of the landscape I was born to—absence
of mountains, dense green, and salt air that smothers
like family, like the waters I breathed penned
in my mother's womb. Hard to say when I
chose this: nothing the hand does
can stitch time back to that place where mind and eye
might mend the world to wholeness. Always
two worlds. What pattern governs this surface
inscrutable as the ocean, my mother's face?

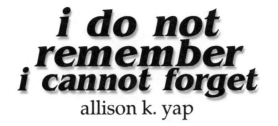

i do not remember i cannot forget

allison k. yap

For my parents, both known & unknown.

I remember
that I do not remember
anything

No quaint stories about the first time that she felt me kick. No retelling of the moment she knew I was coming. No tales of the labor of delivery. No pictures of mother cradling just born baby still wet with womb juice. Nothing.

i was created and carried by you

> *i do not remember*

of your flesh and blood born

> *i do not remember*

given up, given away

> *i cannot forget*

I am a woman born of a woman I do not know. A lost lineage. A history, her story, hidden away. Buried in the (mother) earth. Rich and moist and warm. I am one of the many who reside in the diaspora of adoption. Away from the terrain, the body, the truth of who I am. This knowledge denied to me by law and closed adoption records. I long to return from exile. I have no map to lead me to this lost territory, but perhaps this is for the best. Despite their accurate precision, maps can never capture the feel, the scent, the texture and taste. We must each construct our own multi-dimensional maps from the truths and silences of our own lives, hearts, and imaginations. A map of ourselves. Using whatever tools we have at hand. There are no experts to trust on this matter, for it is a matter of our matter. Our bodies. Our lives. Our blood. Our connections. Our dreams. Making our own trails. Home . . . .

* * *

I yearn for a trace. An outline. An imprint. A fragment. A hint. A semblance of similarity. Are my bones a skeleton of you? Teeth. Hair. Tongue. Hands. Nails. Nose. Who knows what resemblance, if any, there is. I want to tattoo you. Your body. Onto me. My body. One. Two. Me to you.

My mother, myself. My mother, myself. I have two mothers. I love the mother I have been given. But there is another mother. The first one. Blood and bones and skin and flesh and pain and labor and she is it.

I seek recognition. Embodied. A thin-lipped, lopsided smile. A raised left eyebrow. A long, thin nose. Dry skin. Fire in the blood. The inability to whistle. Double joints. Does she share any of this with me? I wonder constantly what she looks like. What words and gestures belong to her. What do we have in common? Maybe nothing. This is the real fear. I long desperately for recognition. For acknowledgment. To finally see a face that looks like mine. To be able to trace myself through the body of another.

Mother.

Starving for pieces of her, I want to know everything . . . What does she look like? What does she do for fun? What was it like to give me away? What is her favorite book? Does she sometimes think of me? What makes her laugh? Did she see me after I was born? What does she dream of? What does she do for a living? What makes her cry? What is her favorite thing to eat? Who is my birth father? If she had to be a fruit, what would she be? What kind of music does she listen to? Did she hold me before she gave me up? Is she impulsive like me? What is her favorite color? Why did she give me up?

I look at my list of questions and laugh at the profound intermingled with the everyday. Yet it is all profound to me, because I have nothing of her. I want to know everything. I feel the deprivation of her so deeply. She who is mother. She who is stranger.

I cannot forget.

* * *

I examine my "CERTIFICATE OF LIVE BIRTH" which attests that the information provided "is a true and correct copy of the original record on file in the research and statistics office, Hawaii State Department of Health."

File Number 151 69 009118 records that I was born August 14, 1969, in Honolulu, Hawaii at 11:41 AM. Sex: Female. Child's Name: Allison Kelly Yap. Mother: Marilyn Anne Gray Yap, Caucasian, age 31. Father: Kenneth Kam Yung Yap, Chinese, age 42.

I always knew that I, like my sister, was adopted. At age 26 I petitioned Family Court for my closed adoption records. I completed, notarized, and mailed the requisite forms to the appropriate agencies. I waited the required 60 days while the court tried to contact my birth parents at the last known addresses on file. When that was unsuccessful, I paid the required

$300.00 to the court appointed searcher to continue the process. I patiently waited the 180 days the searcher had to find and make contact with my birth parents. At the end of 240 days, since neither birth parent could be found, I was legally entitled to inspect my closed adoption records. I went to Family Court and paid the $28 necessary to xerox my records.

It is only then that I see my original birth certificate, over which is stamped in large, red letters:

VOID:
AMENDED BY COURT ORDER

I discover that what was certified "true and correct" is a lie. I learn the name of my birth mother, the 19-year-old, Caucasian, "minor unmarried female," and "sole legal parent." My 22-year-old, Japanese birth father is unnamed. My eyes jump to box #20:

LEGITIMATE: NO.

I do not remember.
I cannot forget.

* * *

After 29 years, I make contact with her again, and we begin to write to each other, I hold her letters in my hands and devour every word, every sentence, every paragraph that she offers me. True gifts. I read and re-read and re-read her words over and over again. My hunger is so insatiable, I am afraid I could eat her whole. I would like to swallow all of her. I long to have her in me. With me. A part of me.

me. her. us. one. again.

i long to return
to when
she
was me
i
was her
we
were one
two
too
we
were
together
i
belonged

I long to recall a time when she was space and I was matter. And she was all that mattered to me. My universe. A world womb enclosed. Blood and water and skin and I am floating within. Growing. Becoming.

* * *

I do not remember.
I cannot forget.

THROUGH YESTERDAY
TO GRASP HER WHOLENESS

The Canyon that took the place of a Couch
Kim Yasuda, 1999

CHRONICLE
Mei-mei Berssenbrugge

I was born the year of the loon
in a great commotion. My mother—
who used to pack $500 cash
in the shoulders of her fur gambling coat,
who had always considered herself
the family's "First Son"—
took one look at me
and lit out
on a vacation to Sumatra.
Her brother purchased my baby clothes;
I've seen them, little clown suits
of silk and color.

Each day
my Chinese grandmother bathed me
with elaboration in an iron tub;
amahs waiting in line
with sterilized water and towels
clucked and smiled
and rushed about the tall stone room
in tiny slippers.

After my grandfather
accustomed himself
to this betrayal by First Son,
he would take me in his arms,
walk with me

by the plum trees, cherries, persimmons;
he showed me the stiff robes
of my ancestors and their drafty hall,
the long beards of his learned old friends,
and his crickets.

Grandfather talked to me, taught me.
At two months, my mother tells me,
I could sniff for flowers,
stab my small hand upwards to moon.
Even today I get proud
when I remember
this all took place in Chinese.

MOTHER AND OTHER HAPA DENIALS

Cristina Bacchilega

"Kneel down and thank the Lord," your father commands.

You feel the blood trickling down the inside of your thigh as you bow your head in terror, in sudden silence, no longer screaming, "Am I cut? Where is this cut?" Your sister will show you how to fold yellowish cotton rags, and you will know what to do soon enough, but you will no longer climb up the magnolia tree in your yard for fear of showing onlookers the red wetness of your insides.

He is tall and tanned in the only photo I've seen. I imagine him, a slim, smart Englishman walking to the bank in the hot Bangalore sun. You say he would not pay attention to you, his fifth or sixth daughter preceding his only son, not even when you went to college, not even when you were the only one left sharing that big house with him. Punctual for dinner, he'd drink and curse the times; drink some more, and curse "that Black Beetle," his father-in-law: how could India be trusted on her own? You'd let his contempt soak your dark skin, wash it away in white muslin. You split when he died: 1947 saw you in London; then, later it was Italy.

Two boys have stopped me on the way up to my classroom; their blue smocks sport immaculate starched bows. *"Sei cinese?* Where are you from?" "Italy! I'm Italian," I burst out, my chin high, my voice like a bell. At home, my father holds me on his lap, a sparkle in his eye as he repeats: *"Cinesino.* They used to call me *cinesino* when I was in first and second grade. You see how narrow my eyes are when I smile? You're just like me." That means Italian, I smile in my heart, running off to play.

I know you are there, you must be there, in that kitchen scene, smoking your after-dinner cigarette. But you are not the one to speak. After all why should you, since you are "Anglo-Indian" and I am being called "Chinese" by little boys who have never really seen slanted eyes? Do you believe I'm safe in my father's lap? Are you so grateful you cannot get yourself to say, "Look at me: eyes are not it . . . "? Grateful for my sake or yours? Because when my father walks you to the center of his small-town piazza, it's as if he were holding exotic flowers out for his people to behold. A thrill for all these rose and lily people. "And, you know," they whisper, "she's not really . . . Well, her father was English and she's been living in England; poor thing, an orphan." Delighted, they inhale an imagined fragrance of magnolias, and my mother's darkness turns into mystery.

"The Queen drinks a glass of warm water first thing every morning, and look at her complexion!" you would tell me when I was nine or ten; you'd never tell me in the mornings, and I did not ask myself why. I could not. I invented: mummy, you have fiercely wished me to have what you chose to give of yourself—the English language, the stews, a dislike for sunbathing, advice for improving one's hair and nose, an education. Though you'd also mention Indian dances, tell a story about rabies injections, and we'd all sniffle over chicken curry on Sundays, I see you clearly only in London, purposeful, alone, at ease. We have not been there at the same time, but there you are, offering me a trying blend of formality and passion. No dressing on over-cooked spinach; salt and pepper on sliced, juicy oranges.

DANDELIONS AND SEAWEED

Mira Chieko Shimabukuro

These two halves
lie in my stomach.

My mother, born Iowan
raised Montanan
planted the first.

She pulled the dewy stem
from between two cracked cement squares.
"Remember not to step on the cracks,"
she smiled at me
motioning towards her lower back.
The dandelion had popped up
in front of the old Henderson house.
It had withstood tricycles,
summer feet and that mid-August
100 degree heat.
The wind blew in her eyes but I knew
they were smiling. "Mira," she said.
"Watch," and she blew
fluff and seed
this way, then that
only to point my laughter
to another yard
where seeds would land
and start again.

My father,
the *Nitengosei*
Uchinanchu
by way of Manoa Valley
handed me the second.

The rice never stuck to his fingers.
He'd comb his hands
in and out of the pearl grains.
Over and under sweet vinegar
would coat his nails. After he was done
he'd set it to cool under a dust-coated
electric fan. He told me
if he wasn't so lazy he'd fan it by hand
but the Red Sox were on, so
"you know how it goes."
After the game, Dad brought out
the *nori*, black seaweed
pressed into paper-thin sheets,
good for munching if you liked
paper melting on your tongue
or black specks on your teeth.
It was brittle, that *nori*
but the sweet rice softened it as Dad
rolled the two together into a perfect circle
with egg, pink tuna and spinach to color the center.
"Now you do it," he said and I smiled
as I dug my fingernails into the rice.

CHRISTA

Sigrid Nunez

Twenty years passed between my own first and second visits to Germany. The second trip took place soon after I graduated from college. By that time already it had become a fad: digging up one's roots, traveling to the land of one's parents, describing how it felt to set foot for the first time on the soil trod by generations of forebears. That tingling of the blood, sense of homecoming, and always, and perhaps most important, pride. Imagine feeling that way about Germany.

I met Germans, young Germans, who had been born in or after Year Zero. On being German, every one of them agreed: It's a drag. On the New Germany: It is boring. Jokes about impenitent old Nazis gathered in the day rooms of nursing homes, watching *Triumph of the Will* over and over again. The young people were all saving their money to go somewhere else. Paris, Rome, San Francisco, New York. I would see some of them again when they came to live in New York.

In the tourist publicity, the words used most often to lure visitors to Germany are *romantic* and *fairy tale.*

I was in the Old Pinakothek in Munich when it occurred to me: Germany was like an Old Master that had been given too many cleanings.

But what had any of this to do with my childhood?

People who remembered said, "When your mother brought you here that time, the children called to one another up and down the street, 'Come and see the children from China!' We got a kick out of that."

But we didn't look that Chinese.

"Well—compared to them."

Taunted in the schoolyard once when I was a child, I went to the teacher who was on recess duty. "Those boys are calling me a half-breed." The teacher said, "Well, you aren't one, are you?" I paused, uncertain. Uncertainly, I shook my head. "Well, then, it shouldn't bother you."

The last thing I would have believed back then was that one day it would be fashionable to be Chinese; or that I had only to wait a few years, till I reached adolescence, to hear people say that they envied me my exotic background.

Myths.

Being of mixed race makes you immune to many diseases.

Women of mixed race are uncommonly lustful.

A famous conductor, introducing a half-black, half-Jewish pianist to a concert audience, suggests that the pianist's talent is a result of his being mixed.

In college, at the beginning of every semester I received an invitation to join the Asian-American Student Society. A Chinese-American man I met much later said, "I got those in school too. That's what I hate about the Chinese: so damn clannish. You can't be yourself, you have to be one of them." He admonishes his brother, who arrives to lunch wearing a short-sleeved white polyester shirt and dark polyester slacks: "Do you have to dress so damn chinky?"

Another time, at a party, a different Chinese-American friend asks me to play Ping-Pong. I have never played before and I tell him I don't know how. He says, "Don't be silly, of course you do: It's in the genes."

Genes. Blood. Soil. Why should I feel a deeper pain on hearing that the Black Forest is dying than on hearing about the dying forests of the Adirondacks? And what is this surge of feeling inspired by a photograph in a magazine: a group of smiling Asian-American children: *Those Asian Whiz Kids!* Pride?

Memory of another teacher, on her knees, hugging me and pleading, "Promise me you'll never forget that you're just as good as any other little American."

When I talked about my mother and father people often said things like, "Only in America." People called their story "a real American story."

The apartment in the projects had a kitchen, a living room, a bathroom, and three bedrooms. The linoleum on the kitchen floor buckled here, curled up there. The windows were the kind you have to crank open, and they had mustard-colored shades that were replaced by the housing authority every three years, though long before that they would have torn or lost their spring. Winter. My mother lays a hand against the radiator. "Freezing!" She pulls her navy-blue sweater tighter around her. "If I don't get out of here soon, I lose my mind!"

For a time when I was very young I used to wind my hair around the fingers of my right hand and tug. I did this mostly in my sleep. When a small bald patch showed on the back of my head, my mother made me wear one of her nylon stockings as a nightcap to bed.

At that early age I often dreamed that I was being crushed by some—Thing. A living, heavy-breathing Thing, covering my entire body, bearing down, crushing, smothering. Murdering.

Older, I had many dreams about trying—and invariably failing—to rescue someone. It might be a child in a burning house, or someone about to fall off a roof or get hit by a car. These dreams persisted into adulthood. In a foreign, war-stricken land—jungle or bush country—I come upon a group of starving natives. I sign to them that I am going to get food, and that they should wait for me. I go and come back, lugging a big steaming pot. But in my absence the enemy would have come and slaughtered them all.

One morning an old woman who lived alone on the top floor of the building across from ours was found lying dead on the ground. Because she was clutching a rag in one hand, some people thought she must have fallen while trying to wash her windows. Later, one of the maintenance men reported that they had found nothing in that woman's apartment when they went to clean it out except a mattress on the floor and a single spoon.

What is a home? In the ten years after I left my parents' house I lived at fourteen different addresses. This constant moving taught me not to accumulate or to set too much store by possessions. (Yet I am someone who is incapable of traveling light; I want to take everything with me. Traveling in general causes extreme anxiety in me.) I have never had much success at establishing a proper domestic life. (Home economics: the only high-school course I truly hated.) For years I ate off paper plates. I don't cook. I can't sew. If there is a leak I stick a pan under it and leave it there. ("I don't know how I could have raised a daughter like that.")

But I am always happy in a nice house. I am in awe of those who know how to make things homey. Comfortable chairs in rooms with sun, flowers in a vase, clean sheets, home cooking—no one could be more appreciative of such comforts than I.

The trouble I have traveling goes beyond the shyness and vulnerability felt by most people when taken out of their familiar world. What I feel is something closer to bereavement. This feeling is associated with the memory of two fictional scenes that have haunted me since childhood, one from a book, the other from a movie. Which book, which movie, I cannot now say, but both scenes are set somewhere in Europe, in train stations, during wartime.

In the scene from the book, a man puts a little girl—his daughter—on a train. He is sending her off to safety somewhere. Father and daughter wave to each other as the train leaves the station. The man watches the train until it is out of sight: "And in his heart he knew that he would never see her again."

In the movie, which I saw on television, a man is seeing a woman off. He is wearing a soldier's uniform and he is on crutches—he has only one leg. The man and the woman wave to each other as the train leaves the station. As the train picks up speed, the man hobbles along the platform, faster and faster, until he stumbles and falls.

Since that trip to Germany I have been back to Europe, but not to Germany. I have never been to China.

So not everyone lives as if a sword were hanging over his or her head! The discovery came with growing up, with going out into the world and meeting people to whom no harm had ever come and who lived, to my endless astonishment, as if no harm would ever come. I didn't know what to make of such types (I am thinking now mainly of people I met once I got to college). They seemed to me to be lacking something, which I often mistakenly thought was intelligence. Many of them came from reasonably happy, prosperous families and from a kind of order that my mother, for all her passion for order, could never achieve. Over my childhood hangs the memory of perpetual violence: quarrels, fits, punishments. Threats and curses rang through those years. It was imperative to escape.

Once, struck by a slamming door, I lost consciousness briefly, and when I came to I saw something I was sure I hadn't seen before: the face of maternal anxiety. In that moment I remember surprise and joy at this undeniable proof that she cared.

Long after that first day of kindergarten, I would still think about it. I never could figure out how my mother managed to disappear so fast when my head turned. It was as if she had vanished into thin air.

Fear of impurities, love of obedience, preference of animals to men. Like my father, my mother also seemed at times bent on conforming to stereotype. She got a dog, a Doberman pinscher, and she named him Woden.

It was on one of her visits back to Germany that she learned that Rudolf, who would have turned sixty that year, had died of a heart attack. She reported this months later, in passing, with a simple shake of her head. It was no big thing to her.

When my mother and my father appeared together in public, which was very seldom, people stared.

No wedding photographs in the family albums.

But this: from the same box that contained the picture of my grandmother's cousin Albrecht, a picture of my parents, taken just before they left Germany for America. A candid shot, catching both of them with their mouths open. They have linked arms and they are leaning into each other, as if for support—so hard are they laughing. Arm in arm, laughing. No, I would never have imagined my parents like that. But even more incredible: One of my sisters insists that she remembers a time when she came upon them kissing and kissing. (Of course one's memories of one's early life are not reliable. It is possible that I have got innumerable things wrong. It is not impossible that one day I will have to write my parents' story all over again.)

That sister would in time find herself trying to persuade my mother to get a divorce. The marriage had been a mistake—who could deny it? No one was happy—why let it go on? My sister believed that my mother owed herself another chance; it was not too late for her to find happiness with someone else. My mother said that even though she wanted to she could not leave my father; she said her conscience would always bother her if she did. As for someone else, again: "One husband was enough!"

Secretly, I imagined that she had lovers.

She could laugh at herself. She often did laugh at herself—sometimes even through tears. Wiping her face with the back of her hand, crying, calling herself a fool, laughing, making jokes about her own stupidity.

One wants a way of looking back without anger or bitterness or shame.

Resemblances between her face and mine became more obvious with the years. I have her voice and her handwriting.

Sometimes, when I am tired, say, or upset, or drunk, I may start to speak with a slight accent. My first year in college an English professor asked, "Why does your writing read like something translated from the European?"

I don't believe there is much Chang in me.

That first day of kindergarten, after she vanished, I did not go through the door that my mother had pointed out to me. I just stood there in the hall, breathless, trembling, staring at the door, until at last it opened and a pretty young black woman who would find a place in my heart forever as Miss Lord appeared. Smiling, bending forward from the waist, holding out both hands to me.

Now that I recall, in those dreams, it was always a woman or a child needing to be rescued, never a man.

There are times when I seem to remember my mother as though she were a landscape rather than a person. Those blue eyes filled the entire sky of my childhood.

I think I know what *Heimweh* means.

It was Nietzsche's idea that when one has not had a good father one must create one. But of course he was thinking only about men.

Time and again I discover that I have not completely let go of the notion that salvation will come to me in the form of a man.

Once, when I was driving with my mother, another car skidded and came hurtling toward us, missing us by a hair. At the moment when it looked as if we would die, she said, "Mama."

What is love? In yoga, there is an exercise in which you close your eyes and try to imagine a bright white shining light, then to think of someone and to send that light to him or her and imagine it pouring down, surrounding and protecting that person. I have never been able to do this exercise without my eyes filling with tears.

One wants a way of looking back without anger or bitterness or shame. One wants to be able to tell everything without blaming or apologizing.

Message on my answering machine: *Mom fainted again today. Please call.*

Freud says the most important event in a man's life is the death of his father.

Oh, Mother.

ISHIN DENSHIN

Teresa Williams-León

For Mom & Dad

no-word woman
falls in love
with verbose masculinity

gaps and barriers
only to fill
and furthermore
to tear down

never say i want
always say for you
a language nurtured
through paradoxical love

no-word woman
speaks to her children
with her deep brown eyes

no gestures
not even a smile
language with no words
pours out of her soft face

verbal-man
learns to speak little
with his gentle blue eyes

misunderstanding
only to lessen
and moreover
to resolve

never say me too
always say for us
communication fostered
by dichotomous love

no sweet nothings
not even a frown
words without sound
flow from his handsome profile

verbose-woman and no-word man
intertwine in a language
with no words

COAL MINER'S GRANDDAUGHTER

Teresa Williams-León

For the two Tracy J. Williamses in My Life

There was once a mountain boy whom for the story's sake we will call 'George.' George emigrated to a distant city in another state where by hard work and application to duty he became quite successful. One day in his office with vacation time rolling around, his thoughts turned to his boyhood home in the West Virginia hills. Homesick for the hills, he shortly thereafter returned to West Virginia for a nostalgic visit.

Granville A. Deitz
Mountain Memories

Introduction:

Growing up in Japan as a *gaijin* (foreigner) and a *haafu* (half), I always longed to "go back to the States," where I believed I would enjoy full membership and equal participation in my "real" homeland, although I had only spent about three and a half years as a baby in California and one year in Virginia as a child. Since I began my public exploration of naming and understanding my biracial, bicultural, binational reality, I have spoken on numerous panels, been interviewed by newspapers and magazines, and appeared on television and radio programs. In the United States, I have learned, it is the ancestry of color—my Japanese heritage—that brings about great curiosity and vast interest. My European American ancestry gets cast aside and then forgotten. For European Americans, I am only special and exotic for my Japanese otherness. Afterall, what is there to being "white?" In the European American-centered imagination, being white has been recoded "American" and "human" to which everyone else is referenced and every other group is made "ethnic" or even worse, "racial." People of color, on the other hand, have argued that white America would never accept me because the rule of hypodescent (i.e. the "one-drop" rule)[1] pervades and therefore, I shall always remain a stigmatized racial minority: a Japanese-American *period*. Thus, within the United States' unequal binary racial structure, my radical subjectivity has necessarily depended upon a disjuncture with white privilege and sole affirmation of the devalued ancestry of color.

As one who grew up in Japan for eighteen years, knowing and loving my Japanese relatives and ancestors intimately, I have longed to know and embrace my European American relatives' ancestors in the same way. It is not the desire to be white or to be better than people of color that has driven me to affirm my European American ancestry. Rather, in order for me to be whole, I had to know my truth in all of its forms—its ugliness, beauty, pain, joy, advantages, disadvantages, contradictions, and paradoxes. Everyday, I feel a dire sense of urgency to reject the false, either-or, zero-sum construction of America's social reality. In learning about my dual ancestries, their unequal relationship, and their respective socio-political locations within a hierarchically-constructed world, I am on my way to the lifelong search for personal liberation.

In My Grandpa Lonnie's Shadow

My father, the youngest son and third youngest child of eleven siblings, was born in Cranberry, West Virginia and raised in the town of Beckley until he was sixteen years old. As the "baby boy," my father has come to be affectionately known by his hometown-folk as "Buddy" and "Bud" because he was the perpetual "tag-along." He was everybody's "buddy." His father, Lonnie Winton Williams was born in 1896. Grandpa Lonnie was a career coal miner, a union man, and a die-hard Democrat. Although he has remained in the background of our family history, it is *his* name I bear with great pride and honor. He is a direct descendant of "Lonesome Dave" Williams, a well-known patriarch of Raleigh County, Virginia and a U. S. hero of the War of 1812.[2]

My father's mother, Tellie Miller Williams, was born in 1902. She was a remarkable woman, a loving mother, devoted wife, and a born-again Christian. I grew up knowing very little about my "American" grandparents, except for the stories my parents relayed to me. My first visits to West Virginia took place months after my birth and again when I was three years of age. My Grandpa Lonnie passed away in 1965 of "black lungs" before I could ever know him the way I now long to.

At the start of the year 1971, my father had been talking about taking a family trip to see Grandma that summer. I would finally be able to know my American Grandma. I was excited just thinking about how I would get to know her the way I knew my *Obaachama* (Japanese grandmother).

Will she teach me songs? Will she tell me stories? Will she play with me?

While Japanese society did not always embrace me, my *Obaachama* showered me with all of her love and attention. I cherished each moment with my *Obaachama*.

My *Ojiichama* (Japanese grandfather), on the other hand, never revealed his true feelings for me and took them with him to his deathbed in 1982. I never really knew how he felt about me, except for when he punished me. He was well respected and highly revered by his community for his successful business and political ventures and was put on a pedestal by all of my Japanese relatives. When he left or returned home, his employees and family members all lined up and greeted him at the entrance-way. Although I participated in this ritual of *Ojiichama*-worshiping, I did not share in my relatives' adoration of my *Ojiichama*. It was my *Obaachama* whom I loved, respected, and adored. I did not want my *Ojiichama's* approval or attention for which the rest of my relatives and his employees competed. I just wanted to be *Obaachama's* little girl. My family was the only one who favored *Obaachama* over *Ojiichama*.

When I was four years old, my father was called away to Korea for thirteen months. Not wanting to be in the U.S. without my father, my mother took me and returned to Japan, after having been on lukewarm terms with her father for marrying my dad.

One day, I had committed a wrongdoing, (although to this day, no one can recall what I had done). *Ojiichama* and his son, my uncle, stripped me down to my panties and tied me up outside for all the neighborhood to see, (perhaps to instill shame in me), and were about to take turns whipping me with a switch. In her father's presence, my mother was left powerless. *Obaachama* threw her body over me, crying and demanding that they kill her first before they ever touched her granddaughter. To everyone's disbelief, this was the first and only time my *Obaachama* had ever stood up to her husband and her son. I often wondered if *Ojiichama's* severe punishments and lack of open affection for me had to do with my being a girl-child, being part *hakujin* (white), or both. Sometimes, however, *Ojiichama* could be humorous and kind, although I tried to stay away from him for fear of any mood transitions.

In the late 1960s when my family moved to Grant Heights Housing Complex in Narimasu and then to Tachikawa Air Base in Tokyo, my *Obaachama* would often sneak out of the house away from *Ojiichama's* watchful eye, catch the express train, and come visit me and my brother. I used to love to go with my Dad to pick *Obaachama* up at Narimasu, Ikebukuro, and Akishima train stations. Dad and I would go several minutes early, just sitting in the car, anxiously waiting for her to appear, while Mom stayed home and prepared some food and my brother cut, pasted, and drew a picture for *Obaachama*. I would always spot her first. I always looked for her neatly set silver grey hair in the sea of black hair. Her thin arms would be carrying boxes and bags filled with our favorite goodies, overwhelming her small, frail body. My *Obaachama* was the epitome of beauty, grace, elegance, and humility even as *purinsu meron* (prince melon) dangled from her already full arms. She almost never wore western clothing because *Ojiichama* preferred her in traditional Japanese *kimono* fit for each season.

We would spend all day talking and playing as my brother constantly interrupted us. My *Obaachama* would bring paper and string to teach me *te-gei* (hand crafts) and *origami* (folding paper). After we finished, she would tell us *otogibanashi* (fairy tales) and sing *doowa* (children's song). After we took an *ofuro* (hot bath) together, she would look at the clock and regretfully say that if she did not get back home, *Ojiichama* would scold her for *abura o utteiru* ("selling oil," a phrase that means "out wasting time"). My brother and I would beg her to stay and Mom would tell us to stop giving *Obaachama* trouble. Then, Dad, Mom, my brother, and I would reluctantly drive her back to the train station.

I cannot say that I have truly resolved my anger, hatred, and pain for what my brother and I had to endure in Japan at the hands of Japanese individuals and institutions, yet our *Obaachama's* unconditional and overflowing love made up for any cruelty, rejection, or exclusion we suffered. When I would tell her how a Japanese kid called me names or beat up my brother, she would sing the popular post-war song, *"Aoi Me No Oningyo,"* about a blue-eyed American doll left behind in Japan, that cries tears of sadness because she longs to go back to America.

Although my *Obaachama* did not fully share my phenotype or my experience, she identified with my pain of being an outsider. Unlike others who told my brother and me that we needed to be bigger and better than those who vomited such hatred upon us, or simply dismissed my brother's and my experiences of prejudices and discrimination as complaints or hypersensitivity on our part, *Obaachama* let us know in her magical way that it was okay to hurt. We never had to explain. She simply understood.

Obaachama used to always say that she was very grateful and eternally indebted to my Grandma Tellie Williams for loving her daughter, my mother, like she were her own. In return, she welcomed my Dad and loved him as her own, showering him with her warmth and kindness until she passed away in 1986. One day, *Obaachama* said, she hoped Grandma Tellie would come to Japan. I hoped so too. I wanted my *Obaachama* and my Grandma Tellie to meet. I was convinced they would become the best of friends. Their hypothetical friendship that my *Obaachama* had planted in my childhood imagination became the bridge that connected my paradoxical, contradictory, and oppositional worlds as I grew older.

In the early 1960s, my father took my mother and me to West Virginia for the first time. My mother's first impressions of West Virginia were not too favorable. She was often made to feel like an *uchuujin* (an alien from outer space), yet Grandma Tellie welcomed her to the family without hesitation and openly embraced my mother as her daughter-in-law, whom she boasted had her first baby at the "old age" of twenty-four. My mother told me how Grandma Tellie's gentle touch and care instantly cured me when I became terribly ill in my new environment. Only with Grandma Tellie did my mother feel that she was not wearing her "racial uniform."[3]

As my father increasingly talked about our re-visiting West Virginia in the early 1970s, the more excited we all became. Before my father's plan of our visiting Grandma Tellie had come to fruition in 1971, she had passed away from a heart attack one day before my brother's second birthday on May 7th. Only if she could have waited one month before departing this world. . . I was only eight years old, but I remember it as if it just happened moments ago.

My father's friend and co-worker, Mr. Balchunas, who had married a Korean woman and had a daughter a year younger than I, came to our house in Grant Heights, Japan with a serious look on his face. I thought it was odd because this man was usually very nice and cheerful. After completing a night shift, my father was sleeping on his bed in his white underwear and t-shirt like he always did. His friend then woke him up and broke the news—the news that we all must one day hear, but can never accept—that his mother, the woman who brought him into this world, the woman who raised him and loved him unconditionally even though he worried her sick with his adventurousness and mischief; this woman, his mother, my grandmother, had passed away.

Suddenly, my brave, strong, invincible father, who would kiss my cuts and bruises when I banged myself up and would hold me tight when I awoke from my nightmares, broke down into tears and began wailing. My father, who held back his tears when his father died, according to my mother, stayed in my parents' room just weeping for hours. I stood leaning against the doorway wanting to console my father like he had always done for me, but my father's friend told me to let my daddy be.

Now that I am an adult, I often wonder about the pain my father felt that day he was told of his mother's death and the lament he carries with him to this day. While he cried for hours in my parents' room that day he learned his mother died, was he asking for her forgiveness for having caused her so much worry and for moving away from home? Was he thanking her for 35 years of love and patience? All of us—especially my dad—have carried that deep sense of longing and regret for not having gone back to West Virginia sooner so we could have thanked her and told her just one last time that we loved her so deeply.

I believe this is why when my father visits West Virginia now, he goes to his parents' grave site *every single day*, washes their tombstones, trims the weeds, and talks to them. My dad looks like a little kid playing in the dirt and grass. "Bud, did you go to Mom and Dad's cemetery again?," his brothers and sisters would tease in their thick, slow, southern drawl. The first and last days, my Dad brings them flowers. When he brought flowers to his mother while she was still alive, his parents would often say, "Save them for when we're dead." He spends more time at his parents' cemetery every other year than do his siblings, who live only five minutes away from where their parents are buried in what is ironically named the Prosperity area of Beckley, West Virginia.

My father used to tell me that even though his family was poor, he never knew it as a child because everyone else around him was poor, too. While his family's poverty and his father's alcoholism brought him much heartache, sadness, and anguish, his mother was always there giving her baby boy, "Buddy," the priceless gift of unconditional love. Though his father was an unexpressive and peculiar man, he too let his children know that they were loved in his own way.

When my parents used to visit West Virginia when Grandpa and Grandma were still alive, Grandma Tellie was the one who gave the big hugs and cooked the delicious down-home country meals. Grandpa Lonnie just sat at his chair and hung around in my parents' company with a poker-face, not uttering much. When the time came for my parents to leave, Grandma

Tellie gave her big-bear hugs, cried sweet motherly tears, told them to come back soon, and apologized for Grandpa's absence. Grandpa Lonnie, who hung around like a shadow during my parents' stay, was always nowhere to be found when they were about to leave. He was never good at saying "Good-bye."

My White America

The white America from which my heritage comes is not upper middle class, educated, wealthy, or polished. My father's people have lived in poverty and economic despair for generations. Young girls got pregnant at early ages like their mothers had, and the young boys went to mine coal like their fathers did. The winters were brutally cold and the summers uncomfortably humid, yet the natural, rural beauty of Appalachia could momentarily soothe any unhappy child's soul—like that of my father's—caused by worldly temptations. After all, it had been given the name, "the little Switzerland of America" by a visiting foreign head of state.[4]

When I was ten years old in 1973, after both Grandma and Grandpa Williams had already passed on, our family moved to the United States. We stayed in West Virginia in my grandparents' house on 800 Ewart Avenue for a month, before moving to Hampton, Virginia for another six months. (Later we returned to Japan.) My cousins, aunts, and uncles warmly welcomed us and seemed to like us a lot. Many of the stereotypical, fictional images I had formulated in my mind (e.g. poor, rugged kids who spoke funny English, listened to weird music called "country" and "hillbilly," and basically had no future unless they took up music and formed a band) often seemed to mesh with reality. I realized very soon that although they possessed racial privilege to which I was not fully privy, my father's humble but stable military career allowed for my family's middle class status to concretize. Unlike my European American relatives, my family enjoys class privilege and international status.

West Virginia was neither the "America" that I was taught in the Department of Defense schools on U.S. military bases in Japan nor the "America" from where the Japanese people thought I came. My relatives were not anything like the white officers' families on the U.S. military bases in Japan, who did not associate too closely (fraternize) with enlisted folks, the European and Euro-American diplomats' families who resided in the exclusive areas of Tokyo and sent their children to private, international schools, or the Stevens family from *Bewitched* and the Bradys from *The Brady Bunch* we so religiously watched in dubbed Japanese voices and tried to emulate.

The next time I visited West Virginia was in 1979 at age sixteen for a family reunion. Conditions had improved, but rather slowly. Unemployment, teen pregnancy, drug and alcohol abuse, and crime among white West Virginians in some ways seemed to escalate each time we visited as the coal industry sharply declined to virtual non-existence.

My most recent visits were in the summers of 1991 and 1993. Many of my relatives, although still living humbly and simply, have reached a level of economic security. Moreover, in a one-week period during my 1991 visit, my dad and I saw and took note of six black male/white female interracial couples, several Asian Americans, and two Latino young men. Although our kinfolk did not share in our excitement, Dad and I enthusiastically documented the "ethnic diversity" we witnessed of this once exclusively white part of Beckley with our camcorder and camera.

During this visit, I decided that it was time for me to do genealogical research on my European American history and to uncover this part of my heritage of which I knew so little. I still had two great-aunts alive. One was 91 and another half-great-aunt was 101 years old at that time; both of them are my Grandma Tellie's sisters, who could tell me about the Miller-Wiseman families. My father's older cousins from my Grandpa Lonnie's side were also still around to share with me stories of the Woolwine-Williams's families. More than ever before, it was imperative for my own personal liberation and de-colonization to learn about my white ancestors, who were as removed from the white power structure as I.

I began to understand why my father had hung out with African Americans, dropped out of high school, hitchhiked out of Beckley at age sixteen, and tried to join the Air Force at age seventeen but was rejected, because the recruiter thought he had forged his birth certificate. During his pre-teen years, he went to live with his older sister in Baltimore, Maryland off and on until he was old enough to enlist in the Air Force. His father, my grandfather, who was an alcoholic, as the song goes, "owed his soul to the company store." In *Night Comes to the Cumberlands*, Harry Caudill has explained how industrialization had under-developed the people and robbed them of dignity:

> Though fabulous wealth has been generated in Appalachia, the mountaineers' share in it has been held to a minimum. . . . To the industrialists who opened the coal mines, set up the great saw mills, operated the quarries, built the railroads and hauled away the resources, the population was a made-to-order source of cheap labor. . . . The debasement of the mountaineer is a tragedy of epic proportions.[5]

The grueling, exploitative, dangerous, life-threatening working conditions—not knowing from one day to the next if my Grandpa Lonnie would come out of the coal pits alive without getting blown up—were enough to make any miner want to drink away his worries, fears, and sorrows. One of Grandpa

Lonnie's "drunk songs" that used to make my father cry went something like:

> Farther along,
> we'll know all about it.
> Farther along,
> we'll understand why.
> Cheer up my brother,
> live in the sunshine.
> We'll understand it all
> by and by.

My father would often steal his father's money to prevent him from buying moonshine and give the money to his mother. Grandpa Lonnie knew who took his money. He would always ask, "Bud, did you steal my money again?" My dad would always reply, "No Dad, I didn't." During our visit to West Virginia in the summer of 1993, my mom, dad, and I went to the New River Coal Company Store, which has now been turned into an antique store, where we searched through dusty old coal miners' time books and pay stubs, hoping to find something with my Grandpa's name on it.

How excited I had become, after hours of flipping through dirty, coal-stained artifacts, when I came across my Grandpa Lonnie's pay stub dated January 15, 1949! Sure enough, at the bottom of the pay stub, my dad's still developing fourteen-year old signature was inscribed in pencil after my Grandpa's name, indicating that he had been the one who picked up that week's paycheck. There I was in *the* company store, where my dad used to pick up the money his father's exploited labor had bought to feed his family, to pay his rent, or to buy a bottle of moonshine. As if thrust back into time, feeling a firsthand connection to America's white working class history and experiencing an important part of my missing past, I exclaimed, "Mom! Dad! It's Grandpa's paycheck! *My* Grandpa's paycheck!"

My dad used to shop at the overpriced company store. As a child, he did not know how the scrip worked so he became a prime target for exploitation. His mother would have to remind him constantly not to spend the scrips before his father got paid. During Christmas, the children could not wait for the storekeeper to take the toys down from the loft and put them on display. They would beg the storekeeper to bring the toys out weeks beforehand. Most of them could not afford to buy them, but got pleasure from merely viewing their colorful presence.

As my dad got older, he would check the prices at the company store and other commercial stores, trying to outsmart the company store. Even though the company store was over-priced, it took credit so he continued to get suckered into shopping there. Sometimes, he would beg the storekeeper to let him sweep the floors or stock the merchandise in exchange for some candy. He would hang around and beg until the storekeeper finally agreed. Because my dad was a resourceful hustler, he earned the title, "Jew-boy."

To erase her worries, answer her family's needs, and provide them with salvation, Grandma Tellie desperately turned to a God filled with wrath and judgment. If they could not have salvation here on earth, then at least, she prayed, they would achieve it after death. Grandma Tellie came from humble farming origins herself. Her father, Marcus Cicero Miller, a harmonica player, was an "illegitimate" child raised by a single mother, Marinda Miller. When I asked my grandmother's sisters about him, they did not want to discuss his background in depth. His wife, Ida Jane Wiseman, was the daughter of two first cousins who had married so they were not thrilled about delving into her incestuous past either. All I got from my great-aunts, my Grandma Tellie's sisters, was that my great-grandmother, their mother, Ida Jane Wiseman, was a dark-haired beauty who expired from breast cancer at age 43. When I asked about ethnic origins, I was told that Grandma Tellie's people were British and Irish, although no one could give me any specifics.

As the primary caretaker of her children and the home, my Grandma Tellie provided her children with the kind of love and compassion needed to survive the adversities of life in West Virginia. Grandma Tellie, like many of the white West Virginian coal miner's wives of her time, who "took their strength from the mountains and from living day to day,"[6] lived the real life stories "of human weakness, of betrayal, of domination——stories without heroes and happy endings, but also without self-pity or defeat. Life as it is."[7]

Most of my grandmother's sisters had married fairly well. That is to say, "well" for poor white folks. Their husbands were considered "professionals."[8] In other words, they did not have to rely on the coal companies for jobs. They were carpenters and artisans with skills. They were registered Republicans and proud of it. They each had very few children, unlike my grandmother, who bore eleven. My grandmother, according to her sisters, not only married too young and had too many children, but worst of all, "married down."

They disrespected and loathed my Grandpa Lonnie, euphemistically calling him a "funny" man.[9] He was poor and unskilled. He worked day shifts as a pumper, who pumped the water out of the mines, and then as a fire boss, who checked for gas leakages before having the miners lowered down into the mines for the New River Coal Company. He also volunteered as an usher at the Union meetings. He and my Grandma Tellie lived in the poor (white) section of town. He was a Democrat. He equally hated his sisters-in-law's "uptown" attitudes, and most of all, their Republican politics. He disallowed all Republicans from entering his house so when my great-aunts wanted to visit my grandmother, they had to do so when my grandfather was out. Although I certainly would not support the pre-1960s Democratic party that my grandfather knew, his allegiance to the Democratic party has informed much of my electoral politics.

My grandfather's mother (my great-grandmother), born Rebecca Jane Woolwine, was an impressive woman. My father and his older brothers remembered her as a "small, old, mean, and hateful lady," who stood barely five feet tall.[10] Her father, "Grandpap Woolwine," a long-bearded man, owned a little store in Fayetteville County. After interviewing relatives who knew her more intimately and understood her struggles, I learned that she was widowed at an early age (her husband, Charlie Williams died while she was still in her forties) and left to feed the hungry mouths of eight children.[11]

She lived to see her eighteen-year-old "baby boy," her youngest son, get mangled by a train as he tried to jump the cars, and another son kill himself by putting a shotgun in his mouth after returning shellshocked from World War II. She worked as a maid for a wealthy white doctor and took in boarders to make ends meet. In the early 1940s, she was printed up on the front page of the local newspaper for fighting developers from demolishing her front yard to build new roads. Her life experiences were enough to make a little woman "mean" and "hateful." Decades after her death, some of her grandchildren pulled their money together and bought her a tombstone, which now reads, "Rebecca Jane Woolwine Williams/ March 27, 1862 - April 2, 1946/ Gone But Not Forgotten" at Wierwood Cemetery in Pax, West Virginia.

The Color Line

The African American experience in white America has represented for oppressed peoples around the world an anti-establishment alternative to oppression (especially at the hands of European/European American colonialism). However, progressive whites have often failed to or have refused to make connections across what W.E.B. DuBois had called, "the color line." In *Black Looks: Race and Representation*, bell hooks points out how the movie, *Hairspray* uniquely attempts "to construct a fictive universe where white working class 'undesirables' are in solidarity with black people."[12] She explains how the working class white female character in the movie connects her struggle for freedom with African Americans:

> When Traci says she wants to be black, blackness becomes a metaphor for freedom, an end to boundaries. Blackness is vital not because it represents the 'primitive' but because it invites engagement in a revolutionary ethos that dares to challenge and disrupt the *status quo*..., Traci shifts her positionality to stand in solidarity with black people. She is concerned about her freedom and sees her liberation linked to black liberation and an effort to end racist domination.[13]

Traci, which is also my father's name, in *Hairspray* reminds me a lot of my father in his youth before he became comfortable in his whiteness. When my father was barely twelve years old, he began to cross over into the other side of town and hang out with black kids. West Virginia was geographically part of the "North," yet psychologically and socially it has been unquestionably part of the white South. In those days, football was a sport for the wealthier "uptown" white boys. My father and his brothers neither had the money nor the prestige to win over the coaches' favor. They turned to boxing and playing baseball and softball.

My father became the first and only white kid on an all-black team in West Virginia's Negro League during that time before "reverse integration" began taking place. My father's ballplaying, which has become legendary in the U.S. military community in the "Far East," (earning him the title, "The

Legend") was my father's first career and the U.S. Air Force his second. My mother used to say resentfully that she was "a softball widow," because my father was off playing in tournaments all over the world when the summer seasons came. My father explained that he would play ball anytime, any place, and with anybody. It was his escape—an escape from the real world into another world, the game world, where poor whites and blacks had an equal chance to achieve victory. This was my father's boyhood "fictive universe."

My father began to travel all over West Virginia and sometimes out of state with his all-black team. When I asked my dad how he was received by his African American teammates in those days, he replied that among his circle of friends and ballplayers, all were so poor that whether they were black or white did not mean much back then. However, among my father and his teammates, it was implicitly understood that blacks and whites lived in separate parts of the town and that their friendship could be interrupted by the harsh realities of racism at any moment. Even poverty was differentiated along the color line.

After a game one evening, his team went out to an all-black club. A couple of African American guys in the club began to harass my dad about how he was just a white boy "slumming." His team members immediately intervened and cleared up any questions the other African Americans may have had about my dad's presence there. When I asked if my dad would have done the same for his black teammates in an all-white club, my dad replied in a regretful tone that the black players would have been denied entry into an all-white club in the first place. I pressed my dad harder, asking what he would have done if they had tried to enter the white club and were refused. My dad just simply replied, "We wouldn't have even tried (to enter)."

On one level, as a poor white boy in West Virginia, my dad shared a closeness with African Americans because he too experienced marginalization and exclusion based on his socio-economic status. Yet, he understood at a deeper level that he was born white and that meant no matter what his affinity was to African Americans, they would never be the same. It was only a matter of time, that this racial difference would manifest itself and lead my dad to take a different life course from his teammates.

In the national imagination, West Virginia has been a poor white state, yet its "proud and immensely colorful forbearers"[14] came from various places in the U. S. and the world for economic opportunities that industrialization seemed to offer. At one of the tourist attractions we stopped off at before going to Kingwood, "Home of the Buckwheat Festival" and Morgantown, where WVU is located, both in the northern part of the state, we found a poster reading,

> **New River People:**
> They came from many parts of the United States, the British Isles, and Central and Eastern Europe to work the mines, railroads and logging camps. They brought their cultural diversity and adapted their skills to create a new way of living in the deep gorge environment.
>
> *No, we never had no trouble. We got along pretty good . . .*
> Mr. Bill Gibson
> Sun, West Virginia

This poster's description of the "New River People" who came to mine coal and eventually settled in West Virginia did not include people of color, although according to my father's memory, people of Chinese, Mexican, and African American descent lived within the various coal mining communities. When I asked my father to tell me more about the Chinese and Mexicans, he could only vaguely recollect some racial epithets that were used to refer to them, a game played using these epithets, and a murder of a Chinese laundry owner that had taken place when he was still a little boy.

As images of student protests and police brutality cover the television monitor in the video, *On Strike!*, about the 1969 San Francisco State University Strike, an anonymous voice boldly states, "A society divided by race is easier to control than a society divided by class." In America, both racial and class structures co-exist, sometimes simultaneously and other times separately. However, whenever feasible, America lays out the white racial safety net, exacerbating the structural differences between poor whites and blacks. Many scholars and political activists have often questioned why poor and working class European Americans cannot simply connect their conditions to those of people of color in order to create the powerful coalition necessary to end class exploitation and racial oppression. The racial politics and history of America have created a false schism between black and white such that the social consequences of this division have stubbornly persisted, enabling this nation to claim, "Mom, Apple Pie, and Racism" to be quintessentially "American." Derrick Bell has written,

> Black people are the magical faces at the bottom of society's well. Even the poorest whites, those who must live their lives only a few levels above, gain their self-esteem by gazing down on us. Surely they must know that their deliverance depends on letting down their ropes. Only by working together is escape possible. Over time, many reach out, but most simply watch, mesmerized into maintaining their unspoken commitment to keeping us where we are, at whatever cost to them or to us.[15]

As poor and disempowered as my father's ancestors had been, a few of my cousins' fantasies of white privilege could instantly give them historical amnesia, ally themselves with their oppressors (the wealthy white landowning, capitalist class), and boost their esteem. The adherence to racism is what allows my cousins to make ignorant statements like the reason why so many African Americans have the name "Williams" is because "our forefathers" owned so many slaves. In essence, they are saying that despite "our" oppression, no matter how poor, how exploited, how uneducated, and how deprived "we" are in these United States of America, "we" are part of the "white race."

No matter where poor whites stand in the social hierarchy or no matter how low they spiral downward, they would always be white. This is their safety net—a social contract of being born white in America. My father and his people have often been made invisible and silenced as most people of color have been, yet it is their allegiance to white supremacy that has kept them from appreciating their own working class resilience in the face of exploitation and oppression. It is my European American ancestors' resilience to overcome and survive, not their allegiance to white supremacy, that I claim and take with me.

The Defiant Stem

My father chokes up each time John Denver's "Almost Heaven, West Virginia" comes on F.E.N. (the Far East Network, the U.S. military broadcasting network in Asia). It has become his favorite *karaoke* song. Even though my father likes living in Japan far more than he does the United States, I always felt sorry for my father who "gave up" his homeland for his wife and children. Beckley, West Virginia will forever remain my father's "hometown," yet it is not his "home."

As a young child, my father saw pain and suffering that drove his father to drink, his mother's anguish and worry over her husband's drinking that pushed her further into born-again Christianity, his sisters' and his brothers' similar economic dependence on the coal companies and addiction to alcohol, respectively. The quality of life in West Virginia hinged on the coal mines, alcohol, and fundamentalist, born-again Christianity. My dad's only complete escape was to respond to Uncle Sam's call. And thanks to my father's decision to join the Air Force, he met my mother in the late 1950s while assigned to duty on Tachikawa Air Base, Japan. *The rest*, I have been told, *is history.*

In 1991, my brother and I went to visit our great-aunt, my Grandma Tellie's half-sister, who now lives in Kern County, California. At the time, she had just turned 102 years old. Because she is the second closest person alive to my Grandma Tellie (her 94-year old full sister lives in Beckley, West Virginia), I wanted her to tell me everything she remembered about my Grandma Tellie. I wanted so much to see, hear, and feel my Grandma Tellie through her half-sister.

Whenever we had visited her in the past, our great-aunt would ask us, "So, what is it like in *your* country? How do *your* people feel about such-and-such?," referring to Japan and its people. During this visit, her daughter, my second cousin, finally broke the news to her that I was a genuine U.S. Citizen by birth. As if she had heard the most absurb claim ever, she replied in her thick West Virginian accent, "I don't believe that!" I was left speechless. She also asked my brother and me what kind of car we drove.

Thank goodness she did not ask us if we were Christian, because I did not have the strength either to lie or to tell the truth. I could just hear my mother's voice from when we were little kids. We were always supposed to answer, "Yes, we accept Jesus Christ as Our Savior." At times, our great-aunt complimented us for studying hard and going to college, because after all, *"your people,"* she emphasized, "are very smart people."

Initially, I was not too annoyed by our great-aunt's innocent questions and ignorant comments. Since she was very old, I wanted to be respectful. However, our great-aunt's comments and questions became sharper and more mean-spirited. Although several times she referred to us as "kin," it became apparent that in her eyes, we were only kin by association, not by blood. After having introduced us to some of her house guests as her nephew's children from Japan, she then cheerfully said, "Yeah, my nephew met their mama during the war when we whopped them Japs so bad!"

I stood in shock, feeling my face flush and trying to crack a friendly smile without tears pouring out of my eyes. How could such ugly words come out of a sweet, old, country woman? I could not believe this woman was the half-sister of my grandmother, "Saint Tellie," whom I had heard about all my life as the sweetest, kindest, most open-hearted, open-minded woman, who had welcomed her Japanese daughter-in-law and biracial granddaughter with open arms?

At times, our great-aunt spoke about us as if we were not even there. I sat paralyzed and silenced among these white people. After several long minutes, I collected myself and pretended that I had heard nothing. I just could not bring myself to call my Grandma Tellie's 102-year-old half-sister on her racism. I was more affected by this than my brother. He seemed not to take anything she said personally because he did not feel a sense of kinship with her from the get-go. She then asked my brother and me where our *real* father was. At first, I gave her the benefit of the doubt. I thought her senility was impairing her choice of words so I repeated the question back to her, but this time more precisely so she would understand exactly about whom we were talking. Slowly, loudly, and clearly, I said, "YOU MEAN, MY FATHER, TRACY WILLIAMS, YOUR HALF-SISTER TELLIE'S SON?"

She boldly restated, "NO! Your *real* father. Where is he?" What does she mean by my *real* father? I thought to myself, what a stupid question, he's in Japan, of course, with my *real* mother. I did not even know how to answer this accusatory interrogation. Throughout the visit, I kept trying to convince myself that she was a good person and meant no harm at all. I kept telling myself I was being "too sensitive."

However, on the way home in the car, I became enraged. Why was *I*—the victim of this woman's hate, humor, and ridicule—left feeling ashamed and disgraced? Whether she can handle the truth or not, I *am* her half-grandniece! Moreover, I *am* my Grandma Tellie's granddaughter! I *am* my Grandma Tellie's granddaughter! I repeated over and over again as my brother and I drove across the Mojave desert to get back to Los Angeles.

I have tried to dismiss my great-aunt and her ideas as products of a racist society, and moreover part of an older— much older—generation when racism was far more undisguised. However, my immediate relatives (my father's siblings and close cousins) in West Virginia accept (or have come to accept) that my Japanese heritage is an important and inextricable part of my identity, yet it in no way contradicts or conflicts with my *working class* European American ancestry. While my great-aunt has never liked or even accepted the working class "Williams" part of my so-called "whiteness," it is the non-European ancestry that makes her question the validity of our true kinship. In fact, as far as she was concerned, I was not even worthy of being related by blood to that poor, working class "Williams" family.

It is these moments in life that joltingly remind me that I am a woman of color in America. However, my great-aunt's or anyone else's classist, racist outlook on poor whites, the Japanese, and people of color as a whole cannot make me turn away from both of my heritages. To claim both of my ancestries boldy and defiantly with knowledge and truth is my only weapon against racist and classist ideologies that attempt to deny them from me. Strangely, I still feel compelled to drop my great-aunt a line or two periodically. She always writes back, telling us how she would love to see us. I enjoy receiving her letters, but sadly, find myself reluctant to visit.

White racist domination has kept me from loving and embracing my European American heritage as much as it has my Japanese ancestry. In the United States, acknowledging, claiming, and loving European America have been in opposition to affirming, claiming, and loving Japan, Japanese culture, and Japanese people (my heritage of color). It is highly probable and possible that within my working class European American heritage exists Iberian, African American and Native American ancestries.

I honor the memories of my ancestors, from whom my history, my livelihood, and my identity have originated and continue to flourish—not the glorious past of the conquerors, rapists, murderers, thieves, founding fathers, industrialists, or capitalists, but the simple, ordinary folk who suffered pain, rejoiced in their happiness, who acted in a world they created as well as got acted upon by a world created before them. My Japanese and European American ancestors—both living and dead—are the "xicay," as the Cakchiquel Indian name for "stem" has denoted for over 500 years in the onslaught of European conquest, that connects my past with my present.[16]

Notes:

1. See F. James Davis *Who Is Black? One Nation's Definition.* University Park, Pennsylvania: The Pennsylvania State University Press, 1991; Maria Root. *Racially Mixed People in America.* Newbury Park, CA: Sage Publications, 1992; Teresa Kay Williams. *The Mulatto Metaphor: The Embodiment of North America's Racial Contradiction.* Paper Presented at the Pacific Sociological Association Conference, April 1993.

2. Haga, Pauline. "Monument Pays Tribute to Patriarch of Raleigh County Williams Family" *The Register Herald*. (1993)

3. Ronald Takaki. *Strangers from a Different Shore: History of Asian Americans*. New York: Penguin Books, 1989.

4. Deitz, Granville. (1981). Mountain Memories I: True and Folk Stories of the Hills. South Charleston, WV: Mountain Memories Books, 1981, p. 5.

5. Flam, Eli. "The Appalachian Voice," from (ed. John Kromkowski). *Annual Editions: Race and Ethnic Relations 1991/1992*. Guilford, CT: Dushkin Publishing Group, Inc. 1991, p. 136.

6. *Ibid*, p. 133.

7. *Ibid*, p. 133.

8. Personal Communication. Myrtle Stover. June, 1991. Beckley, West Virginia.

9. Personal Communication. Myrtle Stover. June, 1991. Beckley, West Virginia.

10. Personal Communication. Fred Williams. June, 1991. Beckley, West Virginia.

11. Personal Communication. Marji Tyree. June, 1991. Beckley, West Virginia; Personal Communication. Della Wade. June, 1991. Pax, West Virginia.

12. hooks, bell. *Blacks Looks: Race and Representation*. Boston, Massachusetts: Southend Press, 1992.

13. *Ibid*

14. Deitz, 1981, p. 2.

15. Derek Bell. *Faces at the Bottom of the Well*. New York: Basic Books, 1992.

16. Luis Alfredo Xicay-Santos. "Reconcilable Differences: Soy Guatemalteco! Soy Mestizo!" Interrace Magazine, (April, 1993), pp. 28-30.

GREAT GRANDMOTHER MAUDE

Karla Brundage

hanging clothes in the summer
that's how I remember her
white sheets
yellow
sun
hot Alabama
shining
beating down on her
disguised behind
a celebrating sky
symphony of clouds
lemonade
and southern hospitality

they are billowing
in the breeze
starched and white
she is
in an apron
it is white
and her dress is yellow
her long black hair is pulled back into a bun
but it keeps slipping out
and she
uses her free hand to brush it back

hair
sheets
white
black
billowing
and she hums a love song
Dinah Washington
hums to herself as she remembers
not her children
or her job
not her husband

working in the mines
to feed them all
but she remembers
last night
the sweetest shadow
the slightest sound
and the deepest pleasure
in between these same sheets
which she is washing only because
the evidence must be hidden

her man
not the first or
even the second
she acquired
he is the young one
fiery and lovely
from across the way
he is the one who is really going someplace
his skin is black as
well as black as the Alabama sky is blue

and his kisses are so hot that she shivers in
the relentless sun
she is humming a tune
that only a lady who flirts with death
knows how to sing

and that is how I first remember her.

the next memory is of her
dead
there on those same sheets
laying on the ground with the laundry basket still on her
hip as if stuck
there is blood staining the sheets
red evidence of passing
her throat is slit
and her life
seeps away into the ground in shame
a no good woman
left to be remembered by no one
this is my great grandmother
the woman no one spoke of for years
the woman who
marked the beginning
of what
I don't know

WALKING IN THE BEAST

Lo Ri Ly Griffin

Her grandmother had been dead for ten days and been in the ground six when Perrin received the phone call from her mother telling her to come back to claim her part of Danielson history.

"Your father wants you to go over to the house and pick something you like," Saphin said, her metal-tinged voice vibrating in Perrin's ear. "You like that bureau upstairs, don't you?"

Perrin's grandmother had willed one piece of furniture to each of her seven grandchildren. Gary and Heather, Uncle Ernie's children, had already taken claim to their pieces. "Killing two birds with one stone," Gary had told Perrin at the funeral the week before. Uncle Franklin's three children were planning on driving from the Quad Cities together the next weekend, maybe get together for a barbecue with Uncle Wil and Aunt Sophie, as they called Saphin, finding her Vietnamese name too difficult to pronounce.

Saphin watched as the house was slowly being divided between the sons and the other grandchildren and she was getting worried about her daughter's inheritance.

"I heard that Gary already got the tea cart and Heather got something, I think the chest in the upstairs bedroom. Somebody's already claimed the table and living room furniture. They aren't waiting for you," Saphin was saying, her disembodied voice rising, calling up the crackle of interference. "If you don't hurry, all the good stuff'll be gone."

Perrin's first reaction had been to tell her mother that she did not want a part of Danielson history, a history of people who could not even learn to pronounce her mother's name. She wanted to tell her mother that she was content to live off the memories already seared into her head about this grandmother and her house. About the wall she felt between herself and the other Danielsons. An invisible wall which told her she wasn't accepted, not fully, anyway. That was why she did not go through the house with her cousins following the funeral even after her father had prompted her to go.

"It'll only take you a few minutes," Perrin's father had insisted before Perrin got into her car to make the ninety-mile drive back to school.

"Your father said you should have taken something when you were here," Saphin was saying now over the telephone. "You left so soon."

"Ma, I have school work," Perrin said, using an excuse she knew her mother would not argue with. But Perrin heard the tone in her mother's voice and finally agreed to make the drive up that weekend. "I'll be home before lunch," Perrin added. "I promise."

And that night, Perrin was awakened again by the dream that she had been having ever since she learned her grandmother had died. The Asian woman clad in black shirt and pants, head leaning down toward the field in which she stood shin-deep in water. Across her forehead, she wore a faded red headband with blue diamonds set in larger purple diamonds. The knot sat just behind her ear and the excess material hung to her shoulders. At her feet, a child stood pulling water up to her small face in palmsful, watching with awe.

The child's brown eyes glittered as the water escaped through her fingers back to the paddy field below. And Perrin could feel the woman's heart racing as the brush shook with haunting noises. And before Perrin could see what was breaking through the foliage, the child would scream as the woman crushed her body down upon the child's. And Perrin found herself surrounded by bubbles as the child tried to scream again.

"Run!" Perrin wanted to yell but could not, her voice just as lost as the child's underwater. Each night, Perrin would feel the threat from the jungle and each night she struggled futilely to discover the identity of the attackers. But each night, Perrin would wake up, always before she knew whether the woman and child were safe. And she would sit up, look around the dark room unable to get back to sleep and wonder why the woman and this child began visiting her after her grandmother's death and now would not go away.

That weekend, Perrin drove along the two-lane highway surrounded by Illinois farms and small towns wondering with what piece of furniture she would drive back home. A desk? A lamp? Something that would represent the times she spent with her grandmother. She thought about the first time she had met her grandmother. Wil, Saphin, and a three-year-old Perrin had just arrived in the United States from Vietnam.

"You'll meet your grandmother," Saphin had said as Wil pulled the big green station wagon off the highway and headed toward Forrest, Illinois.

"But what about Gahnie?" Perrin had asked, remembering her grandmother standing in the doorway of their home in Vietnam, waving. "Take care of your mother like your mother took care of me," she had whispered in Perrin's ear before kissing her on the cheek and placing something soft in her hands. Gahnie looked very sad and Perrin remembered her mother calling out the window of the cab, "We'll send for you, Ma." But that seemed like such a long long time ago.

"This is another grandmother. Your new one," Saphin had told her, trying to smile.

But Perrin did not want a new grandmother. She had Gahnie. And when Perrin's father pulled the station wagon up to a small white two-story house, Perrin was still searching for the shacks and the dark-skinned neighbors walking down the dirt streets toward the marketplace. She did not find these things. Instead, there was a plump white-haired white-skinned old woman standing on the sidewalk with her arms outstretched.

"Wil!" the woman cried and hugged Perrin's father when he stepped from the car. Her father's tanned skin had not prepared Perrin for this woman, his mother, who had skin like plastic sheeting. "And who do you have with you?" the woman added, winking at her eldest son.

"This is my wife, Saphin," Wil said, holding his wife by the arm. "And our daughter, Perrin."

And Perrin remembered being lifted up to her grandmother's chest and given a great big hug that smelled like baby powder. "Perrin, what a pretty name. Did you know you had such a pretty name?"

She did not answer the question because her new grandmother was already asking another one. "So-fing, did you say?"

"Saphin," Wil corrected.

"Sore-fing?"

"Saphin," Saphin said.

"Oh . . . Saphin." And the girl squirmed in her grandmother's grasp so she wouldn't have to look into the old woman's face as it twisted into a grimace. "Sophie. That's what we'll call you."

"Mom . . ." Wil said, following his mother who still carried the child and was now heading toward the house. "Her name is Saphin. Not Sophie."

And Perrin continued to squirm in her grandmother's arms and she fought against her hold until finally her father took her from his mother and she could breathe again.

"I want to go home," she said.

"In English," her mother hissed. "We're in America now. We speak their language."

"Sophie," the old woman said with a smile. "Let's get your things inside and let you freshen up a bit, huh?"

And Perrin remembered hearing her mother respond to this foreign name in strained English and watched as she followed the woman who smelled like baby powder into the house. And in her hands, Perrin still clutched the brown package, neatly wrapped in string.

That had been twenty years ago. Now, she exited the highway and made her way to her parents' home. When she arrived, she found Saphin out back pulling down crisp towels and sheets from the clothesline. Saphin was finishing filling her basket when she looked up.

"Don't be sad," Saphin said as they hugged. "We all miss your grandmother." And Perrin's heart flickered with uncertainty as she hugged her mother, her love for the woman shadowed by the guilt for what she felt, or could not feel, for a dead woman.

"Grandma would want you to get something nice," Saphin said. "Go now. I checked. There's still a lot of good stuff."

Perrin nodded in agreement and followed her mother into the house, the younger woman carrying the heavy basket propped up on one hip bone as if it were a child.

"Go by the cemetery," Saphin said while Perrin got something to drink for them out of the refrigerator. She saw that her mother's eyes had grown wet. "I brought out some flowers from her rosebush. The one outside her bedroom window. But that was a few days ago. They're probably brown by now."

Perrin promised to go, promised to visit the house and the grave. She turned from her mother then, her mother never wanting anyone to see her cry. And Perrin had only seen her mother's eyes tear twice since they left Vietnam. Once, a few years before when Perrin's father fell to the floor, hand to his chest, head hitting the door frame separating the kitchen from the dining room as he crumpled in a heavy mass, his face turning ashen.

"Don't worry about your father," Perrin remembered her grandmother saying while the two sat in the elderly woman's living room waiting for news of Wil Danielson's condition. "If there's anyone you ought to worry about, it's me. I'm next in line. You know, we Danielsons always die in order."

Which was true for even the women and men who married into the clan as far back as the elder Danielsons could recall. They always died in descending order of age. And in Perrin's lifetime, Death inched its way down the line taking all of her grandfather's older siblings, one by one, until it finally took Clugg Danielson, too. And Perrin saw Death continuing to reach out, toward her grandmother, all the while eyeing Wil Danielson, the next generation. And that got Perrin thinking about promises. Promises she had made to her father. Promises she had made to her Gahnie.

"Take care of your mother for me," her father had said three days after his collapse, his green eyes coated with a haze before the sedative took him away again. Took him away until his heart had healed, its surviving mechanics compensating for the lost functions of the dead tissue hardened by lack of oxygen. Perrin was standing in that doorway now and shook away the memory and stepped back into the kitchen. She turned her back to the doorway and glanced past her mother's profile. A tear still glistened on Saphin's cheek. And Perrin recalled the second time she saw those tears, when she was six, when Saphin got her first letter from Vietnam. The one telling about her father.

Now her mother wiped her cheek dry. "She was like a mother to me," she said, sitting at the table with her glass of iced tea. Perrin knew that her mother was thinking of her own mother back in Vietnam, alone, neglected by her oldest. "I tried so hard," Saphin said. "I tried so hard."

Perrin did not respond. Could not respond. She only stood awkwardly, afraid that any sound she would make would be wrong. Her mother's showing of emotion paralyzed her for a moment, making her unsure of a reaction. She had seen her mother's efforts to take care of her mother-in-law, trying to drive away the guilt of leaving her own mother behind. But what Perrin saw in her mother's face was not just guilt. There was something else. Pure grief. Perrin's heart pulsed and she closed her eyes and tried to imagine the woman in her dreams, standing on dry land, holding the small girl in her arms.

"Go. Before lunch," Saphin said, moving with the laundry into the living room. "I'll make some fried rice for lunch. You like fried rice?"

Perrin began to leave her mother who was sitting now on the sofa folding the clothes into neat squares. But she hesitated at the door. Looking back, she saw the trail of the tear down her mother's left cheek and a shiver passed up her back. "I'll take care of you," she thought, hoping her Gahnie would understand she was trying. Saphin looked up from her folding and smiled.

Outside, Perrin made her way along the sidewalk toward her grandmother's house three blocks away. Halfway between her parent's house and her grandmother's grew a mammoth lilac bush standing about thirty feet high and twenty feet long. It always had looked like an elephant to Perrin with its round middle and a dollop of leaves and blossoms at the top. Heavy blossoms hanging from the head produced African ears in the late spring and, toward the approach of autumn, the elephant was Indian, its ears short and cropped. In the winter, the animal had no ears at all, or a distinguishable head for that matter. During the growing season, a morning glory vine would twist its way up the spine of the elephant to the head, winding its way upward until it hooked on and ran along the telephone line above to form the animal's trunk.

Perrin could see the elephant's trunk swaying as a squirrel scurried across the wire then paused when it sensed Perrin's presence. The rodent watched her, head cocked, then darted across the line to the pole, and scampered downward, head first, following an imaginary peppermint stripe to the ground.

The bush had long ago grown out over the sidewalk and was still inching closer and closer to the road. Instead of cutting down the bush after it had spread over the concrete, someone, long before Perrin had been born, had cut away a walkway through the elephant's stomach right along the bush's twisting stems where the sidewalk would have been if the roots had not buckled it to gray pebbles and powder.

As she neared the green and violet underpass, the overripe smell of the lilac bush heavy with blossoms met her.

The scent clung to the air making it difficult for her to breathe. Broken concrete crunched under the soles of her shoes as she walked within the beast. Around her she could hear the chittering of sparrows and the rustling of leaves and she could almost see the birds through the intertwining branches resting on the elephant's spine, flitting from rib to rib, from vertebra to vertebra. As a child, the passage was a game, a daring adventure into a deep, dark jungle. But now, the noises within, the churning of the animal's stomach, seemed so menacing. The awning produced a dark blanket over her head, surrounding her with noises that grew louder and filled her head and heart. And she saw once again the little girl and the woman in her dreams, unable to see through the branches to the source of the noises rumbling, threatening.

As she walked, the smell was beginning to give Perrin a headache when she passed through to the other side. Over the tops of the maples along the street she could make out the rooftop of her grandmother's house.

Perrin stared at the house and she remembered standing there twenty years before, reaching out with the small package. A gift, she recalled. From her Gahnie. The package was soft and brown. Brown paper wrapping with string. And she could see her new grandmother taking Saphin by the arm and leading her into the house, leaving Perrin alone on the sidewalk, package still in her outstretched hand.

And then she saw an image of her Gahnie, standing in the marketplace, fighting for lower prices with the apple merchant and the sugar vendor. But she was older now. Tired. Living still in the small house with the dirt floor where they had left her with the promise that they would send for her. But the governments of the still bitter countries would not accommodate their plans, or Saphin and Perrin's obligation. And when Saphin got the news that her father had run off, had found himself a younger woman he found more pleasing to his needs, Perrin was six years old. That was the other time Perrin had seen her mother cry.

"I should be there for her," she had heard her mother whisper. "I should be taking care of her."

Perrin slowly walked up to the house.

"If she was good to him, he would have stayed," she remembered hearing her grandmother telling Saphin, the girl sitting on the floor of the old woman's kitchen with a fat gray tabby on her lap. She had looked up then at her mother and grandmother sitting at the opposite ends of the kitchen table, each with a cup of coffee. Saphin's hands, smooth and brown, circled around the mug, her left thumb hooked in the handle. Her grandmother's hand, white, wrinkled, and knobby at the knuckles, clutched a magazine, swaying it gently back and forth to cool herself.

"Are you warm?" she kept asking Saphin, who would shake her head slowly, dry eyes lowered. "I'm warm. Are you warm?

"I always say, you've got to keep your man happy," the woman continued, her head rocking back and forth like she was really sorry about something, her face lined with worry. "I gave my husband three sons. Thank God for my sons, especially Wil, just living down the street. That was his duty, though, I guess. Being the oldest and all. Aren't you the oldest in your family, Sophie?"

And that was when Perrin saw her mother's tears, marking her face; the streaks on her brown skin like polish on teak wood. The drops glistened, then fell, rolling down her cheeks. She saw her mother put out her hands, brass-colored palms facing upward, trying to catch them as they fell. Saphin watched them slip through her fingers onto her lap. The cotton of her pants soaked up the tears greedily.

"If only I could be there . . ." Perrin heard her mother say.

"One thing though," her grandmother said then. "You people know how to treat the elderly. That's one thing I wish I had. Someone to take care of me like that. You'll take care of me, too, won't you, Sophie?"

Perrin walked up the sidewalk and up the front steps to the porch. She could see through the windows of the front door to the shadows within. The knob turned and Perrin let herself in. She walked through the dining room, making her way around where the dining table used to stand. She wondered in which of her relatives' homes it now stood. The shades were drawn, keeping the cool of the morning still trapped within the walls, the soft brown wallpaper with its tiny yellow roses with green stems holding onto the chill and the darkness of the room. Then she stood in the kitchen.

"Are you warm?" she heard her grandmother say again as Perrin watched the tears roll down her mother's cheeks.

She looked around the empty room. The smell of her grandmother, baby powder and Mentholatum, still lingered in the air. The house creaked once then settled again into silence.

"Don't cry, Sophie," her grandmother had said then, patting Saphin's black coarse head of hair with her bony fingers. "You don't have to worry when you get old. You have Perrin to take care of you, doesn't she, Perrin?" The old woman looked down at the six-year-old on the floor, the child's fingers parting faint lines through the hair of the tabby. The girl had gotten to her feet, gently pushing the purring warm lump of fur to the floor, and went to her mother.

Perrin left the empty kitchen and made her way up the steep stairs, steps her grandmother had ceased using once the arthritis grew deep between the bones in her ankles and in the cartilage in her back. She looked into the storage room and saw the neat stacks of boxes labeled "Christmas," "Halloween," and "Bar-B-Que;" boxes she had oftentimes been asked, over the seasons, to run up the stairs and bring down to her grandmother below. In the next room, Perrin noticed the bright blue square on the faded carpet where the cedar chest had sat for forty years but was now in California with Heather.

Perrin looked past the matching twin beds and past the nightstands each topped with its own green marble lamp with age-stained shades. Her eyes came to rest on the bureau snuggled up against the wall between the two long windows overlooking the street. Perrin walked across the room and fingered the brass handles, darkened around the raised designs in the metal. From outside, she could hear the sound of a lawn mower running, idling.

Pulling open the top drawer, she slowly began to examine the contents. Bed linens, old summer shirts, and boxers that used to belong to her grandfather; clothing she used to slip on over her own clothes when she was little, play-acting like the fisherman/camper that family stories made her grandfather out to be. The sound of the mower grew louder. Perrin leaned over to look out the window and saw her father's figure jouncing across the lawn atop his riding mower. He steered the machine in a wide circle around the front of the yard and slowly rocked and bounced, disappearing around the other side of the house, the sound of the engine fading away to a hum. The hum of soft wings.

The child stood in the paddy field, glistening water around her knees reflecting the sky and the clouds. A dragonfly darted across the surface of the water dipping into the marsh periodically sending circles outward, growing larger until they disappeared into the ripples created by the woman beside the child, her arms buried to her elbows, fingers caressing grassy leaves. The child began to laugh, pointing at the insect whose wings were beating rhythmically, buzzing slightly as it hovered over the child's head, darting from one ear to the other.

"It's whispering to me," the child said, still laughing.

"Shh," the woman commanded, standing straight, water dripping from her fingers back into the field.

"I can hear it whispering to me," the child asserted. "It wants to play with me."

The woman squatted quickly, the water wetting the seat of her pants. She grabbed the child's arm. "Shh," she said, looking directly into the eyes of the child and Perrin, too, saw into the child's face. Eyes brown and small. They looked back with comfort. The fear that Perrin felt for the pair did not reflect back from the eyes of the child.

"It told me we'll be all right. You'll take care of us," the child persisted and the woman continued to shush her. And a sound came from the brush one hundred feet away and Perrin tried to call to the two. They were coming. The snap of branches and the crunching of leaves grew. And the child began to hum, louder and louder. "Shh," Perrin whispered, kneeling beside the bureau.

The child smiled and her face loomed in Perrin's vision. She could see the pores on the child's nose. The dark brown of her eyes with flecks of black and copper. Her lashes, short and sparse. Her nostrils, round and flat against her full face, glistening in the sun like polish. Like polish on teak wood.

The humming grew, drowning out the sounds coming from the brush and Perrin looked out the window again to see her father circling on the mower. Her father lined up the left tires of the riding mower to overlap with four inches of the trimmed strip that circles the house and the machine continued to follow the path around the silver maples and the crabapple tree. "You'll take care of your mother for me, won't you?" Perrin heard her father say again, lying in the bed in the ICU, Perrin taking his hand and nodding. "Just get better, Daddy," she said then, standing tall and holding back her tears. "I promise. Just get better."

And the dragonfly was gone and its whispering had stopped but the child still insisted that it had talked to her. "It said we will be all right. As long as you're here," the child said, putting her hand up to the woman's face, patting her skin wet. Perrin looked down. "I don't think I can . . ." she whispered sitting beside the bureau. "I just don't know . . . ."

"But you promised," the little girl said. "You said you'd come back for me."

And the sounds of the vines and branches ripping erupt-ed and the woman clasped her hand over the child's mouth and she pushed her into the water, laying her own body solidly against the girl's. Perrin couldn't see clearly. Could only see the blurred image of grassy leaves through murky water. And her head grew light and her chest tight when she realized that she was not breathing. The hum returned, growing louder, when she finally gasped, leaning over into the open drawer of the bureau. She breathed heavily and saw the woman pull out of the water, water pouring off her head. And then the child emerged, crying, sputtering through the cascade over her face from the water off her bangs.

Perrin's father steered the lawn mower around the dark trail of cut grass, bouncing around the side of the house again as the room grew silent. Perrin raised her head out of the drawer and looked around the room and she knew that her father, though out of her view, was continuing his path, in circles, around his mother's house. She felt something soft in her hand and looked to see her fingers clutching a silk scarf. It was red. Ruby red with blue diamonds set into larger purple diamonds lined corner to corner in a formation four diamonds high and four feet long. On one end of the scarf, the material was soiled. A soft brown stain marked the silk.

"Sorry, Gahnie," she whispered, draping the scarf across her raised knees. Her fingers folded and smoothed the colors until the material was four layers deep with one row of dia-monds running the length of the material, the discoloration hid-den within the folds.

And Perrin could see Gahnie pulling the beautiful pur-ple and red scarf from around her neck, folding it into a square and wrapping it in paper. Brown paper with string. "For your new family," Gahnie said, her eyes moist, as she handed over the small package to Perrin. Then Gahnie turned to Saphin. "May they take care of my oldest and may you never forget," she said before she turned and disappeared into the house.

"That's one thing about you people," Perrin heard her grandmother say again as Saphin sat at the kitchen table, palms catching falling tears. "You sure do know how to take care of the elderly." And Perrin was standing next to her mother's chair, her small hands reaching out, trying to rub away the tears from her mother's hands, to erase them.

"Damn," her grandmother spat as she put down, with shaking hands, her coffee mug still dripping brown liquid. And Perrin watched as her grandmother looked around the room, finding the soft silk material in the hallway hanging on the coat rack. She watched, in horror, as the purple and red diamonds grew brown as the coffee was wiped from the table. The six-year-old reached up, linked her fingers around her mother's neck and pulled herself up into her mother's lap and held her until she felt the woman's arms around her back and could feel the flow of her tears mix with the rocking motion of their breathing.

The child looked into the woman's eyes, brown and small with flakes of black and copper, and watched as they slowly grew calm. Grew dry.

Resentment presented itself and was just as quickly hidden in the child's heart as she heard the exhausted exhale of the old woman, her withered mouth pressed in a frown creased with years and overuse as she took the cloth to the sink and rinsed it haphazardly. Somehow, the scarf, still stained, found its way into a bottom drawer of a bureau upstairs.

The lawn mower returned and Perrin looked out onto the front yard and to her father below. His balding scalp was scarlet and moist with sweat as the sun kept pounding away at his unprotected head. Perrin's breath was labored as she felt the itch of lilac blossoms once again in her nose and a familiar feeling swelled in her chest. She could feel the dark blanket of leaves, hear the whispering of birds grow louder and louder in the blackness until the feeling brought Perrin quickly to her feet. She grabbed an old fishing hat from the hall closet and ran down the stairs to the front door.

"Dad!" she called through breath hindered by her sudden movement and emotion. She waved the hat at the man but his head was lowered, his eyes watching carefully the path that he was to follow.

"Dad!" she repeated louder, making her way toward the mower, the engine much louder without the wall's insulation. He looked up and smiled. His green eyes were still covered with the haze that had never left them since his stay at the hospital. She could hear the beating of his heart, labored and strained, weakening and slowing as she forced a smile. He smiled back at her and took the hat and fitted it atop his head. Slapping it down with the flat of his hand, he grinned, waved a thanks, and rolled off around the house again. Perrin stood watching her father's back disappearing down the side of the house and circling off toward the alleyway, the hum of the engine and the tired rhythmic beating of his heart slowing fading away.

The little girl stood, soaked head to toe, in the paddy field. She was laughing. "We'll be all right because you'll take care of us. You'll come back for us," she said. And the woman took the child by the hand and they turned and slowly walked out of Perrin's vision.

Perrin stood alone in the yard. Taking the scarf she still clutched in her hand, she threw it over her head and raised her hair so the cool silk could lay against her neck, the tassels hanging over her chest. She raised the ends and tied a knot at her forehead and turned the fabric until the knot sat securely behind her ear and the band of silk tied her hair back from her face. She turned and made her way down the street to return home.

And up ahead, just a block and a half away, she could see the lilac elephant, its shadow laying down, sleeping on the grassy lawn, and she closed her eyes and could still smell the scent of lilacs on her sleeves and she could still hear the chittering of sparrows hidden deep in the body of the beast.

REFLECTION

Jolyn M. Yamashita

for my Father

Dawn in a white T-shirt and cloth diapers
in a jungle of green army blanket
trying to get her gums around a large red apple
reminds you of another time . . .

Coming home!
        from Vietnam . . .

Me, two months old
a dark swatch of hair
swaddled in a stampede
of pink and blue elephants.

"Vietnamese orphans?"
strangers had asked my mom
before your return.

You study her
blond brown hair
and sea green eyes
as she hands you your "Second Daughter"

You smile with a different face
angled cheeks, almond eyes,
and vana hair soften suddenly.

I scream as you hold me
my red lichee face
and open papio mouth
a reflection of the hurt and anger
you hide in the many pockets
of your green army uniform

STORIES

Kyoko Katayama

I

A story!
No, stories.
A story within a story.
Story within stories.

Theories are stories.
Paintings tell stories.
I am a story.
When my story meets the story of a painting
we create a story, and another, and another . . .

Aren't we all, in some shape or form or voice or texture
trying to make sense out of this existence by collecting little
        stories,
hearing the big story (trying to put that in the background),
so we can make up a singular story called "my life"?

Am I a story in progress?
Am I many stories unfolding at different speeds?
Does the story end when I drop this body?
Will you pick up the many shades of my story
and wear them like a ribbon around your straw hat?
Or tie them like a woven belt close to your heart
when I die?

When I was young and the world was so big and endless
          around me
I wanted to know my story
From the beginning
(Maybe so eventually I could figure out the ending.)
I wanted to know why I was born
who I was
to whom I belong.

My mother
who looked liked everybody else that my little eyes could see,
green-black hair, narrow slanted eyes, short and small, said
that the story was that everybody starts with a Mama and a
          Father.
In my case, Father died,
whatever that meant.
Other than that, my first story was that I was supposed to be
          like everyone else.

This was before I started school.
My mother, my aunt and my big uncle and my little uncle
and my sick grandpa,
we all lived in this one room.
I thought everyone else lived like that
since all the neighbors around us lived like that.

At night, the bare bulb turned the square room into a circle of
          light
Dark corners whispered memories of the war and deaths
          unattended.

One day, I was alone with Grandpa
who was forever lying on the futon on the tatami floor.
On this morning, his sleep was different.
I called my aunt outside
Her hands were all red and raw from washing clothes
in the February well water
She ran in to see grandpa.
A doctor came and knelt by grandpa
and said something to my aunt.
Next day, grandpa was inside a wooden box
Lots of people came to our room
that was filled with the incense smoke
and the Buddhist priests chanting day and night.
Then everything disappeared and everyone went away
I waited for my mother for a long time as usual.

I was so excited to see her come back
carrying a white box by her chest
I knew she was bringing me a cake
for being such a good girl while I waited for everyone to return
"It's a cake for me, isn't it, mamma?!"
holding on to the edge of her black kimono.
Mamma said solemnly,
"No, inside are grandpa's bones."

I felt like fainting
from the terror
that grandpa could turn into bones,
and the shame that I was so childish, ignorant and selfish.

The white box of bones was placed

on the little low table in the little room where now five of us
        lived
for forty days.
For forty days, and even after the bones were taken away
I avoided going to that part of the room, just a few steps away.

The beginning of my first story
of how I got born starts with the sentence
"Your Father died."
It ends with my discovery that Grandpa was dead.
My mother never included herself in the story
There was supposed to be the main character, Father,
but he died.

Mamma was just there
powerfully
as the teller of the story
and I laid my head on her big lap that smelled so nice.

                        III

When I started school
I began to notice that something about me
was quite not like the others.
I didn't know what the difference was
My classmates were not content with the "father was dead"
        story
Then, *they* were more curious about
what had happened to my Father.
Not having a father was a fact of my childhood
but for the rest of the class,
every single one

every single one
of them had a father each.
It must have bothered them to no end
that I didn't have a father to claim me.

I was beginning to get it.
In this land where I got born
when there is no father to declare you
you have no family
then no name
then you are no-body.
It was father who can pronounce your existence
as deserving of occupying a place in this land.

So I urged my mother to tell me more
"Where is my father?"
"What really happened to him?"
"Who is he?"

IV

Stories, stories . . .
How do you tell truth from lies?

I got a brand new story about my Father.
He was an American (whoever they were), a foreigner.
Because he was an American, he had to go live in America.
Because my mother was Japanese, she had to stay in Japan.

The next time I was asked about my father
I told the new story
Now we were going into fourth or fifth grades

and I started to hear rumors about how kittens were born
(by ripping out the mamma cat's tummy!)
So my friends were not completely satisfied
but they put me in some kind of category
whatever that was.

Then I was shy
but not self-conscious
My mother was devoted to me
and my attention was on being her good girl.
After all, she was all I had in the vast, strange world.

V

I am 15 now
I notice how the boys are
looking
looking
looking
at me.
What are they noticing about me?
I
look
look
look
in the mirror
for the first time
with the fresh self-consciousness
of a just-menarched girl.

The cake in the box turns into grandpa's bones
and I feel like fainting

with the pang of terror
of losing my innocence.

There is no Japanese girl in the mirror
There is someone else,
a stranger from another place
her hair, her eyes, her bones
are not the familiar ones of my mother
Is this why people are looking at me?

All the eyes on me
all the curiosity of my school friends
suddenly make sense.

My face in the new mirror
betrays my mother's old secret
and I didn't even know.
The appearance of the box betrays what is inside.
I should have known.
Grandpa was dead.

I lose another layer of innocence
and I press my mother on for the real story
"Who am I?"
"Why was I born?"
"Who is there to claim me?"
Her lap is so tiny
I am so much taller than her now
Her figure gets smaller and farther and farther away from me
and I am left all alone
stranger to myself in a strange world of
peeping people.

VI

Two years later we came to America.
Many years passed since then.
I got busy trying to learn how to do America.
I got married
and gave birth to a daughter on a snowy day in Minnesota
We moved to Italy and I gave birth to two more children
There, I learned how intoxicating it was
to breathe in the air of the Tuscany hills
in spring
among the ancient olive groves
fields full of crimson poppies.

Many more seasons passed.
For each ripening summer,
there were bitter, no-exit winters.
We came back to Minnesota.
I divorced my wine-soaked husband.
The children grew
and there was space in my life once again.

VII

The old void started to throb painfully.
I discovered that the yearning for my story never died:
It was once again demanding to be told.
So I started a search:
"A 45-year-old Amerasian woman looking for her lost father in
        America."
I had very little information
I only knew his name
and the approximate time he was in Tokyo.

I also started to read books on racism and sexism and culture
    and history.
What historical context and location was I born into?
While I waited for replies from the U.S. Government,
my imagination ran wild
What did it mean that my father was a GI, a conqueror in
    occupied Japan?
Who was my mother to him?
Was she raped?
What power did she have to resist?
To the war
she and her siblings had just lost their home,
their parents,
and most of all, their dreams of future
Her mind must have been filled with the memories of the
    charred bodies

"On March 9, 1945, 334 bombers flew over Tokyo
and dropped two thousand tons of incendiary bombs.
The raid left 83,793 dead, 40,918 injured, and a million homeless."

The starvation that came with the peace
Her heart filled with grief that could not be voiced
What was the price for her survival?
Was she simply exploited as a spoil, a woman of the defeated
    nation?
Did she fall in love, looking for an oblivion and a deliverance
    from her pain?

Who was my father to her?
Was he attracted by her exotic innocence?
Was he encouraged by his buddies to exercise his entitlement?

Was he lonely?

Eight thousand miles away from home for the first time in his
young life

Did he fall in love, looking for comfort and chance to look
gallant?

Were they both hurt by the war?

Was there a deep yearning to connect, to reconcile and heal

between my father and my mother?

Japan and America

man and woman

White and Asian

rich and poor

Christian and Buddhist

victor and the defeated

What if I am a child of rape?

What if I am a child of hope and yearning?

VIII

I received letters back all saying that they could not help me
find my father

But I needed to know where I came from

What are my roots

Which of my fantasies and nightmares are true?

More I became obsessed, more I realized the impossibility of
the task

I felt that the world all around me

the authorities, the American government of my father,

my mother as my sole parent

were all screaming at me, telling me that I didn't deserve to
      know,
that I was forever abandoned
going through this life without roots,
floating without a name
without a story.

I was desperate and that made me determined.
If I cannot retrieve my story through the ordinary means
then I will find ways to enter it through extraordinary means.
So I started to look in places that are very deep
or very high
or very close.
I looked to my body
my cells, my blood and bones for the stories of my father
The key to my story was perhaps inside of me
Voices said that I have all I need to know
I wanted to have conversations with my veins
my muscles
my innards
and my heart.
Half of my body knows my father and that is a lot of
      information.
I conjured images of my forebears unseen
I drew them and invoked their oracles for their forgotten child
I taught myself to pray before going to sleep
that I might meet and speak with my father in the midnight
      dream.
In that lucid dark my soul will make contact with his
for no other reason than my coming to claim my birth right
to *know* him
to unfold my story,
our hundred thousand stories.

And so I began my long apprenticeship
with the archaeology of future
weaving shapes
pulsations
whispers
of the ancestors of my heart,
the threads that guide my journey
in the dense labyrinth of my lived life.

A DRAWBRIDGE TO A DESTROYED HOMELAND

Mira Stout

My uncle from Seoul came to stay with us when I was 14, my first year of boarding school. It was winter in Vermont. Beyond the window the pines would have bristled sparsely against the hushed, white snow. The grey, swelling sky would have been as vast and lonely as a northern sea. But I can't recall Kwang-ho's arrival. His presence was ghostly at first, so alien that he scarcely left an imprint. Yet now, years later, when I remember that emptiness, Kwang-ho's face follows. His slash eyes, wide-boned pallor, and shock hair gave him an outward ferocity. Although I had met my mother's friends, my uncle was different, more Korean somehow, like a wild animal compared to a domestic one. Even his gestures required translating: a sneeze was a violent "YA-shee," rather than a tame "ker-CHOO." And he walked in Korean, too, arms stationary and body canted forward. He rather stuck out in our redneck town.

My mother must have looked equally oriental, but I noticed less—she was a mother, already a separate species. Besides, they didn't look alike. My uncle's face was paler, and round like a moon. There was something remote and masked about him, as if he were stranded in his skin.

Despite our kinship, I felt little for this new relation. Though he was young enough to be a brother (I hadn't any siblings), no reassuring sympathy for him welled up, and no rescuing tug of filial loyalty helped me pretend otherwise. Kwang-ho was a spaceling to me. The rapid, guttural language of clucking, hacking noises that he and my mother spoke sounded ugly and comical to my teenage ears. It separated us like barbed wire.

As a child I had refused to learn Korean. I had even blocked out most of my mother's worn stories of Seoul, which were as unreal as fairy tales, but with tragic endings. The gilded family sagas finished in divided lands, ruined diamond mines, betrayals, and executions at the hands of Japanese invaders even before the beginning of the catastrophic war.

Since my mother had returned home just once in 30 years, the narrative store could not be replenished. By default, Korea had shrunk to meaning little but my mother's iron discipline, and eating dried squid after school instead of marshmallow fluff.

Until now, I had only known my uncle from photographs in our album. In an old sepia-tinted family portrait taken before the war, Kwang-ho was a small, doll-like boy in a sailor suit, shyly holding my grandmother's hand. (She is dead; I never met her.) The family looked grave and distinguished: tall men in wire-rimmed spectacles, high collars and buttonholes, and women, fragile but assured, wrapped in stiff silk *han-boks* seated in a shadowy, peony-filled garden. My mother, chubby-faced, with a severe bob, stood protectively next to her brother.

I daydreamed secretly about them, especially about my great-grandfather Bong-lae, the wastrel poet so vain that he would only be seen in public astride a white horse—which sometimes returned empty-saddled, its master having passed out in a ditch. In a later black-and-white image, dog-eared from handling, Kwang-ho was grown up, dressed in military uniform, leaning against a wooden footbridge before a pagoda, smiling confidently at the camera—roguishly handsome. I had looked forward to meeting *him*. But this full-colour, three-dimensional stranger seemed jarringly unrelated to those glamorous photographs. For a start, he was here in our kitchen, rather than safe-ly *there*.

But during his visit my mother became more alive and fluent than I had ever seen before. They would stay up late together drinking ginseng tea and talking excitedly. Years had passed since their last meeting. Sometimes they spoke with a raw, almost animal pain that frightened me. Gradually the sound became less exclusive, and flowed generously, like water freed from a dam. This awesome current bypassed me and my Boston-Irish father (who spoke no Korean), but neither of us remarked upon it. I was content to pretend they were discussing dull mat-ters like jobs in Boston. (Kwang-ho was to attend university there in the autumn.)

During those evenings my father and I tactfully watched ice hockey on television but neither of us could really concen-trate. Although we were silent, we were acutely aware of Kwang-ho's presence. I would sneak glances at him from the sofa as if he were a surprise package delivered to us which I hoped someone else would open. While I had decided he was to be a marginal figure in my life, I kept a self-interested eye on him anyway during those first winter nights, sensing, with some dread, that he contained secrets I might some day need to know.

One morning after Kwang-ho first arrived, we drove out through the snow-banked woods for an educational breakfast at the Timberline Restaurant, renowned for its 16 varieties of pancakes and "Famous 100-Mile View" over Massachusetts.

Lavender-haired waitresses in white uniforms and orthopedic shoes delivered the orgiastic fare with medical brisk-ness; cranberry banana-dot pancakes, blueberry French toast, waffles with melted butter and hot maple syrup, sausage patties, bacon, steak-and-eggs, eggs-any-style, oatmeal, homefries, toast and muffins. They refilled your coffee cup instantly, and offered second and third pancake helpings on the house.

That sunny morning the dining room was crowded with skiers, bunched around the colonial wagon-wheel tables in pneumatic, technicolour anoraks. They roared with pre-sport gusto, clanking their cutlery uninhibitedly, as if their appetites might extend to the creamy blue mountains which beckoned beyond the plate-glass window like a majestic frozen dessert.

At first my uncle looked overwhelmed, but soon glanced about delightedly, taking tiny experimental slurps from the coffee cup he held ceremonially in both palms. People stared baldly at us, jaws momentarily disengaged. Orientals were rarely seen in the New England countryside.

We ignored their dismay—led by my mother's well-practised example—but I felt scalding embarrassment. Although we had begun by speaking in English, my mother and Kwang-ho soon broke into voluble Korean as if my father and I were not there.

At last our breakfast arrived. Still feeling unwell after his long journey, my uncle faced a modest fried egg. Kwang-ho hesitated a moment, but with a sudden scowl of concentration he seized the sides of the egg white with his fingers and crammed the whole object into his mouth in one piece. Head bowed and cheeks bulging, he chewed the egg penitently, as if ridding his plate of an obstacle. My father and I froze, stupefied. Never having seen an egg dispatched in this way, I began to laugh, but my mother's eyes caught me like a pair of bullets.

The next week my mother urged Kwang-ho to look for a job in Starksboro—the nearest big town—to improve his English and relieve cabin fever. As his classes would not begin for several months, he acquiesced, but found nothing.

In the mornings, after a bit of coaching, my mother and I would drop him off in the icy parking lot on Main Street, *The Starksboro Reformer* help-wanted ads folded neatly inside his glove. Yet by noon he would be waiting for us dejectedly at the counter of Dunkin' Donuts, attracting hostile stares from berry lumberjacks grimly chewing their jelly doughnuts, puddles forming on the pink linoleum beneath their snowmobile boots. After a week, his only offer had been a part-time window-washing shift in the sub-zero February winds. (Dad said they must have thought he was Eskimo.)

Struggle was foreign to my uncle. He was the pampered youngest son of a noble family, raised in a big house in town with servants, and estates in the country. My mother even claimed Kwang-ho was renowned in Seoul as "a happy-go-lucky playboy"—inconceivable though that seemed to me as I examined him critically through the gap in the car headrest. Here, he was assumed to be a refugee.

I saw Kwang-ho again at Easter. At home, snow still scabbed the fields, but the ground had thawed. Wild gusts of fresh, spring wind roared through the bare treetops. Unpacking my duffel bag, I resolved to be kinder to my uncle, providing it was not too painful.

But I had forgotten little things about him—like the way he chewed spearmint gum with smacking gusto, and sang corny songs in the car. And his sense of humour! It seemed he seldom laughed, but when he did it was a razor-edged soprano giggle. At moments of unanimous family mirth he was isolated in his silence. He thought most American food was disgusting, and I never saw him reading an English book or a newspaper.

Kwang-ho was like unconvertible currency: he refused to be tendered or melted down. There was no western equivalent for his value. Sometimes I suspected he was simply saving himself so he would not have to change again when he returned home.

Yet in my absence there were surprising developments. One afternoon as I studied for exams, I looked out at the faithful view of sloping fields, towering Scotch pines and immense sky and noticed something peculiar about the younger trees opposite. Their lower branches had been brutally pruned as if to resemble topiary, but their trunks looked disastrously bald, like shorn poodle shanks. When I protested to Mother, she smiled and insisted, "Now they look like Korean bonsai."

Kwang-ho then reappeared from Starksboro with a red and white striped parcel from Sam's Army-Navy Store, and went off to his room. As I was reading, something caught my eye out of the window; there was my uncle, zipped into a new track suit, vigorously touching his toes in the waist-high weeds as if in an indoor gym.

Then he stopped, approached a pine bonsai and playfully shook its slender trunk. After an interval of staring bull-like at the tree, he suddenly charged at it, yelling murderously and raining side-kicks and karate chops upon it.

I rose from my chair. Had he gone mad? I heard my father laughing in his studio, and ran off to confer with him. He had left his easel, and was standing at the window watching Kwang-ho. Without speaking, we observed him warily circling the tree like a shadow-boxer, delivering the odd kick-chop. Dad rapped at the window and my uncle whirled round, red-faced with exertion, and waved at us enthusiastically. We laughed and waved back, marvelling. From then on, my uncle performed his *tae-kwon-do* exercises on the lawn without interruptions.

After this, the atmosphere was lighter between us. Attacking trees seemed to relax Kwang-ho; he smiled more readily, looking quite as handsome as his photographs. This unexpected glimpse of him lent a wider radius to his character.

Still, an unnegotiable distance separated us. I regarded him more as an exotic zoo animal than as my only living uncle. It was safe to observe him through bars, to admire him wryly from the window, but I couldn't begin to relinquish those barriers. The schoolyard bullies who had kicked me behind the apple trees with their pointy-toed cowboy boots might come running back through the years to punish me again for having Korean blood.

Kwang-ho's foreignness could be contagious; I might be ostracised not only for harbouring an alien, but for becoming more of one myself. With my loud sportswear and Celtic freckles, I could pass for Caucasian, but my uncle's incriminating features would give me away. It was smarter to stay clear of him, my Korean half exiled to a remote inner gulag that even I was unable to find.

I remember one final episode that Easter holiday. As I studied for exams one afternoon at my usual place by the window, Kwang-ho entered the kitchen to toast some seaweed. After offering me a warm, sulphurous black square—which I ate grudgingly—he left to join my mother in the garden.

Then I heard a yell, and saw Kwang-ho transfixed, his eyes locked to the ground. Running out to see what was wrong, I found him down on all fours, stabbing spasmodically at the earth with a trowel. Inured to his ways, I asked casually what he was doing.

"A grass snake," explained my mother. "But they're harmless," I said, popping my eyes. "Maybe. But to him serpents are a symbol of evil, and must be destroyed."

My uncle had lost sight of the snake, and was shouting at my mother in Korean. "What's he saying now?" I piped.

"He can't believe we allow snakes to poison our land," she said neutrally, as if unsure about where she herself stood on the matter. Still muttering, Kwang-ho crouched in a combat stance in the dead asparagus patch, gingerly parting weeds with his trowel.

Wishing him luck insincerely, I went inside. Minutes later my parents left on an errand.

Kwang-ho came indoors, and began rummaging angrily through drawers and cupboards, changing into his new jeans, my father's too-big rubber boots, wood-chopping gloves and a fireman-style hat. Then he left without a word, carrying a long, fat stick he had found beneath the porch. I looked around reflexively to see if anyone could confirm what I was seeing, but I was alone. Shaking my head, I returned to the hygiene of my algebra book, now and then looking up expectantly at the field.

My parents returned from town with the groceries, and asked after Kwang-ho, smiling when they heard about his hunting preparations. We watched a muted sunset, and took tea and Chinese steamed buns in the sitting-room, half listening to the news on the radio.

Just then the front door opened, and Kwang-ho stamped in, displaying a small green snake by the tail as if it were a ten-foot swordfish. Dutifully we admired his catch, but the pride brimming in his eyes was much more remarkable and disconcerting. His delight was so intense that I almost found myself wishing I could see the snake as he saw it. I stared hard at it, hoping for something magic to happen; but nothing did. My doubt remained and divided us.

Kwang-ho soon went back outdoors to dispose of his quarry. I watched from the window as he scaled the stone wall and stood there, surveying the woods below. He whipped the snake round his head like a lasso, and cast it high into the air with a defiant shout.

For many years I carried that image with me: Kwang-ho, snake-slayer of Vermont, arm raised against the darkening sky like a warrior throwing his sword into the spokes of the universe, hoping to arrest its wheels upon his victory. At least, that's what I wanted to see.

Now I recall it differently. The sun had set, and my uncle was mostly in shadow. After he'd flung away the snake he looked so small and vulnerable and alone on the ledge that I could hardly bear to look at him.

Kwang-ho spent the following few years at university in Boston, one of 10,000 freshmen. To his own surprise he was not quite the star he had been in Seoul, though he had plenty of friends. My mother, fond of making oracular judgments from hundreds of miles away, pronounced him bright, but lackadaisical.

Yet Kwang-ho was hardly lazy. He took a night job as a taxi driver, though he barely knew the streets beyond Copley Square. He was almost immediately robbed and beaten at gunpoint on a midnight fare to Roxbury.

Next, he took on odd shifts as a waiter in Chinatown. He felt safer there. He studied business administration by day, and on free nights gambled away his earnings, making extravagant barroom loans to friends.

My uncle then had a pretty Irish girlfriend called Mary. He was crazy about her. "Irish and Koreans are so alike, so sentimental," he would tell my mother over the phone. One day Mary told him he was a worthless male chauvinist pig, and left him forever. Then he found a rich Korean girl, and drove all the way to California in his cab to escape her. Six months later they were married.

News of Kwang-ho came secondhand from my mother, often months after events had passed, subtly filtered by her own approval or disappointment, distorted by translation into English. Although Boston was only three hours away, trying to follow my uncle's progress was like monitoring conditions on

Mars through a faulty satellite link. He became an abstract fuzz, composed of long shadows and receding footprints.

Next I heard that Kwang-ho had set up a small shipping firm in New York, and moved to a model home in Fort Lee, New Jersey, with his wife and two babies. Reportedly, he now wore a solid gold Rolex watch and drank lots of whisky with golf cronies—all Korean. During my uncle's Fort Lee tenure, we saw very little of him. He didn't much care for Vermont. He preferred neon night life and the siren call of near-fatal business schemes. Yet unexpectedly, when I moved to New York myself after university, I began to see Kwang-ho quite regularly.

We would always meet in a Korean restaurant off Fifth Avenue and 34th Street. Young Bin Kwan was his favourite. He was often outrageously late, but I didn't mind. The mean-faced maitre d' would bring a dish of exquisite dumplings and barley tea, and I would luxuriate in the suspect glamour of floor-to-ceiling fish tanks and Las Vegas chandeliers like someone in a spy-thriller. Anticipation of the ritual feast ahead and the denouement of my uncle's life story put me in a buoyant mood.

When Kwang-ho finally arrived, he was the playboy, clapping imperiously for more beer and *kimchi*, and barking commands at the traditionally robed, twirling waitresses with breathtaking but good-natured arrogance. They served him adoringly, swiftly replacing empty celadon dishes with fresh *bulgoki* and cauldrons of demonically spicy *mae-un-tang*. My uncle grinned, slurped and chewed with abandon.

Once, as I watched him stuff a rolled lettuce parcel into his mouth in one bite, distending his cheeks like a chipmunk's, I suddenly recalled the fried egg episode that first week he had arrived, and understood. "The custom," he explained, motioning me to do the same. When I'd packed the *bulgoki* into my straining jaws, we both laughed achingly, my eyes swam with tears, and the juices exploded in my mouth and ran down my chin.

Kwang-ho showed me how to hold my teacup deferentially, like a proper Korean lady, and taught me heatedly about Korean history and Confucian philosophy. Railing about the ignorance of the West, he would glare at me unforgivingly, as if I were no longer his niece, or even anyone he knew, but a symbol of the entire "West" and its calumny.

One night he became pleasantly sentimental, and drew the ying-yang circle of the Korean flag for me on the tablecloth with a metal chopstick, explaining its integrated symbolism. Then, smiling cruelly, he drew a diagram of himself and me, comparing our closeness to two independent circles overlapping only slightly at the farthest parameters.

I wanted to protest that he was being harsh, and that there was more between us, but I could not. Perhaps it was true that only this segment of tablecloth joined us; perhaps we had never succeeded in meeting before. But if we were not intimate as some relations, we had come a long, painful way to our present distance.

Over melon and toothpicks, Kwang-ho would listen entranced, but uncomprehendingly to my hopes and woes, then smack my shoulder encouragingly at the end, whatever I had said. Perhaps he couldn't quite follow the language or my way of seeing things, but it didn't matter. The smack made me laugh.

Then my uncle would grandly pay the stiff bill, and drive me home to unfashionable West 100th Street in his plush blue Chevrolet Royale with the amazing shock absorbers. During those nocturnal rides I felt a rare, childish joy, as if no danger or sadness could reach me there within that safety of new-found blood kinship, padded vinyl and electronic locks. It was not to last.

A couple of months later Kwang-ho's beloved business partner vanished in the middle of the night with all the firm's assets. The investigators could not trace him. Ruined, Kwang-ho sold his house and moved his family back to Seoul for good.

On our final evening together before my uncle's departure, on the way home I glanced at him in the driver's seat. Neon lights from the Broadway marquees washed over his tired face. He ignored the crowds and the limousines, and focused blankly on the red traffic light ahead. A ghostly feeling emanated from him. I recognised it from years ago when he first came, as if his body had landed but his spirit had remained behind. Now there was a similar emptiness about him, as if his soul was already in transit and had begun the long journey home.

I wondered if Kwang-ho had really dreamed of success in America, and if it grieved him to see it eluding him now. Perhaps he was glad to leave; I still hadn't learned how to read his face. There were many things I did not know about him, and it seemed now that I might never know them. It was too late to ask those questions.

The chance had arrived that winter, ten years ago, when he had come to stay, and I had not taken it. I had been neither kind nor unkind to my uncle, but saved up knowing him for a future time, when it would be easier. I had thought he would always be there to discover, like a locked family treasure chest, too substantial to be moved. I would surely inherit it one day, and be given the key. A sick, black feeling welled up in me, and I realised then that the key had been inside me all along, and I hadn't known it was there.

The streets flowed quickly past the window, bringing our farewell closer. Through my uncle, Korea had become almost real to me. But I suspected that when he left the floating embryo of coded dynasties, diagrams, religious precepts and war dates might perish. He would exist only in the unfinished monument my mother's memory had carved, in the transient taste of bought *kimchi*, and in visits to greengrocer immigrants, whose faces, behind bountiful rows of fruit, were closed with forgetting.

I didn't see it then, but my uncle was a drawbridge to the destroyed homeland my mother had left. Through him I visited the mansion with the green gates where they were born, the northern estates, and my great-grandfather's temple on Mount Sorak surrounded by the thousand chestnut trees he'd had planted for longevity. Although the Japanese had burned down these homes, and the lands were divided on the 38th parallel, I felt I had walked through these places, and breathed them. All this still existed inside him, intact and beyond reach. The drawbridge was now closing.

I forget what we said when we parted. The glare of oncoming headlights numbed me. The car door slammed, a reflection of the street facade obscured his face, and he was gone.

Later I stood in my apartment and looked down on the myriad changing signals and dim taillights below that formed an endless, sweeping canyon of arrivals and departures. With pain, I imagined Kwang-ho at the window of his aeroplane, returning to Seoul, contemplating the same city.

What would he be thinking of as the brutal streets of New York contracted into cool, glittering grids? What would he recall of his years with us? Eating fried egg with his fingers, or an afternoon's serpent hunting? Perhaps a dinner at Young Bin Kwan. These incidents seemed meagre, but I hoped he would remember them. I wanted to be there in the background, and to appear across the table from him, years later. But I couldn't break into his memories. Too much glass, and flesh, and time sealed them. I had to be content just to picture him thinking, suspended somewhere over the Pacific.

I remember being seven years old and the smell of apples. A boy was twisting my arm behind my back just for fun.

"Say 'uncle!'" the boy taunted as a crowd gathered. For some unknown reason "uncle" was the word American bullies used to torture you. I wouldn't say it. He twisted my arm harder and harder until my shoulder was shooting with pain, and my face was red and sweating. "Uncle! Uncle!" I cried out in furious shame.

YOMESAN

Cathy Kanoelani Ikeda

How you must have dreamed,
Most venerable father,
Of the perfect *yomesan*
Who would bow deeply before you each morning,
Hand you the steaming, milky miso soup
With ribbons of *konbu* dancing in the broth
And open your drapes
To chase away the insecurities of aging.
You had three sons,
A lucky number,
Surely, one of them would bring her home,
The daughter-in-law from your dreams.
Instead, eager to break the mold
Of your *nisei* expectations,
They brought home only *gaijin*
Or worse, the half-breeds,
Poi dogs with Japanese faces
and *katonk* aspirations
Of moving in the fast lane in the big city.
But how well you have adapted,
Most aged father,
To eating lasagna with your rice,
Poi with your *sashimi*,
And brushing away cobwebs
Of past dreams
With *lauhala* fans
Made by your mongrel grandchildren.

LOVE CAN BE ARRANGED

Usha Lee McFarling

My eldest cousin Ritu is marrying a girl who is the wrong color. She is white.

Ritu's mother and six aunts refuse to attend the wedding. I, too, have been forbidden from going.

"I don't want my blood mixing with hers," my grandfather says.

Papaji wants Ritu, his eldest grandson, to marry an Indian. Preferably Punjabi. Preferably warrior caste. Preferably trained in radiology.

Margie has never had a job. She is 23 and has twice modeled bras for newspaper department store ads. Ritu is 30, bald and overweight. He sells computers and is good at convincing people he knows what they need. Ritu has a lot of money because he has lived at home for so many years.

Margie's mother is on welfare, my aunt says, crying. We don't talk of these things, but I know what she means: Margie is of the wrong caste. Too often touched, perhaps, untouchable.

Papaji says: I don't want my blood mixing with hers.

One year ago, Papaji arranged a marriage for Ritu with a girl from Delhi. A fair-skinned Punjabi medical student who cooked her grandfather's vegetables every afternoon.

Ritu was 29 then, my age. The family thought it was time for him to marry. Ritu flew to Delhi one month before the wedding to meet his bride. She wouldn't look at his face. He looked at hers, at her body under the loose *kurta* pajama. He looked at her thick black hair, dark hands, the maroon *bindi* on her forehead, her jewelry. Her gold, he thought, it looks yellower than the gold at home. I don't like it.

At dinner, Joginder's grandfather spoke quickly in Punjabi. Ritu didn't understand. He just nodded and ate. Then he went to sleep.

The next night, the family left Ritu and Joginder alone. He walked toward her, took her hand and placed it on his penis. She ran from the room. For three days, she wouldn't come out of her room, or eat, or speak. Finally, they let Ritu leave, apologizing for Joginder's inexcusable behavior. In a month, she would be fine, they said, ready for marriage to such an honorable husband.

In a month, Ritu announced his engagement to Margie.

Papaji has lost this battle before, has lost it eight times. He has lost eight daughters.

He sent them away to get the American medical degree he never received. He thought they would return home, marry well and give him many grandsons. But my mother, the oldest, surprised him.

She wrote: Papaji, I want to marry an American.

Papaji's letters came furiously back across the Atlantic. You disgrace the family. You will breed monsters. You are no longer my daughter.

She wrote: Father, please give your blessing. Please arrange a wedding in Delhi.

Papaji's wrote, You will not marry in India. Make this filthy union in your new land. Make it in America.

Then his letters stopped.

Mother and father married in Kansas, wed by an Episcopal priest in a ceremony organized by my father's oldest sisters. The sisters, tall and blonde, wore borrowed saris as bridesmaids' gowns. Each wore a bindi on her broad midwestern forehead. The only other sari in the church was my mother's.

My mother says she ignored Papaji's rejection, but I think she's lying, or her memories have changed. She won't talk back to him even now. And she waited to have a child until her younger sister bore Ritu. Mother was the first sister to see the new baby. Ten fingers. Ten toes. The child was not a monster. Weeks later, mother was pregnant.

Grandfather acknowledged our births by demanding that we be given Indian names. But he never left India to see us. Only when his left kidney had to be removed did he come to the States. Came, finally, to his daughters and the many half-breed children they created.

Papaji loves us, I know, but it hurts him to look at us. We are not pure descendants, but detours. We are dilutions of his warrior blood. He wants to stop us before we weaken the blood further, before there is no trace of India left in our children's faces, in their skin. He has waited 19 years to reroute his bloodline. This time he won't lose.

And you, he says when he forbids me from attending Ritu's wedding. You, my only granddaughter, you are next.

Papaji has never said anything to me about my white boyfriends. Papaji has told my mother we can date Americans, but we will marry Indians. Everyone knows my cousins, the boys, laugh about Papaji and imitate him behind his back. Everyone knows they will do whatever they want.

The one time I imitated Papaji, mother slapped me.

I don't invite my boyfriend to Ritu's wedding. He wonders why. You'll be bored, I say. Jeff knows, though, why he's not invited. If I married you, would your family boycott our wedding? he asks. Don't be stupid, I say. I can do what I want.

But they would, I think. They would.

Papaji has been fighting weddings all his life. Each younger daughter heard the same curses as my mother, felt the same cold boycott. Yet each wedding party grew larger as the older sisters, with white husbands in tow, filled the churches.

Finally, only Papaji's youngest daughter, the most beautiful, remained single. Rani loved Papaji best. So she agreed to marry a man Papaji found for her. The boy was the nephew of a Delhi surgeon. He was already in the U.S., living in Houston.

He's been there three years. He must be very American, Papaji told Rani. You will like him. He's an engineer—something very complicated. I can't understand it. Must be he will become very rich. You will like him.

From California, without ever seeing the man, Rani agreed. They married in Delhi, under Papaji's gaze, then flew back to Houston. There Rani learned her husband was not an engineer. Instead, he washed dishes in a bar. There Rani learned her husband wouldn't return home until after two in the morning, long after her curry had congealed into butter and spices, long after her *gobi aloo* had gone too soggy to eat. There Rani learned her husband would come home smelling of other women, cheap American perfume, sweat and sex.

After three days, Rani went home to California and had her marriage annulled.

Rani lives alone now, laughing at the widower Punjabis who come to court her. She has not spoken to Papaji since her wedding.

At Margie's bachelorette party, her friends joke about her fetish for Indians. Margie had a lot of Punjabi men before Ritu, maybe ten. One of the men was Ritu's younger brother. Ritu knows, but he won't admit it. No one's brought this up since the wedding was announced, but we wonder, we all wonder how Ritu can marry a woman his brother has tasted. I think about the fights to come between them: Gurpreet will win every fight from now on. All he'll have to say is, You know, Ritu, I like what your wife does with her tongue. You know, Ritu, she's not so good in bed after all.

My mother says Margie has no fetish, that it's money that she really wants. These lusty Punjabi men, mother says, are just easy targets. Lusty? I laugh. These Indian boys? They are men, my mother says. You just don't notice it.

I don't know why I never chose an Indian, or let one choose me. I don't know how I learned what to desire. My mother chose my father, his white skin a birthright to this America. Papaji chose a fair-skinned wife, planning the skin of his children. Now I am surrounded by the fairest skin, the skin of the north, shades of mountains and pure air. The gradient has shifted so far I can't even see the darker end. Sometimes, I can't even see myself.

When I was 15, I stayed in Ritu's room for three months while our roof was being rebuilt. In Ritu's room with its baseball trophies, KISS poster, balsa wood racing car. Ritu was at boarding school.

When I opened his closet to put my clothes away, I found Ritu's magazines, stacks of them. A naked woman looked up from each cover. That night, I began flipping through the magazines, seeing the cheerleaders, the farm girls, the starlets. It took me three weeks to get through the piles, through the thousands of blonde heads, huge breasts, palest lipstick smiles.

I didn't see a single Indian face. No brown breasts or thighs. No one even slightly dark. No one like me.

I remember those women now: their twisted bodies and glowing white skin, the positions the same page after page, month after month. They all have the same face in my memory: it is Margie's.

Two hours before Ritu's wedding, Papaji summons me. He says grandmother will be going to the wedding and I must drive her. So, he's known all along I was defying him. I rush to dress and drive to their house. I know we will be late, but I have to obey Papaji. I wonder how Bibiji got permission to go to the wedding. She probably threatened to stop cooking.

When I get there, Bibiji calls me to her door. Nice, she says, feeling my flowered dress, but don't you want to wear one of my saris? No. This blue bindi will match. No. Bibiji looks ready, but says she isn't finished with her makeup.

Papaji makes me sit, though I'm nervous about being late. He begins telling me a story. I wonder if he's just talking to delay me so I'll miss the wedding. He tells me about Rani, a girl from his village—the most beautiful in the village. I watched her grow up, he says. I waited for the day I could marry her. When I asked, my father just laughed. Her family was poorer than mine. My father found your grandmother's family. Her dowry paid for my medical school.

I can't believe I've never heard this story. I hope grandmother can't hear us.

Child, Papaji says, It would make me so happy if I could see you in a sari.

Okay, I mumble.

Today.

Papaji is using his I am the patriarch tone of voice. I know I'll never get to the wedding if I argue.

Okay.

Bibiji brings in a red sari, bordered in gold. A sari like the one my mother married in, I imagine, although her wedding pictures are black and white. The sari and the slip are ironed, ready. The blouse has been taken in to fit me. I wonder how long the sari has been ready for me to wear.

In the bathroom, I step out of my flowered dress. I hook the blouse over my bra and tie the slip around my waist. I have no idea how to put the sari on. I don't want to ask for Bibiji's help but the wedding is in 20 minutes.

I let Bibiji wrap the silk around me. She leans on her walker as she pleats the extra fabric into gold-threaded folds at my waist. She takes the loose end of the sari and drapes it over my shoulder.

How beautiful, she cries.

I like the way the silk feels on my skin, but I won't admit it.

Bibiji reaches for her makeup case.

No! That's it. I am not wearing a bindi.

Okay, but you must wear bangles. You must.

I leave the bathroom, my dress crumpled on the floor near the shower. Bibiji's still not ready to go, so I find Papaji, who says nothing about my sari. He knew I would wear it.

Papaji, what happened to Rani?

I would be working in the dirt if I married her.

But you think of her. You named a daughter after her! You must have loved her.

Love, Papaji says as the doorbell rings. Love can be arranged.

It's Paviter at the door, the grandson of my grandmother's best friend. He's in a suit. He looks nervous. Oh Pete! my grandmother says, speaking too loudly. What a surprise! We're just on our way to Ritu's wedding. Why don't you come?

Paviter, who is constantly trying to be more American, makes everyone call him Pete. It's easier to pronounce, he says.

Hello, Paviter, I say, pronouncing every syllable. He asks why I am wearing a sari. I tell him to shut up. Pete offers to drive. My grandmother asks to sit in the cramped back seat, even though it means keeping her stiff knees bent through the 45-minute drive. She wants Pete and me to sit together in front. I refuse to talk to him or my grandmother. We ride together, silently, pulled by the undertow of my family's desires. It feels like my sari will fall off any minute. I should have brought Jeff.

In the church, my cousins all sit in pews with their white girlfriends. Each girl is whiter, blonder than the next. Our new land: we hear its invitation to merge.

My cousins whisper to each other as I walk in with Pete. The wedding is about to start. The only noise in the church is the creaking of Bibiji's walker. An usher helps her to the first pew, next to Rani, and I slip into a seat between Gurpreet and Pete.

Gurpreet keeps whispering in my ear through the ceremony: Arlina's with an Indian boy. Going to marry an Indian boy. Looking for some dark meat. Pete's next to me, smiling stupidly. He wouldn't marry a full Indian, but he'll take me.

You're next. It's Gurpreet's whisper, but I hear only Papaji's voice. You're next. You're next. The youngest girl, the only girl. You're next.

I can't see myself in the white dress. I see only my dark arms emerging from this red sari. I see *mehendi* patterns imprinted on my palms and on the soles of my feet in these gold sandals. The *bindi* on my forehead itches. I'm sweating under the weight of the wedding sari, giving off the smell of sandalwood soap. I can't lift my wrists, burdened with heavy gold bangles. I'm next. I'm next. I'm next.

Looking for some dark meat . . . Shut up! I say, too loud. Three pews of people turn backwards. Gurpreet looks stunned. Just kidding, he says, God! Pete takes my hand, touching me for the first time. At the altar, Ritu bends to kiss Margie, and I watch them through the metal bars of my grandmother's walker.

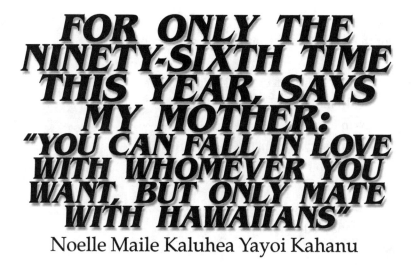

FOR ONLY THE NINETY-SIXTH TIME THIS YEAR, SAYS MY MOTHER: "YOU CAN FALL IN LOVE WITH WHOMEVER YOU WANT, BUT ONLY MATE WITH HAWAIIANS"

Noelle Maile Kaluhea Yayoi Kahanu

The valley
is alive

I waited at home for the call—
the call from Palani to go into the valley

But the call came not from him
but from the valley itself

Persistent
but quiet

I felt a longing
in my body
in my sex

But I, too was afraid

For the second time, I entered the valley alone

It is there that I can feel the akua's heartbeat
his breath moves each leaf
his groan found
in the bending between two bamboo stalks
his warrior in pili grass dancing in the rain

I am followed
soft breath on the small of my back
bare shoulders
the tightening of my na'au
the beating of a frightened heart

I persist, held by this longing
this yearning
for the clearing up ahead
for the heiau where I leave a perfectly formed
granny apple and round sweet orange

At the heiau I can feel the mana's pulse
I envision a heiau
before Hewahewa
before foreign contact
before the coming of the bamboo

I ask, as always, for guidance
and strength
and wisdom
sufficient to sustain me
in my travels
and paths that take me

away but always return me here
to this valley

As I leave, movement amongst the low dry groundcover:
he is dark brown, almost black
he is not in front of me but to the side of me
a mo'o

I walk guietly from the heiau
holding my keys to silence their rude jingle
listening intently
for footsteps

In the midst of fallen bamboo leaves, he moves again
not in front of me but to the side of me
he is nearly black
the mo'o

I emerge from the heiau's path, relieved to once again
be in the sun
to hear the buzzing of modern civilization
I greet and chat with another young Hawaiian woman

I am now almost out of the valley
feet walking on soft green grass
I do not hear his rustling
but rather see him
not in front of me but to the side of me
this dark brown black mo'o
my mo'o

And this yearning persists
in my body
in my sex
and now in my veins
in my pilikoko

for a dark brown black Hawaiiian man
with feet that can walk on heiaus
on dry crusty bamboo leaves
and green green vibrant green grass

(my mother would be pleased)

MY MOTHER SITS
LIKE A GEISHA

Jacquelyn Kim

On days off,
she becomes a witch at her stew
busying all four burners.
The floured chicken
fries to gold in the puddle of oil,
pumpkin soup simmering.
Plump grains form a clean surface
in a new pot of rice,
steam rising when she lifts the lid.
She's half-akimbo,
humming Korean folk songs.

She tells me about philosophy at the marble table
eating short strains of white meat,
forkfuls of myulichi, crisp fish edges,
black-eyed, inch-long, salty as pigs.
She describes her last life over apples.
Our bites sound like logs
cleaving along the grain.

After this, she brews me lemon tea in a sauce pan.
The red seeps from the bag,
a dense cloud in hot water.
Soon, the whole pool's burgundy.
She brings me the golden drink on a tray,
her love, rich as my gluttony.

A CONSERVATIVE VIEW

Cathy Song

Money, my mother
never had much.
Perhaps that explains her life's
philosophy, the conservation of money,
the idea of money as a natural resource,
the sleepless nights worrying
whether there is enough of it.
According to her current calculations,
there isn't.

I used to think it was because she is Chinese,
proud of the fact that her practical
nature is due to her Chinese blood.
"We do not spoil our children"
she is fond of saying as an explanation
for never having given in to our demands.
"Take care of the needs but not the wants" is another.

Place a well-behaved child
in front of her and my mother will say,
"Chinese, eh?"
She believes Japanese and Korean
parents spoil their children.
"Doormats to their kids."
And the bok gwai?—well,
they ship their offspring to camp or boarding school, right?

For the Chinese discipline begins at home.
And it begins with teaching the value of money.

There are two things in life
my mother vows never to pay for:
gift wrapping and parking.
It hurts her to cough up change for the meter.
Lucky is any day she can pull
into an empty space with time still running.
I was convinced my friends knew
that the birthday gifts I presented at parties
were wrapped in leftover sheets of our bathroom wallpaper.
—"Eh, how come dis paypa so tick?"

My mother's thrift frowns on the frivolous—
like singing in the shower
(it's a waste of water).
Her clear and practical sentences
are sprinkled with expressions
semantically rooted to the conservation of money.
They pepper her observations like expletives—
"Poho" if we bought something we couldn't use.
"Humbug" if we have to go out and buy
something we don't need.
"No need"—her favorite expression of all

On shopping trips to the mall
she'll finger something soft and expensive,
letting her fingers linger on the exquisite
cut and fabric of a garment
when suddenly she'll exclaim,
like a Kung Fu battle cry,
"Pee-sa!"

(the one word she borrows liberally
from her Korean in-laws),
shuddering and releasing the price tag
as if she'd been bitten by a snake.

My sister and I agree
she takes the price of things too personally.
Every morning there is her wake-up call—
"Diapers on sale at Longs."
"Price of lettuce up at Star."—
as though she were reporting the Dow Jones Industrial
        Average.
If I answer in the negative
to her interrogative
"Did you use coupons to buy that?"
—*that* being chicken thighs or toilet paper,
I feel guilty.

My father doesn't help matters.
He has heard enough from Mother
about Koreans being big spenders, show-offs—
"champagne taste on a beer budget"—
to have his revenge.
He thinks Mao Tse-Tung is the best
thing that ever happened to China.
"How else are you going to get those damn pa-kes to share?"

SHRINKING THE UTERUS

Cathy Song

After the birth of my son, my mother moves in.
She enlists the help of her sisters, my aunts
who appear in full force
with chicken broth drenched in whiskey
to tide me over, a preliminary
dish to the masterpiece
they spend days in my kitchen
preparing—ju gerk, pig's feet soup,
which I can hear rattling on the stove top
as if the pig's feet were tap dancing
to a simmering frenzy.

The stew is sickeningly sweet,
vinegar and brown sugar
boiled down to a thick caramel tar.
I am ordered to eat it—
or else in my old age
I'll have "plenny pilikia"—woman's trouble.
Pig's feet helps shrink the uterus,
which after birth is a flabby bag of muscle.
Pig's feet helps get rid of the old blood.
So I am told.

I am told a lot of things.
My mother scares me with a string of wives' tales
and my aunts concur.

I must keep off my feet.
I must keep them warm.
I must keep away from windows.
I mustn't under any circumstances
wash my hair for a month.
Ancient Chinese birth control,
my father says with a wink.
My mother gives him the-what-does-he-know-look.
And already, tsk, tsk, I am spoiling the baby.

The wind is howling
when commandeered by my mother
I shuffle in my house slippers toward the kitchen,
my hair matted with the sweat of labor,
of my mind rice gruel from lack of sleep.
Who would find me
desirable in this hour of my life?
She leads me to the table,
offers me at last the triumphant gelatinous hooves—
silent pearly knobs of cartilage
bobbing like dentures in a porcelain bowl.

SURFING AND OTHER FORMS OF LOVE

Mindy Eun Soo Pennybacker

Tory's first memory was of her great-grandmother's naked breasts.

"Jesus love me, this I know
'Cause the Bible tell me so . . ."

All the English Hulmone knew was contained in hymns.

The old woman lived downstairs in the back room off the kitchen.

"Yes, Jesus love me
Yes, Jesus love me . . ."

Unobserved, in empty rooms and hallways, Tory still crawled. When they found her, they plucked her up by the armpits and made her choo-choo on her feet as she leaned on furniture and walls. But they hadn't found her yet.

This time, she made it as far as the room of the old woman. It was filled with radiant light and cigarette smoke. The old woman was a cone shape, in her full white skirt, sitting cross-legged on her flat square zabuton pillow on the floor, sewing by hand as she sang. Her silver hair was loose. Bound by a rag at the forehead, it flared out, down her shoulders and back. Sunlight poured through the windows onto the naked breasts, white and vast as icebergs, flowing down her chest and over Hulmone's thick sash until the nipples rested in her lap.

In that house, no one ever intruded on another's nakedness. And, for all Tory knew, no one was ever naked except herself or Henry, springing from the bath into the shelter of a towel.

Hulmone was always prim, a strict moralist, quick to punish you with a blow from her gnarled hand. Tory had never imagined the old woman's breasts before and here they were, the forbidden sight, huge beyond imagining and flat as pancake batter poured with a free hand until it fills the griddle.

The old woman caught sight of Tory—frozen, one hand raised in mid-crawl—and laughed out loud. She held up one of her drooping breasts and shook her head from side to side, making a "tsk-tsk" deprecating sound. "Too many baby," she said.

That was Korea, Tory thought, years later. A ruined matriarchy. Sagging, empty breasts. That was why they had all left.

They all lived together in their grandparents' house: Hulmone's room was in the back. Tory and Henry shared the sunny front bedroom with its six windows on three sides. Across the landing, their grandparents' room tunneled deep into the shade of the Douglas firs. Their parents, Janet and Jim, slept in the front bedroom downstairs, with its own bath and the windowed closet that served as a study, where their mother sat and corrected papers.

Their father never had papers to correct because he was a rover, a substitute teacher. Tory and Henry heard them fighting, sometimes, late at night and in the morning. Other times, the children heard the bed bumping against the wall in the room below, and afterwards low, confidential talk and gentle laughter. The parents often talked of moving out, but they were trying to save up money to buy a place of their own. "And besides, we couldn't afford even to rent a place by the beach. These kids are already spoiled," their father said.

Their father, Jim Murphy, was a Southern Californian, a golden boy: tall, straight-shouldered, with stone-green eyes, a small nose, turgid-lipped, toothy smile and curly blond hair. He was a man of few words. He knew the beach best, and that was where he spent most of his time, easy and relaxed, with his children. His faded swim shorts hung low on his soft belly with the hairs clustered about the navel. His arms and legs were lean, long muscled, hard. When she was cold, at the beach, Tory curled up on his warm chest and belly.

Henry had the green eyes, but Tory didn't resemble either parent. Tory could have been a twin to Alice Liddell, the wild-looking, dark child who looks out, unsmiling, barefoot and tense, from the Reverend Charles Dodgson's photographs, the child who was rendered blond, sentimentalized—made safer—in Tenniel's illustrations.

"She sees right through things," Tory's father said to her mother. "She sees through all the bullshit. She wants the truth. Don't cha. Hah? Don't cha." Tory charged him and he fell to the ground, holding her over his head, his arms so long that her flailing limbs couldn't touch him. He laughed and laughed as their mother looked on frowning.

"Well, she'll never get it from you," said Janet.

"What's that?"

"The truth."

"Hey—that's what I'm trying to tell ya. She already knows it!" He lowered Tory and blew air against her stomach, then rolled over on her, pretending to crush her, holding back his full weight.

"Crush me. I like it," Tory said, giggling.

"Jim, that's enough."

"No!" said Tory, but he got up, obeying their mother, and brushed the grass off his knees. His face was red. Tory got that from him, that inflammable skin. It burned bright with embarrassment as well as sun. She knew her gorgeous parents were unhappy with each other. It was her fault. She was in the way.

Now he leaned over, lazily tickling her belly where her shirt rode up, and her neck until she made her sputtering sound. "What is this, 'Crush me, I like it? Crush me, I like it?' I never heard of such a thing. You crazy little mite."

She giggled and squirmed like a puppy.

Henry, diaper sagging, arms open, toddled towards him with a big, unhooded smile.

"Oh, no! It's the Atomic Baby!" cried her father, and he flung himself to the ground again to receive Henry's assault.

Later, her father was serious. "It's okay, Black Eyes," he said to Tory. "See what you have to see. Think for yourself. Make up your own damn mind, pardon my French."

She held his fingers bunched in her small hand. "Mom gets so mad."

"It's not your fault, Sweets. Hell, it's my fault. Adult stuff. Don't worry, we can handle it."

The world of the yellow alligators was happy, sunny. Tory painted beaches, forests, streams, ancient temples and great castles. The alligators made links, tooth to tail. They made hoops and letters, looking out of the pictures with their sly eyes and serrated smiles, proud in their ochre skins, secure in their awkward reptile limbs. At the end of the year, Tory's teacher wanted to keep an alligator painting, but Tory would not give one up. They were a family, each alligator alive and unique to her.

"But dear, we have stacks and stacks of them," said her mother.

"They belong together," said Tory.

Her mother and the teacher were silent for a moment. Tory watched dust motes float in shafts of sunlight.

Miss Reyes sprang back. "This one is still wet, however. And it's such a big painting. Why don't you leave it here to dry, and you and your mother can come back for it next week?"

"No. We have to take it now," said Tory. She writhed as the teacher put a hand on her arm, and gave Miss Reyes a good swift kick in the belly.

"Ouch," said Miss Reyes, and burst into tears.

"Now you have hurt her feelings, Tory. Now you must give her the painting," said her mother.

Tory wept. Her mother gave her lickings, and still she wept. That night she lay awake, contemplating the word "infinity." She pictured the universe as it appeared from the ground, dark space with pinpoint stars, through which yellow alligators traveled, with their pointy noses, until they came up against a brick wall. This they clambered over, only to find the same stardusted vault, and traveled on to the next brick wall. She found it useful to have markers. It had to end somewhere, she thought. She could not conceive of space going on and on forever. Yet in subsequent nocturnal travels, she and the alligators never got to the end. And they were always painfully aware that one set of alligators was missing, held prisoner by Miss Reyes, forever.

"I'm going to eat you up, Grandma!"

"Oh, please don't, Tory dear!"

"I am going to eat you now."

"Ouch! Don't you get too wild, or I'll have to shut you up in a cracker box," said her grandmother, who had soft, golden skin and hooded eyes that crinkled with amusement at the corners. She had thinning hair and dentures, but she looked glamorous, to Tory. Grandma had poise, and a no-nonsense, geometric sense of *chic*. She was not a frilly, fussy person, not a wearer of pastels. Her dyed dark hair was blunt cut to the jawline, with just the slightest wave. She favored orange or red lipstick, and her glasses had thick, rectangular tortoise rims. And Grandma was gentle with Tory, her long face often crinkling with amused smiles. She had not been so gentle with Tory's mother, Janet.

"Mom says you used to lock her in the closet, Grandma. Why?"

Grandma shook her head and worked her tongue over her upper teeth. "Nothing else to be done with her when she was having one of her tantrums—just like a wild animal!" Lips closed, she gave her wry, contained smile.

"Why did Mom have tantrums?"

"She wanted everything her way," Grandma said. "She was selfish. Good girls are not selfish."

"I'm too big for a cracker box."

"We'll see," said Grandma. Grandma had long legs and liked to sit, while working in the kitchen, on a high stool. She was preparing short ribs, slicing each piece of meat vertically and horizontally, almost to the bone, and then, with the blunt end of the knife, pounding it tender before she plopped it into its soy, garlic, scallion bath.

Tory's big black eyes were riveted on her grandmother. "Are you planning to cut me down to size?"

Grandma chuckled. "What do you think?"

Tory laughed, sharp white teeth parted, head tossed back, the warmth rising to her face. "I don't think so!" She turned her head and looked at her grandmother from the outer corner of her eye and poised on the balls of her feet, about to run.

Grandma nodded, smiling back. "Less trouble to find a big cracker box. Just big enough to hold you and keep you from growing. So you'll always be my little Tory darling." And just as Tory began to dart away Grandma caught her in her strong arms and pressed her to her big, soft belly and bosom. She smelled of garlic, honey, chilis and peanut oil.

"It was wrong of Mom to give away my alligators."

Grandma looked worried. "It is customary to give the teacher a gift at the end of the year."

"But the alligators were a family!"

Grandma gave her a long look. "You don't have to worry about our family. We love each other and we're all going to stay together. Certainly, no one will be given away."

Immensely relieved, Tory hugged her grandmother and gently bit her wrist.

In the summers, their father worked in their grandparents' store and her mother taught summer school. But they still had a month at the end, and that was their beach month. The August Tory was six, they camped in a beach park on the North Shore, cooking on a hibachi and hanging out their wash on a line between the trees, "Just like the Hawaiians and Samoans," their mother said.

"You've gotten black as a Samoan," their father teased her. He was late. He'd just got back from town, and forgotten the milk. All he'd brought was beer, and he was drinking one now.

Their mother looked up. She was crouched over the barbecue; she gave a howl as the wind drove the oily smoke into her eyes. With the tongs, she picked up a hot coal, straightened up and fired it at him. With a *smack*, the coal appeared to lodge itself in their father's chest. His eyes and mouth opened wide.

He brushed the coal away. There was a red-purple hole and the acrid smell of singed hair and flesh. He ran across the park, leapt over the low stone wall and dove into the sea.

"What if you'd hit one of our kids, or someone else's? You could have put out an eye," Jim said to Janet later. He lay on his back on a towel beneath a *hau* tree as she cleaned his wound with hydrogen peroxide and covered it with gauze. "What's wrong with what I said? The beaches are covered with people trying to get your color."

"It was your tone. You were putting me down," Janet said.

"The put-down's in your own head. I'm supposed to apologize to you? After you battered me with a burning coal?" He grinned. "I don't believe it."

Janet sighed. Beads of perspiration shone on her upper lip. She blinked rapidly, and brushed her forehead with the back of her hand. "I'll admit I overreacted," she said.

The children noticed that she didn't say she was sorry.

"I've always been dark. When I was small, the other kids used to call me 'Samungi.'"

He nodded. "I know. You Orientals look down on Samoans."

"Well, you haoles look down on everybody else."

"It would be so much simpler if you looked up to me as I deserve!"

Janet flung herself on him, but Jim caught her by the forearms and lifted her above his supine form, tucking his knees under her hips, the way he wrestled with Tory and Henry.

The children cheered.

Janet fought, but even as she clamped her lips shut in a frown, her slow smile emerged, revealing her big front teeth with the gap between them.

He lowered her down and hugged her as she lay on top of him, hiding her smile against his bare chest, and he kissed the top of her head.

Later, after the bonfire and the marshmallows, the children, lying in their small separate tent, heard the sounds of heavy breathing and the rustle of quilts against the canvas sides of their parents' big tent. Still later, as the moon threw the trees into puppet silhouette against the walls, Tory heard her father say, "You've got to watch it, Janet. You think it doesn't hurt because I'm bigger. I know I'm a numbskull, but I do have feelings."

"Plenty of feelings, and no self-discipline."

"God. You were such a cute little shy chick at Berkeley. Never gave me any backtalk. What happened, hah?"

Silence.

"Hah?"

"I thought you didn't want any backtalk."

"I'll show you what I want. Come here."

Because they always made up, sooner or later, and because her grandmother had promised the family would stay together, it came as a great shock to Tory when her father left them. She was six. Henry was three. The adults muttered late at night when the children were supposed to be asleep. But Tory sat silent and tense on the shadowy landing.

"That whore—" It was an aunt speaking.

"What do you expect from that kind?" said Grandma. "Get nothing from 'em. Okies, the whole lot."

"Fresno," said Janet.

"I thought San Diego," said Uncle (*Doctor*) Pae.

"That was all an act. He worked in a cannery there once," said Janet.

"Better cut all the ties now. Less pain that way. Don't write, don't ask for money," said their grandfather.

"They haven't got any, anyway," Janet said. "I think Jim was the first in his whole clan to go to college."

"Don't even say his name again. It makes me sick," said their grandmother.

"Still. What about Henry? Boy needs a father," said their grandfather. As if a girl didn't.

"He's got you. You're still young," said Grandma.

"Too old for some things," said their grandfather in a heavy sigh.

"Thank goodness for that," said Grandma briskly.

They thought it was poetic justice when Jim Murphy, surfing off Santa Cruz the following winter, was presumably killed by a great white shark. The body was never found. Just the board with a chunk bitten out of it.

A few years later, when their grandmother died, the gloom settled in permanently. Their grandfather remarried and moved into his new wife's house in Mōʻiliʻili, in an island carved out on the flat midlands by crisscrossing highways, a brief oasis of old homes shaded by big trees near the Willows Restaurant, where the small wedding reception was held.

To her father's wedding, Tory's mother wore black. She stood on the footbridge above the lake of carp and frowned. Black was the Korean tradition at weddings, but the family had long since been westernized.

"She looks like a witch," said Tory's grandfather under his breath, through his teeth.

"Never mind," said his new wife, but she looked as if she did.

Uncle Chung came and took Hulmone, their grand-mother's mother, to live with his family. There was so much to load in his car—the sewing machine, the chests and tables from Korea, the baskets of bright fabric remnants collected over years and years from the whole family, with which the old woman could not part—that it got overloaded, or at least wouldn't start. Tory helped push it. She ran down the street, shoulder to hip with the men. She felt useful and strong.

Excited, she ran to tell her mother. No achievement was real until it had been told to her mother. She ran around back to the kitchen and burst in the door. Her mother was standing at the sink with Auntie Hee, washing and drying.

"I helped push Uncle Chung's car!" Tory shouted.

"Shut *up!*" cried her mother, drawing herself upright, and let fly with her wet, soapy hand across Tory's face.

Auntie Hee raised her own hand to her mouth.

"Can't you see I was *talking* to someone?" screamed Janet. "Pushing a car—are you crazy? That's dangerous. Now get out of my sight!"

"We don't need anybody. Fuck 'em," said Janet. She had a beer. She sat back and wiggled her bare toes. She did not say she was sorry for hitting Tory. That didn't matter. What Tory hoped was that the fit of rage had passed. If it hadn't, she would lie awake in bed, waiting for the heavy tread on the stairs, the door bursting open, the livid face and raised fist and recriminations.

Janet's face grew tense. Her lip twisted. She looked angry, stared, not at Tory, but into the middle distance, as if something hovered in the air above the grease spot in the driveway. "I dreamt of your Grandma again last night. She came to the table, wiping her hands dry on her apron, sat down in a chair and looked at us all with oh, such love in her eyes. But she didn't eat, she didn't touch the food. She knew she was dead." Tears welled in Janet's protruding eyes; she wiped at them awkwardly as they spilled over.

Tory touched her shoulder.

"Do you mind?" Janet asked, with a look so mean that Tory jumped back.

In their family, grief was as embarrassing as nakedness.

"Kids, we're smart and self-sufficient. We'll get on fine on our own," said Janet, staring at the diseased panax hedge, the cracked, humped sidewalk.

Soon afterwards, she took up with Louie Cheng, who became their stepfather.

BIGMA

April Melia Coloretti

She does not remember
the lavender rug
or the sheets I gave
her of the same shade.
She forgets the time
we ate Filipino food
in old town Kalihi, the waiters
speaking in *Tagalog*
and broken English
balancing their steaming bowls
of bittermelon or *pansit* noodles.

She can only swear in *Ilocano*
spitting out her words
like *li hing mui* seeds
after all the sweet-sour plum meat
has been grated off by teeth.

Stolen spoons crust in her dressers,
rusted with cheap hair spray.
Crumbs in her nightgown pockets
crush into sand. Half a cough drop
bundled in tissue
molds in the hold of her purse.

In thirty humid summers
of waiting, she recalls a common

gravestone among thousands,
my grandfather's bones as brittle
as her memory,
and the sound of my voice
bringing her back.

LUNA MOTH

Jessica Hagedorn

When I finally come home to Manila to visit, my father warns me not to bother visiting our old house. "You'll be disappointed. Memories are always better." Smiling apologetically, he tells me reality will diminish the grandeur of my childhood image of home. I take his picture with my new camera, which later falls in the swimming pool by accident. The camera is destroyed, along with my roll of film. I decide to visit our old house in Mandaluyong anyway, borrowing a car from Mikey. Pucha goes with me; she loves riding around in cars and doesn't need any excuse. "After that, let's go to the Intercon Hotel and have a drink," she says, a gleam of mischief in her eyes. "Put on some makeup," she bosses me, "you look tired." I laugh. Pucha is up to her old tricks. She applies thick coats of blue eyeshadow on her heavy eyelids, studying her face in the mirror with rapt concentration.

My father is right. The house with its shuttered windows looks smaller than I remember, and dingy. The once lush and sprawling garden is now a forlorn landscape of rocks, weeds, and wild ferns. The bamboo grove has been cut down. "Let's go," Pucha whispers, impatient and uninterested. An old man with bright eyes introduces himself as Manong Tibo, the caretaker. He unlocks door after door for us, pulling aside cobwebs, warning us to be careful. Rotting floorboards creak under the weight of our footsteps. "My bedroom," I say to the old man, who nods. I am overwhelmed by melancholy at the sight of the empty room. A frightened mouse dashes across the grimy tiled floor. Pucha jumps back and screams, clutching and pinching my arm. "Let's go," she pleads. "Wait outside. I'll be there soon, " I say, trying to conceal my irritation. I am relieved finally to be alone, in this desolate house with only Manong for company. He studies me with his bright eyes. "You live in America?" His niece is a nurse in San Francisco, California, he tells me with pride. Someday, he hopes she'll send for him.

I stay another hour, walking in and out of the dusty rooms in a kind of stupor. The shutters in the windows of the kitchen, Pacita's kingdom, are hanging from their hinges. The gas stove and refrigerator are gone. "Thieves, " Manong shrugs, when I ask him. Broken glass is scattered on the floor. He tells me the house will be torn down within the month and a complex of offices built in its place. The property and the squatters' land adjoining it have been bought by the Alacran corporation, Intercoco.

I say good-bye and thank the old man. "See you in America!" Manong Tibo says, waving farewell. Pucha is slumped down in the front seat of the car, irritated, hot, and sweaty. "I wouldn't do this for anyone but you," she grumbles without looking at me, then peers into the rearview mirror. "Look at my makeup!" She gives me an accusing look. I slide into the driver's seat, fighting back tears. Suddenly, I grab her hand. She stares at me, puzzled. "Are you okay?" It seems an eternity, but I pull myself together. Pucha hands me her lace handkerchief, drenched in perfume. "Watch out when you blow your nose—okay, *prima*? She teases. She squeezes my hand, uncomfortable with our display of affection. I start the car, turning to look at her before we drive away. "I really love you, " I say, to her utter amazement.

My cousin will find happiness with a man, once and for all. He is a stranger to us, a modest man from a modest family, someone we never knew in our childhood. The Gonzagas breathe a collective sigh of relief. Pucha lives with her new husband, childless and content; she never leaves Manila.

My *Lola* Narcisa lives to be a very old woman. She is the main reason for my frequent vists to Manila; I dread not being there when she dies.

* * *

I return to North America. I save all Raul's letters, along with my father's cordial birthday telegrams and Pucha's gossipy notes, in a large shopping bag labeled FAMILY. I move to another city, approximately five thousand miles away from where my mother lives and paints. We talk on the phone once a week. I am anxious and restless, at home only in airports. I travel whenever I can. My belief in God remains tentative. I have long ago stopped going to church. I never marry.

In my recurring dream, my brother and I inhabit the translucent bodies of nocturnal moths with curved, fragile wings. We are pale green, with luminous celadon eyes, fantastic and beautiful. In dream after dream, we are drawn to the same silent tableau: a mysterious light glowing from the window of a deserted, ramshackle house. The house is sometimes perched on a rocky abyss, or on a dangerous cliff overlooking a turbulent sea. The meaning is simple and clear, I think. Raul and I embrace our destiny: we fly around in circles, we swoop and dive in effortless arcs against a barren sky, we flap and beat our wings in our futile attempts to reach what surely must be heaven.

IMMIGRANTS

Debra Kang Dean

To be always carrying
this stone whose own inertia
keeps doubling its weight even

as I hold it in my hand—
in truth I would cast it off
if I could
            though it cool the
sweat of my palm, suffer itself to be touched. Know I would

heft it at water or glass
simply to hear one thing
deafen another awake

to hear fragments falling like
stars to wound or baptize
everything
            compassed inside
the arc of its wake—but for
one thing: my grandmother gave

this stone to my mother, and
she to me, saying each hand
need have something hard to fill

its grasping, something only

time and touch can transmute into an object,
                    beautiful,
this stone from Okinawa
where the grains of sand are stars.

THE WEEP LINE

Debra Kang Dean

for my son David on his 18th birthday

Under the trees we paced
and drove Jobe's spikes
along the weep line.
Working clear of roots,
I held the spikes
while you hammered.
I kept looking up at
the trees because,
until rain falls
heavy and steady,
we must imagine it.
Later, when it appears,
an imperfect circle
under the pin oak,
I think of you, still
a child among grade-school
children holding hands,
forming a circle. Caught

outdoors in a downpour
you step inside the weep line.
Leaves on the tree's upper
branches sluice rain down.
Under the tree you can hear
rain drop, leaf by leaf, down to
the weep line. Beyond it

everything's hazy. I know
you think life's like that.
There, under the tallest tree,
here, where often lightning
strikes close by, you know
by now life's currency, and—
if you're the man
I think you are—
you'll also imagine
the spikes, now unseen,
feeding the tree.

MY HEART'S OWN CATHEDRAL

Chonun ("Myself" in Korean)
Lee Williams, 1995

ON BEING MULTIRACIAL

Ai

I was twenty-six before my mother finally agreed to tell me anything about my natural father, other than his name, that he was dead, and a Japanese with some ethnic ties to the Philippines.

My parents met in Denver, Colorado, in 1946. Mother was sixteen, unhappily married, but still a virgin. They had an affair. But when my mother became pregnant, my father told her to go home to her parents. She couldn't. In desperation she threw herself down a stairway. When her husband found out, he beat her. Finally, she told her parents everything, and they took her home. She was on the verge of a miscarriage when her maternal grandparents took her to Albany, Texas, to live with them. I was born there in the seventh month on October 21, 1947.

As I grew up, I was told that my mother's ex-husband was my father. I did not resemble him in any way, but mother would say, "You look like Papa," my maternal great-grandfather, who was half Choctaw Indian and half white. Since my maternal great-grandmother was half Irish and half black, any combination seemed possible. Yet I was shorter than my relatives, and none had eyes like mine.

When I was seven, my second stepfather was sent to Korea, so my mother moved with my stepsister and me to Las Vegas where her mother lived. A Catholic, I was sent to the only integrated school in town, a parochial school. There were seven black children and me. I remember some older white children throwing gravel at me at recess. They did not throw it at the black children. So my mother enrolled me in a black school. All the teachers were white. Mine taught music every day after lunch. We'd march around the classroom singing "Mammy's little baby loves shortnin' bread." This would last the entire afternoon.

In a few months, my stepfather returned and we moved to San Francisco. One day my mother sat down with me and said, "If anybody asks what you are, tell them you're Indian. She admits now that when she saw so many Japanese in San Francisco, she was afraid they would treat me like a freak. As it turned out, Japanese people were always kind to me. But I remember many times when a group of older black girls would call me nigger-jap. I knew what jap meant, but not nigger. Then a family friend made it quite clear: "Nigger," he said, "is you."

In high school nearly all my friends were black. But when I entered the University of Arizona, we drifted apart. A shy person, I managed to make a few friends in Oriental Studies, my major. These were white and Chinese only, since there were no Japanese in the program. Nor blacks.

I was a senior before I realized my natural father was Asian, probably Japanese, but I didn't know how to confront my mother. By this time, blacks were asserting themselves as they had never done before. I was forced to be loyal to myself as a multiracial person or be immersed in the black struggle for identity with which I had little in common. Except a desire to be accepted as I was. But the members of the Black Student Union felt otherwise. When I didn't join them, they began yelling my name whenever they saw me. They hated me and I hated them. I totally withdrew from blacks. My family, which had always been alternately Indians, peripheral blacks, or nothing, adopted the black struggle as their own. I had only myself.

But I was at peace studying Japanese culture, although I had no experience with the day-to-day reality of being Japanese. It was the compassionate Buddha, Avalokitesvara, to which I turned. What I loved was a totally aesthetic atmosphere, fostered by the Oriental Studies faculty, by books, records, and my own fantasies. This was my identity. I had crawled through a dark tunnel, but up ahead, I could see the light and wasn't about to turn around. No arguments, threats, or friendly persuasions could make me deny, hide, or sublimate my complete devotion to being aesthetically Japanese.

People whose concept of themselves is largely dependent on their racial identity and superiority feel threatened by a multiracial person. The insistence that one must align oneself with this or that race is basically racist and the notion that without a racial identity a person can't have any identity perpetuates racism. How else am I to make sense of the whites who say "your people" (meaning blacks); the well-intentioned friends who urge me to apply for this or that job because I have two things going for me, race and sex, never mentioning my ability or achievements; or my stepsister calling me "honky" because she believed the old saying, "if you're not with us, you're against us."

But I have learned well the lesson most multiracial people must learn in order to live with the fact of not belonging: there is no identity for me "out there." I have had to step back into my own heart's cathedral and bow down before I could rise up.

Since I believe that clinging to one's race tears one apart and that letting go makes one whole, I wish I could say that race isn't important. But it is. More that ever, it is a medium of exchange, the coin of the realm with which one buys one's share of jobs and social position. This is a fact which I have faced and must ultimately transcend. If this transcendence were less complex, less individual, it would lose its holiness.

Note: Ai, who received the National Book Award in 1999 for *Vice: New and Selected Poems*, is of Japanese, African American, Irish, Dutch, Choctaw, Comanche, and Southern Cheyenne ethnic background.

(A WOMAN BEGAN)
Irene Small

I lack something
to hold me   together
she said—   have started to look
      for limbs   in my bed
when I wake   secretly
realize universal   truths
such as:
          the sun is whole   in the sky
        my body is the inexistence
           of space
a series of disintegrations
I run into myself   it breaks me
into pieces   a marionette   a psychologist
     you must realize malfunctions
     you must come to terms with atrophy
     you must understand your decay
she answered
     I am continuously erupting
     do not define   my fire

WAR DOLL HOTEL

Kiana Houghtailing Davenport

When we're young, we record things very fast. Life develops the film. Ritual for sleepless nights: shuffle mental snapshots, fan them out like playing cards. Choose one.

Here's a picture of my mother as a child, rollicking in mud of taro patches, her full-blooded Hawaiian mother, dark, stately, beckoning to her. Here's my mother a teenager, chasing mongoose across lava shelves. She's tea-colored and beautiful, broad cheeks, full lips, hair dark, electric. Here's a picture of my father, blonde and pale, a boy in Alabama.

Here's a snapshot that's always troubled me. My father's father, in Decatur, Alabama in 1921. He's wearing a white robe, and a funny cone-shaped hood. Behind him are other men in robes and hoods, and masks with eyeholes. Peekaboo. They're poised, ready for something. You can almost smell the kerosene, hear the crackling wood, the flaming cross. I was twelve when I found that snapshot. Old enough to know. The night I found it, I was afraid to lie down. I fell asleep on my feet like a horse, leaning against the bed I'd barricaded against my door.

This snapshot, too, has troubled me. A picture of Emperor Hirohito and his wife, walking their palace grounds, their dog beside them, leaping and yapping in the sun. It was taken two days before America bombed Hiroshima. I've never understood that dog. Didn't he know what was coming? Aren't animals intuitive? Each time I see that photo in old magazines, that leaping, yapping dog, I think of my father after World War II, taking his Hawaiian wife home to meet his folks in Alabama.

I used to imagine him at the front door of his father's house, puffing his chest out, grinning and proud. He puts his arm around my mother, rings the bell. (Didn't he know what was coming?) They're all assembled inside. Maybe there's a cake, candles lit. WELCOME HOME. Maybe someone sits at a piano, fingers poised above the keys. A window curtain twitches. My father rings and rings but no one ever answers. Finally, he and my mother leave.

This was the late forties, a full decade before Hawai'i became a state. A lot of Americans still weren't sure exactly what Hawaiians were. Maybe my father's people thought they were like Nebraskans, or Canadians, white folks from far away. Until someone inside the house looked out. What I want to evoke here is not my father's shame, not my mother's humiliation. Not even the silence after he rang the bell. What must be evoked, is the twitching of that curtain.

My parents never went South again. They began a life of improvisation and drift. I wonder about my mother in those years, the pain of trying to fit in, her differentness from white, mainland Americans. My father said people saw her as "exotic," which is what one says about those they tend to stare at. By the time I was born, they were living back in Honolulu.

Here's a snapshot of my mother running into the sea. I'm six or seven, watching her arms spin gracefully in their sockets, pulling the ocean behind her. She moves like liquid immersed in liquid, and I swim hard to catch up. I tell her I'm confused. I don't know what I am, Hawaiian or Caucasian. *Both,* she says. *What am I, first?* I ask. She doesn't hesitate. *Hawaiian.* But I don't look Hawaiian. *You will,* she promises. *It works its way out from the blood.*

Here's a snapshot of me at thirteen, looking down at my mother's grave. In a year my father will desert me, too, going back to Alabama. I don't understand why he leaves me behind.

My skin is Anglo-pale like his, I have his pale eyes. In other words, I "pass." Years later, I will understand about this man, that the War took his youth, and my mother's early death finished him. The rest of his life was epilogue. I would see how that journey South with his dark-skinned bride had been an act of hopeless valor. He must have known what was coming. Maybe marrying her had been an act of courage, too, his passport out of his past. But in the end, played out, he went back to what he knew.

So, I grew up in the islands, surrounded by my mother's family, my *'ohana*, dark, handsome husky men, big, graceful women with a buttery cast to the whites of their eyes. My cousins were all mixed marriage offspring: Hawaiian, Chinese, Japanese, Korean, Portuguese, Filipino, dark, tan, yellow, so many hues. I didn't know how happy I was, how secure, locked in the bosom of this large, rollicking, feverish, high-strung clan.

Here's a snapshot of me in summer, working my way through university. I'm standing on the assembly line at Dole packing plant in Honolulu, wearing a steely hairnet, ugly, pineapple rash climbing my arms, swearing to myself, *I'm getting out of these nowhere islands. I'm going to the mainland where I belong.* You see the trouble I was in; I still didn't know who I was. I would lose a whole decade, all of my twenties, before I learned that recognizing who you are isn't the subtext of a life. It's the main point. The week I graduated from university, I boarded a flight for New York City, as far from Honolulu as I could get and still be in the United States.

I arrived in the middle of a snowstorm, stepped out of a cab in Manhattan and started walking toward the brightest lights, which turned out to be the Waldorf-Astoria Hotel. I got as far as the doorman, peered into the lobby of that costly place and saw what a discrepancy I was. Incongruously, half a block from the Waldorf was the YWCA. I lived there a year, in a room so small, I moved around by stealth, by squeezing sideways past the bed. After the shock of those first few days, I was swept up in a blizzard of colors, odors, textures of young women flinging themselves through the door of the Y like splendid rag dolls, like glamorous refugees.

They came from everywhere, high-caste women with Ph.D.'s and women whose parents were gypsies, dragging in their bundles and bags, wearing galoshes and parkas and Chesterfields over shawls, saris, kimonos and Rasta braids. They came bringing the perfumes of the Orient, and the Caribbean, and the veldt. Golden East Indians, pale Finns, twins from Kowloon, a Haitian singer, Cubans, South Africans, an Estonian auditioning for the American Ballet Theatre, even a beauty queen from Manila.

We were the "foreign residents," apart from the transient population at the Y, drawn together by multi-tongued gabfests in the showers, the cafeteria, by fights, and thefts, and midnight wailings that seemed to voice a central ache. And there was something else that slowly emerged: a communal scrubbing-down of identities, eccentricities, as we waited for green cards, a husband, a job, degrees.

This was the early seventies, when the Youth of America was still in the throes of hippiedom—headbands, body paint, ragged velvet, glitter and tat. Yet each morning at the Y, we ironed each other's hair straight, wedged ourselves into cheap high heels and somber-colored little suits that didn't fit the shape of our bodies, then rushed out into corporate New York, hoping to blend. At night, we collapsed in our tiny rooms resembling interiors of gypsy caravans, wherein we wiped away the make-up and dragged off the city clothes, exhausted by a world some of us wouldn't achieve.

In time we learned to dress smart, acquire airs, meeting dates for drinks in the bar of the Waldorf, which the twins from

Kowloon pronounced "War . . . dol." The bartenders started calling us their "war dolls," and the Y became War Doll Hotel, from which we fanned out every morning, aiming ourselves at the city. I think the fact that we could do that, that such profoundly dislocated, homesick young women could buoy each other up, assemble, and take *aim*, well, that was the important thing. New York, the target, was insignificant. Targets change.

Of course for some of us, the city was only on loan, we would have to give it back. These were the women New York broke with blinding exactitude. The suicide, leaping from her window as an afterthought, hair still lathered with shampoo. The student from Caracas who, one night, long sobs tearing from her throat, ran through the halls, scrubbing the walls with her excrement. Paramedics finally pinned her against a door with a needle and syringe, so for a moment she was frozen in the attitude lightning gives its victims. We never saw her again.

Here's a snapshot of that night, five of us huddled, terrified, in someone's room. Sindiwa whacks wet laundry out of the way and calms us down, talking about her three kids left behind in South Africa. White teeth gleaming against her black cheeks and the dazzling bush of her Afro, she tells us how she's going to be a famous journalist. She's twenty-four, older than any of us. She's lived through childbirth, revolutions and divorce, and she's full of such tremor and dreams; I want to be her friend forever.

And Meena from New Delhi, golden in her saris, her beauty, her gestures so fine they can't be analyzed. A secretary at the U.N., she wants to study law, go back to India and fight for women's rights, for young brides burned to death over dowry disputes, for women denied birth control. But Meena has no funds. Her family disowned her when she refused to marry the husband they chose.

One evening I found her pacing up and down the hall. "You'll make it in this city," she said. "You look white."

I didn't know how to respond. At the Y with my friends, I tried to hold in my whiteness, but out in the city, I held back my Hawaiian side. "Does it bother you . . . being dark?"

Meena shook her head impatiently. "First, Americans look right through you. When they finally see you, they stare because you're foreign. When the novelty wears off, they insult you. You're invisible again."

An aunt finally came and took her to New Jersey. Sindiwa moved in with a man she met at an interview, and I moved into an apartment with two women I didn't know, robust, racquet swinging blondes from Massachusetts who'd advertised for a third roommate. Here's a snapshot of me at dinner, describing to them my family's house "on the ocean in Kahala," the millionaire's enclave above Waikīkī. They think my family are Caucasians, rich enough to live out there year-round. I never mention my Hawaiian blood.

In time, my roommates introduced me to men from Brown and Amherst, and very quickly, these new friends formed certain assumptions about me which sealed me off from any genuine human contact, because those assumptions were false, and I had engendered them. I was beginning to learn about secrets, the ones we move fast to keep ahead of, the fear that at some point they'll get out in front.

After a year as receptionist at a public relations firm, I started writing press releases for wigs and hairspray, thinking that was writing. Another year passed. I kept in touch sporadically with Sindiwa and Meena, and my family in Honolulu, took writing courses at New York University, sent short stories to magazines, filed the rejection letters, changed jobs and after several more years, married a lawyer, an older man, pale and blonde as my father had been. I sent my father snapshots, needing to show this man who had deserted me that I'd replaced him. He wrote, wishing me happiness, and just seeing his handwriting triggered a meltdown in my body chemistry, like lovesickness or deathly fear.

Like all marriages, ours dipped and soared. My husband encouraged me in my writing, and seemed to take pride in my Hawaiian background, conjuring for his friends my family in Honolulu as "Dutch with a touch of Hawaiian blood." (In fact, it was the other way around.) I became his "island aristocrat," his tall tale, maybe his tallest. On reflection, I realized I'd married him partly because I saw him as my ticket to the other side, legitimate WASPocracy. Now I wondered if maybe I was *his* ticket out. Maybe some devious code in his family scripture called for an occasional "exotic" marriage, offspring with a touch of spice, a little jazz in the tidepool of stagnant family genes.

I stopped talking about my heritage, felt I'd forsaken it. Increasingly uncomfortable in my husband's world, I buried myself in writing, and let the marriage slide. I meant to have children, I thought I did, but books came out instead. In the next four years, I sold several stories, and wrote two unpublishable novels.

I wasn't writing for pleasure then, and certainly it wasn't for the money. I think I was doing it because I was lost and extremely lonely, and writing seemed to approximate the actions of someone jiggling a key in a lock, which would open a door that led me out of my condition. So I kept writing, jiggling the key, trying to engage all the tumblers. Here's a snapshot of me holding my divorce papers, and in the other hand a letter of acceptance from a publisher. After almost ten years of trying, I've finally sold a novel, and friends take me out to celebrate. I don't think about the divorce; reverberations will come in their time.

The novel was commercial and sold moderately well, and at a book-and-author luncheon, I met a writer from

Mississippi, a soft-spoken, courtly man, terribly attractive because he seemed to lack awe for anything. He took me home to one of those antebellum plantation houses with magnolia trees, and mournful Spanish moss. I was charmed. Each night, we gathered on the front gallery, drinking with his friends, men in law and real estate, gentle with their women. I don't know when I started feeling uncomfortable. Maybe it was seeing Ruth, the black maid, slipping leftover food into her pocketbook. Or, it was the way Marcus, the black butler, served us. Tall, dignified, innate grace of a patriarch, he was over sixty. We should have been serving him.

One night my host and his friends got seriously into drink and telling jokes. As the jokes turned ugly, so did they, sounding like rednecks with callused trigger fingers, sawed-off shotguns in their trucks. Each joke dragged a nail down the length of my spine, "A coon who st-st-stuttered . . ." ". . . A nigger with such big lips, she could blow a man and smoke a Camel at the same time." All the while Ruth sat just inside the door, folding napkins. And all the while, Marcus served us drinks.

That night I woke with a jolt, my skin crackling, my heart trying to leap out of my chest. I dragged my suitcase down the stairs, packing in the dark. Marcus called a cab at dawn before the house woke up, and waved me off, bewildered. On the plane back to New York, I thought of an old snapshot, source of a young girl's nightmares. Men in white robes and cone-shaped hoods. That I had gotten out of there alive, survived brief truancy into the geography of that picture, seemed to me a miracle.

Years bucketed by. I published a second novel that quietly rolled over and died. The story I had hoped would absolutely scald, leave readers barking with shock and recognition, turned out to be a yawn. Insentient characters, anemic little lives. There was something I wasn't catching on to. I was still jiggling the key, still trying to engage the tumblers in that lock, but I couldn't open the door, couldn't get beyond that metaphysical place I was stuck in.

What I hadn't yet learned was that a writer's voice is the sound of her convictions. Lack of conviction is the impulse of death, it sterilizes the writing. I hadn't scrutinized myself, still couldn't define who I was, what I stood for. I stopped fiction for a while, went back to writing about wigs and hairsprays.

One day I looked down and when I looked up, my thirties were over. I understood that, very shortly, what I was, was what I would be from then on. Realizations didn't hit me all at once, some facts take hammering in. That summer I learned that a cousin in Honolulu had become a minister, another a lawyer. I'd missed their transitions, the celebrations. Then my favorite cousin, the one I loved most, the one whose letters I'd stopped answering, suddenly died. A nephew was fatally shot in the face. I'd missed most of their lives. After the paralyzing shock came grief, and I began to see that at a certain age life hits back, that the things we desert come after us.

One night at a cocktail party book-launch on the twentieth floor of the Waldorf-Astoria, I glanced out of a window expecting to see, far below, the YWCA. My shock was absolute. The Y, and the entire block were gone, replaced by an eerie, massive crater, a prehistoric punchbowl surrounded by a tall makeshift construction fence. In two years another glass and chrome monolith would crowd the skyline. I thought of Meena and Sindiwa then, sad that we'd lost touch, and I wondered where they were, how their lives had fared.

Some months later, I read an article in the *Village Voice* on Nelson Mandela, with Sindiwa's byline. Her words leapt out, radiating passion. Yet her views against Apartheid were balanced, restrained, so her argument resonated beyond the measure of the page. She traced me through my publisher, just as I was tracking her through the newspaper, and we floated to each other down the avenue, laughing and crying out loud. Her Afro was very short, and she was wearing stiletto heels and a chic big-shouldered suit.

"Ah, yes, the dashikis, the turbans and beads. That is still my basic dress, but we need variety, no?" She hugged me over and over, squeezing my hands repeatedly. "Remember our gypsy rags? What did they call us? War Dolls! Wasn't it?"

She still had that forceful, physical glow, still full of incredible tremor. Hugging her, I could feel the surge. It had been over eighteen years and we talked through dinner and far into the night. Sindiwa had spent several years on a Cleveland newspaper, then a year on the *L.A. Times*. She went home for two years and, one at a time, brought her children to New York. Now she free-lanced for liberal magazines, and had written a book on South Africa, published in London. It won an award and Meena, living in London, attended the ceremony. Meena had earned her law degree, married a diplomat and went back and forth to New Delhi, torn between the new world and her own.

We talked about my novels which Sindiwa had only recently discovered and read. She said she believed I had the true gift of a storyteller though I had not yet found my subject. She asked if I'd been home to the islands recently, then she looked at my face.

"I never went back." I said. "It's too late."

"It will happen." She took my hand. "It was hard for you, a half-caste. I used to watch you secretly. Your two selves, warring with each other."

The shock of it, of her knowing all those years ago, made me suddenly weep.

"Listen to me," she put her arm around me as if I were her very large child. "In my country when whites stare at me, there's no ambiguity, it's pure hate. I always know who I am. You

are different. Mixed blood, mixed cultures. You have to impro-
vise, hide, take sides."

I talked about my marriage then, and the years of lying.
I told her about my father's father, the Ku Klux Klan, how I was
always aware that my cells contained that man's nuclei. How I
had spent years ignoring my native blood, but ignoring the
Southern blood, too. It seemed I'd spent years of my life denying
all of me, trying to run my genes off, like fat.

"Never mind," Sindiwa said. "We're all hybrids of the
new world. Making ourselves up as we go along. This is why we
write, juggling our little flames. One burns through muck to find
the core."

We talked a lot in the next few months, and that summer
I went home to Honolulu. My family was welcoming but wary,
waiting to see what I'd become. I spent weeks getting my bear-
ings, listening to aunties and uncles "talk story," retelling our
family history. I lay on beaches with cousins and their kids,
catching up on their lives, gossiped with old school-friends and
hiked ancient rainforests alone with a backpack. After a while,
my family stepped closer, took me in completely, hugging, teas-
ing, feeding me foods of my childhood: kim chi, laulau, poi, and
salty little silver-eyeballed fish.

Nieces pinched my arm, playfully. "Oooh, plenny thin!
You need da kine taro fo' make you fat!" They wanted to find me
a husband. "One local man, make good love fo' you."

Here's a snapshot of me surrounded by my clan, my
'ohana. Tradewinds rustle banyans, blowing narcotic sizzle of
ginger through the screens, while I talk about living on the island
of Manhattan. Nephews listen with their mouths open, as if hearing fantastic tales of a shipwrecked sailor. For some things it's too
late. My cousin died feeling I deserted her. She once wrote asking to visit New York, and I had made excuses. I sit beside her

grave. I study my mother's photographs, stunned again by her early death. I think of my father.

One day, I started taking notes, tracing the line of our ancestors who, on my mother's mother's side, came to Hawai'i from Tahiti by way of the Marquesas, almost 2,000 years ago, and the Dutchman on my mother's father's side, who rounded Cape Horn on a whaling ship in 1840, and sailed into the arms of a full-blooded Polynesian. The notes became my novel, *Shark Dialogues*, which took eight years to write.

I do not rush it. I come home more and more now, swimming for hours each day in the sea. Back on the mainland, sometimes I dream I'm still swimming, and wake up with stiff arms, exhausted. Sometimes I feel I'm swimming through the city, stroking through crowds, a city now so multinational, that not to be blonde and WASP is a bearable affliction.

Last year, Meena passed through New York and we had a reunion, meeting at the Waldorf for drinks. She still possessed that slender-boned beauty of a natural aristocrat, floating forward in bangled arms, a tangerine silk sari. Tears stood like jewels on her cheeks when we embraced. Sindiwa had reverted to the embodiment of the Ethnic Ideal, turban, dashiki, head to toe in bold colors, all dimmed by her dazzling smile. I was just back from the islands, a turquoise jumpsuit, orchid in my hair. We were who we were, no longer dressing like children wanting to mingle with the grown-ups.

Still the quiet renegade, no children, and drinking scotch, Meena was divorcing her husband and for the present, remaining in London, helping legislate for more Indian women's crisis centers there. She felt there were enough children in the world and rather than have her own, she said, one day she would adopt. We talked about this dual existence, our adopted cities versus our genesis, the conflicts and tension, the often comical struggle not to disappear into the "mainstream," the sense of accomplishment in holding fast to our identity through our work. At the moment, there were no men in our lives, and I wondered if that part of life was over.

Sindiwa responded in her wonderful Aframericanese. "Ladiees, please . . . it 'tisn't over . . . 'til it's over, isn't it?"

We spent a great deal of that evening laughing, remembering the Y. The "house-warden" discovering a pet monkey in a dress. A man discovered in someone's bed. Someone eloping, someone disappearing. Girls yelling back and forth from windows, like housewives beside a Chiang Mai *klong*. The ones the city rejected and the ones who left, rejecting the city instead. That night after dinner, we strolled up the avenue past all-night Korean grocers and Senegalese hawking watches and scarves. Finally, we turned down the block where the Y should have been. A few boards were knocked out and we were able to look through the construction fence down at the crater.

"War Doll Hotel," Meena said.

We were silent then, and the specter of that year, that place, floated up before us. Memories of the pluck and terror with which we arrived in the city almost twenty years ago, ready to trade in our identities in order to succeed, not knowing that the more we imitated New York, the more we lost the privilege of our uniqueness. That year never taught us all we expected it to. But it gave us an edge, made us alert, helped us understand that survival means the mind's, not the body's, ability to endure. The years in between taught us the rest, to keep one foot in the ideal plain of our origins.

Here's a snapshot of three friends laughing at the edge of a crater, like wondrous hybrid flowers, splashed palettes on the landscape.

SEEING HER AGAIN

Diana Chang

When we run into one another
      on the corner of Madison and 57th
      and I remember her reading mss.
      for *Mlle.* Magazine and Avon Books

      or our paths cross at B'way
      and 116th where we were
      seniors at Barnard

      or later opposite Stuyvesant Park
      at 17th, below a brownstone
      walkup that we knew

When I come across her, surprised
      at her fall of black silk
      which was my hair,

      I marvel how at intersections
      she runs on platform shoes
      in her narrow sheath
      in pouring rain or shine

When I wait on the steps of Carnegie
      Hall and she, approaching, looks
      up eagerly into eyes of a man
      who will soon be a stranger to her,
      yearned for or forgotten

When I see her arm raised to wave
         or is it to embrace,
         or possibly to warn

I do not wave back—
a voyeur now—
among the steepness,
the glitter of New York

I do not wave back,
averting myself,
shy of remembering,

but wave her on
to years that are still to come
for her to live, to know

ALLEGORY

Diana Chang

From the photograph the child
(Dutch-boy bob, cross-stitched yoke,
Sitting on one leg in a pavilion)
Looks out
At the monolithic spread of my view
Over the capital of the Empire State,

And at someone old enough to be her mother,
Who is also the child's child,
Since it is a portrait of myself as I posed
Five-years-old, in Peiping, in quite another story.

The child is translated into our native genre:
American, I am here to attest
To that child I was, misplaced
And found again.

How she remembers all that was to come
Is strange, incredible,
Past my understanding

Though her smile is worldly.
Mine, thirty years later, is skeptical.

From time to time our glances meet:
You are certainly outrageous, I inform her,
While she softly declares tall tales are everywhere.

NOTES FROM A FRAGMENTED DAUGHTER

Elena Tajima Creef

Some Personal Scenes

1. At an art gallery opening for local Asian American women artists, a tall white man in glasses, beard, and big hair bundled up into a ponytail hovers over a table full of sushi, chow mein, egg rolls, and teriyaki chicken. He looks at me awkwardly and attempts conversation. "Did you make any of the food? I notice you look kinda Asian."

2. Marion is half Chinese and half Japanese and I like the way his face looks. We sit and talk about what it means to have mixed backgrounds in a culture that can't tell Chinese apart from Japanese and where McDonald's still serves Shanghai Chicken McNuggets with teriyaki sauce.

3. I am fifteen and am sitting in the backseat of my best friend Doreen's Volkswagen Bug, when her uncle's new wife Clara climbs into the passenger seat and we are introduced. Clara speaks in tongues at the Ladies Prayer Meetings, and has seen angels in the sky through her Kodak Instamatic. She turns to me and shouts in a thick New York accent, "So what are you studying?"

I say, "English."
She says, "Gee, your English is very good.

How long have you been in this country?"

I say, "All of my life."

She shouts, "Are you Chinese?"

I say, "Japanese."

She says, "I admire your people very much!"

I smile and say, "Yes, and we are very good with our hands, too."

4. Katie Gonzales follows me around for one week at sixth grade summer camp, her left arm in a sling from a tetherball accident. "I'm gonna get you, you flat-faced chinaman." I want to tell her that I'm only half Japanese, but the words stick in my mouth and instead, I call her a beaner and imagine I am twisting that left arm right off her brown skinny body.

5. Later, when I am thirteen, I bury my mother once and for all and decide to go Mexican. It makes a lot of sense. I am no longer Elena, I am now Elaina and I begin insisting I am Mexican wherever I go. With my long black hair, my sun-darkened skin, and my new name, I can pass and I am safe. For the next year, I obsessively hide my Japanese mother and deny my Japanese roots. No one is allowed to meet her. I do not let her answer the phone if I can help it, or go near the door if I can get there first. I sabotage the PTA's efforts to get her to come to their monthly meetings, and I conveniently get dates mixed up for "Open House." I live in fear that someone will find out that my mother is Japanese and spread it around the classroom like a dirty rumor. I love it when people ask if I am Español, because it is safe, because it means I do not stand out.

6. My mother and I are getting out of the car at Builder's Emporium when a young, ugly, straw-haired man gets out of his truck and shouts that my mother has stolen his parking space. She says she doesn't know what he's talking about and he tells

her to shut-up her slant-eyed face. My heart is pounding as we shop for light fixtures and nails, but we never say a thing.

7. It is a dark, wet, rainy Santa Cruz night, and I go to see *Tampopo*—your basic Japanese noodle western—by myself. I am in a very good mood and allow a balding middle-aged man with a burgundy plum scarf tied around his neck to make conversation with me in the lobby.

"I really love Japanese films, almost as much as I love Asian girls! I'm going to Taiwan next month to meet this woman I've been corresponding with. I really prefer Oriental women to American because (he whispers) there are so many 'feminists' in this town. You are Asian, aren't you? Don't tell me, let me guess. Japanese? Chinese? Hawaiian? Eurasian?"

Idiot. I am the daughter of a World War II Japanese war bride who met and married my North Carolinian hillbilly father one fine day in 1949 while she was hanging up the laundry to dry. Nine months out of the year, I pose as a doctoral student—a historian of consciousness; the rest of the time I am your basic half-Japanese postmodernist gemini feminist, existentialist would-be writer of bad one-act comedy revues, avid cat trainer, and closet reader of mademoiselle, cosmo, signs, diacritics, elle, tv guide, cultural critique, representations, people magazine, critical inquiry, national enquirer, feminist issues, house beautiful, architectural digest, country living, cat fancy, bird talk, mother jones, covert action, vogue, glamour, the new yorker, l.a. times, l.a. weekly, and sometimes penthouse forum.

So how do you like them apples, bub? If you come near me one more time with your touch-me-feel-you New Age Bagwan male sensitivity, I just may strangle you with the burgundy plum scarf you have tied around your neck.

Deconstructing My Mother as the Other

The headlines blare: "They're Bringing Home Japanese Brides! Six thousand Americans in Japan have taken Japanese brides since 1945, and all the little Madam Butterflies are studying hamburgers, Hollywood and home on the range, before coming to live in the USA."

Although she is not interviewed, my mother appears in one of the bright technicolor photographs in the January 19, 1952, issue of the *Saturday Evening Post*. She is the short one with the funny hairdo, hovering over an apple pie, smiling with her classmates in the American Red Cross "Brides' School" for Japanese Wives. While the article attempts to tell the postwar story of the Japanese war bride in general, it also tells the story of how my own American G.I. father met and married my Japanese mother in war-torn occupied Japan. It is, in essence, my own pictorial origin story.

There are over 45,000 Japanese women who married American servicemen after World War II and immigrated to the United States. I have been meeting and interviewing these women for the last few years for a collection of oral histories I hope to someday publish. I have been told over and over again by many of these women that they despise the name "war bride." There is something dirty and derogatory about this word, but rarely has anyone told me why. "Call us 'Shin Issei'" (the New Immigrants), they say. "Or how about, 'Japanese Wives of American Servicemen.' Don't call us 'War Brides.'" They whisper, "It is not nice."

I am the daughter of a World War II Japanese war bride
who met and married my white North Carolinian hillbilly father
one fine day in 1949 while she was hanging up the laundry to dry.

There is no escaping this body made out of history,
war and peace,
two languages,
and two cultures.

My name is Elena June,
I am the youngest daughter of Chiyohi,
who is the only surviving daughter of Iso,
who was the daughter of the Mayor of Yokoze
and was the Village Beauty
born in the last century to a Japanese woman
whose name is now forgotten,
but who lived in the Meiji era
and loved to tell ghost stories.

OFF-WHITE

Teresa Williams-León

For Jay

Off-white
yeah, that's what I am
when you mix white and yellow
that's what you get
Off-white

Folks tell me my white daddy
gives me privilege
'say my yellow mommy
gives me novelty

But I tell them
I'm Off-white
nothing more
nothing less
yeah, that's Off-white

I'm all right
'cuz I'm Off-white
I mean, just right

If they say
otherwise
I tell them
right off.

ALL-AMERICAN FAMILY

Nanea Hoffman

As a child, I was constantly aware of my weirdness. Not just ordinary weirdness, either, such as being bow-legged or having parents who were about 15 years older than everyone else's, or even embarrassing weirdness that was visited upon me by said parents. Like the time my father, in a burst of artistic inspiration, decided to use food coloring to transform my rather mundane white bread sandwich into a spectacular, rainbow-covered fiesta. A sandwich, I might add, which consisted of peanut butter, Betty Crocker chocolate frosting, and raisins. Sister Juliana, who supervised the cafeteria, thought the bread was moldy and tried to confiscate it. My mother was appalled at the use of chocolate frosting as a lunch food, and Dad was unceremoniously retired from brown bag duty. But stuff like that didn't phase me, much.

Those things, like the orange and purple paisley pants my mother insisted I wear to Summer Fun, made me different and occasionally drew unwanted attention from my peers, but they did not much trouble me. Even then, I think I suspected that every kid had some little thing that made him or her different. To each his paisley. No, what lurked perpetually at the edge of my consciousness was this vague sense of otherness. A feeling of being slightly unconnected from the group, no matter which group I happened to be with. It had to do not with such superficial things as clothes or physical appearance, but with something much more basic. Primal. My blood.

I remember in grade school hearing one of my classmates proudly declare that she was pure Japanese. A couple of other friends chimed in, "So, I'm pure Chinese," and "Well, I have pure Filipino blood!" I was really impressed. Pure—that sounded pretty good. I was a mixture of Okinawan, Hawaiian, Chinese, and German. Did that mean I was impure? In Catholic school, impure was a bad thing. It was confusing. I stared at the blue veins lying close beneath the skin of my wrist. Suddenly the blood in them seemed muddied and weak. What *was* I, anyway?

The Chinese and German parts of me were too insignificant to matter. They were the faint legacy of a thrown-away baby girl (rescued from a garbage heap in China and brought to Honolulu by a kindly Hawaiian family), and a sailor on a whaling ship who must have succumbed, as did many of his brethren, to the charms of a native maiden. Aside from the romantic stories, I felt little connection with these long-dead ancestors. I could imagine after three or four generations, the tiny bits of Chinese and German disappearing into my genetic soup the way the sweetener did in my father's coffee, without a visible trace.

I could have been Hawaiian. Like the infamous One-Drop rule in the old South, which meant that anyone with even a hint of African blood was considered black, regardless of the color of their skin, a drop of Hawaiian blood, however small, meant the Hawaiians would gladly claim you as one of their own. I am just a little over a quarter of Hawaiian, 5/16ths to be exact, which is perhaps more Hawaiian blood than can be claimed by even the most ardent of sovereignty activists or the most traditional of kumu hulas. So I'm more than qualified, but here's the thing: I've always felt like a bit of a fake. It isn't that I felt alienated by my fellow Hawaiians—a more accepting people has probably never existed. I'd just never felt like the real thing, as if my brown skin were a thin veneer that would peel off as easily as a coat of house paint that hadn't been weather-proofed, revealing . . . what? Good question. I only knew what I wasn't.

I knew it the first day of preschool when all the other kids were talking funny. I went home and reported the phenomenon to my parents who laughed and said, "That's just pidgin." It was the first time I'd ever heard it. My parents, who grew up running barefoot through the streets of Kaka'ako and Palama were fluent in this alien speech. Pidgin, or Hawaiian Creole, was the language of cousins and insiders, a shorthand between locals. I liked its abbreviated, casual sounds and rolling cadences. I knew instinctively that to fit in, I'd have to speak pidgin, so I enthusiastically set about learning it the way you would a second language, by mimicking and carefully committing phrases to memory. Still, I never spoke it like a native. Every once in a while an "r" that was too pronounced, a "t" that was too crisp, or a vowel not properly elongated would slip out and betray the fact that I was "trying fo' ac."

My parents were determined that my sister and I would receive a good, Catholic education. They sacrificed and scrimped to pay for uniforms and tuition. They worked long hours to come up with mortgage payments for our three-bedroom house in a nice part of town. We led a sheltered, somewhat vanilla, middle class existence. I learned about Hawaiian history in school and took the obligatory hula lessons for a couple of years (I was, shall we say, rhythmically challenged), but somehow, I felt we were too mainstream to be really Hawaiian. Not that Hawaiians are abnormal—trust me, I'm as proud as the next person of my heritage, and I really am going somewhere with this. It's just that, to me, a Hawaiian lifestyle seemed more laid back. Easy going. A kind of lifestyle where things which would be considered in most other parts of the country to be unacceptable—and sometimes downright sinful, according to the nuns—were simply accepted with grace and equanimity. A child born out of wedlock? No problem, the whole family would help raise it. No job and no place to stay? There would undoubtedly be an extra bed somewhere, say, at your sister's brother-in-law's cousin's uncle's house. Relationships were fluid—who was married to whom and which child belonged to which parent was not as important as the larger sense of family—'ohana. And once you were a part of the 'ohana, you were taken care of. Once, in high school, I went with a girlfriend to visit her family on Moloka'i. Amongst the many cousins, uncles and aunties who streamed in and out of her uncle's house, there was a haole man named Peter. He was no blood relation—just a neighbor from down the road who ended up in paradise and spent much of his time surfing and partaking of the local herbs. Apparently his house had burned down, and in the true spirit of Hawaiian hospitality, my friend's relatives had taken him in as one of the family. No big deal.

These ideas were fascinating to me, and they were totally foreign. I tried to picture my folks taking in an itinerant surfer— no way. Maybe it was because I grew up in a supposedly typical family unit—mom, dad, two kids, and a cat. Or maybe it was because I grew up speaking the language of mainstream America. Years later I would take a sociology class in which I heard language described as the window through which a culture views itself and the world. That could explain a lot. At any rate, I didn't, couldn't, feel like a totally genuine Hawaiian. I must add here that this ever-present sense of otherness was not a big, traumatic, life-altering kind of thing. It didn't keep me from having a happy childhood or drive me to drink when I was twelve or anything like that. It was more of a niggling feeling— a psychological paper cut, if you will. A constant, yet admittedly minor discomfort.

It turns out that my mother, a mix of Hawaiian, Chinese, and German, had almost exactly the same sort of feelings growing up. Her parents, too, sacrificed and scrimped to give her and her brothers a good Catholic education at Maryknoll. Paul and Daisy Umiamaka insisted that good English be spoken in the home, with varying degrees of success; the boys were less than conscientious. Their children were sheltered as much as possible and didn't mix with the "rough" kids who attended the non-English standard public schools.

My mother recently confessed to me that although she was more than half Hawaiian, she often felt like other Hawaiians might think she was *ho'okano* or "stuck-up" because of the way she spoke. I asked her if she felt, well, not as Hawaiian as other people. "Yes!" she cried. "That's exactly how I felt." Of course, for Mom there were other issues associated with being Hawaiian. As a child, she was told by the nuns at school that the hula was sinful. Mom, by the way, is a beautiful dancer. She kept on dancing, of course, but from then on, hula must have been somehow associated with shame. At that time, Hawaiian language was forbidden in school and I doubt very much if Hawaiian history and culture were taught.

At the top of the local economic hierarchy were the whites, and then, later, the Japanese. Mom can vividly recall looking through the want ads for jobs and seeing the words "Japanese only" in many of them. The Hawaiians were lowest on the totem pole. I wonder, though I've never asked her, if that is why my mother never goes out in the sun. It could be that she just doesn't like it, but I have a different theory. The browner you are, the more Hawaiian you look, and not even 40 years and a resurgence of Hawaiian pride are enough to erase the stigma Mom must have faced growing up. So here we are. Mom and daughter—the tentative Hawaiians.

There's nothing tentative about my father. He's one hundred percent Okinawan. He is second generation Uchinanchu, the son of immigrant peasants. He knows his people—their music, their food, their stories. He doesn't speak the language, except for a few bad names he and his siblings used to call each other as kids (*yudayah*—"slobber lips" and *gachimayah*—"greedy cat"). But I can tell by the look in his eyes when he talks about his "small kid time" that he can hear the words in his memory. Like my mother, he experienced bigotry because of his ethnicity. The Japanese immigrants to Hawai'i were scornful of their hairy, darker skinned, pork-eating cousins, and although Okinawa was technically a part of Japan, the Okinawans were made painfully aware that they were not, and never would be, Japanese.

Some Okinawans, however, still craving acceptance, changed their names to sound more Japanese. That's how our family name, Chiyan, became Kiyabu. Dad refused to feel ashamed, though. If anything, this strange prejudice served to crystallize his ethnic identity, and it instilled in him a sort of perverse pride, a celebration of the differences in the two cultures. And he's quick to inform anyone foolish enough to make the mistake that we are Okinawan—not Japanese (*"They* lost the war, we didn't!"). He's always known who he is, and with this certainty comes the luxury of being able to disregard this whole pesky issue of ethnicity. Which is maybe why he doesn't think about it much, except once in a while, to tell my sister and me about our intrepid grandparents who came to Hawai'i from Okinawa.

His mother came over as a "picture bride" but then ran away when she discovered the man she was supposed to marry had lied and sent a much younger picture of himself. Grandma refused to marry the old man and then further scandalized everyone by declining to become a field worker on one of the sugar plantations. Eventually, a position was found for her as a maid with a wealthy local family, which is where she met Grandpa. He was the chauffeur. They raised seven children and ran several successful businesses, but Grandpa and Grandma

Kiyabu died before my sister and I could really know them, so the stories Dad tells are, to me, just stories.

All of my father's brothers and sisters intermarried with other ethnic groups like crazy, so the third generation of Kiyabus is separated by more than just an ocean from our distant relatives back in Okinawa. They would no more recognize our faces than they would the name. I suppose that's one of the reasons I've never identified myself with my Asian heritage, even though ethnically, that's the one I should identify with most. My husband, Bob, who is from New York and is as white as white can be, thinks this is interesting, because to him, and indeed to most Caucasians I meet, my features are undeniably Asian. In Hawai'i, though, they are not Asian enough for me to "belong" to that group.

There was a time, in high school, when I really wanted to be a petite, fair-skinned, almond-eyed Japanese girl. I think that had more to do with being a teenager and wanting to fit in than with anything else. Most of my friends were small Asian girls. I suppose if all my friends were black girls, I'd have wanted to be one, too. The fact that I had dark skin and was about four inches taller than every other girl I knew made me literally stand out, at a time in my life when all I wanted to do was blend. I'm only 5'5", but I still felt like a gangling freak sometimes.

I even had a name for this group that I so desperately wanted to join: I called them the Sharis. Looking back now it sounds dumb and stereotypical, but I swear to God, it seemed to me that every high school had a group of cute little Asian girls that all hung together. They all carried Hello Kitty pencil cases and, for some reason, drove Honda Accords, on the dashboards of which they would have the requisite prom picture displayed, along with one or two tiny stuffed animals. They invariably had names like Shari, or Kelly or Michelle, and their, naturally, Asian boyfriends were often named Brian or Scott. They were so together, in a way that seemed a little more cohesive than an ordinary high school clique, that I really envied them. Here was yet another group of which I was not really a part.

Ironically, I had to leave Hawai'i in order to discover my identity as a Hawaiian. After high school, I went away to Santa Clara University in California. It was a cultural epiphany. For the first time, more blonde heads than dark surrounded me, and as I moved through the sea of strangers, I discovered how very different I was from them. This time, however, this feeling of being different didn't bother me, because every other student from Hawai'i shared it.

And then it hit me: I definitely wasn't haole, so that must mean that *I was one of the Hawaiians!* Only this time, Hawaiian meant anyone from Hawai'i, not just the narrow, ethnic definition. Japanese, Chinese, Filipino, poi dog, whatever—our common identity derived from the unique culture in which we had been raised. Like shipwrecked sailors, we found ourselves unexpectedly thrown together by circumstance. Disoriented and a little startled by the strange mannerisms and customs ("Eew, they wear their shoes in the *house!*") of the mainlanders, we clung with relief to others from home.

Over Spam musubi, prepared with a rice cooker someone had smuggled into the room, we would listen to the Beamer Brothers singing "Honolulu City Lights," and sigh over how meaningful the lyrics had suddenly become. I reveled in this homesickness because it was proof of my Hawaiian-ness.

The forthright speech and in-your-face behavior of the haoles made me just as nervous as it did the other Hawai'i kids. It was weird to look someone in the eye the whole time you were talking to them—offensive, almost hostile even. I was shocked the first time I saw two friends loudly and heatedly arguing, and then ten minutes later, head off to the dining hall together as if nothing had happened. It was equally unnerving to witness the way the haole guys would just go right up and talk to girls they found attractive. Just like that. Even if she were a complete stranger. In the heavily Asian-influenced Hawaiian culture, only a total loser with no friends of his own would do something like that. In Hawai'i social interaction took place within sheltered circles of friends and open conflict was rare. These and other revelations helped me to realize how Hawaiian I really was, and that it had very little to do with ethnicity or lack thereof.

One of my favorite moments from that year happened in the hallway of my dorm, as I and a bunch of other Hawai'i people were preparing to make a midnight run to Denny's. I mentioned that I had graduated from Kamehameha, a high school exclusively for those of Hawaiian ancestry, and a short Japanese boy named Scott—honest to God—stopped in his tracks. With a half smile on his face, he wheeled around to face me.

"Kamehameha? You wen' Kam?" "Yeah," I answered cautiously. "So what?" "So les hear it, girl!"

He waited expectantly. I realized what he wanted, and, crossing my arms over my chest and thrusting out my chin belligerently, I said in my best pidgin, "Why, boddah you?! Get problem o' wot?" Everyone busted up laughing, and I grinned triumphantly. I spent only one year at Santa Clara, but that one year was enough. When I returned to Hawai'i to finish my degree at the University of Hawai'i, I had a sense of comfortable belonging.

The next big discovery would come after I got married and moved to Japan, where my husband had a job as a consultant. This one was even more profound than the realization of my Hawaiian-ness. When I got to Tokyo what I found was this: I was very, very American. Despite the fact that I was half-Okinawan, to the Japanese, I was all foreigner. If living in California had been a bit strange, living in Tokyo was like visiting a totally different world.

This time the feeling of being an alien wasn't vague at all. It was the glaring, defining fact of my existence in Japan. Everything about me shouted that I was a foreigner. I spoke in halting, clumsy, classroom Japanese which earned me stares of mingled curiosity, impatience, and sometimes, disgust. I walked with a swinging, Western stride, rather than the delicate-stepped gait that the Japanese women had, as if they were wearing *geta* sandals. Most of all, I discovered that I thought like an American woman. Japanese language and society were vertical—a system based on in-groups and out-groups, superiors and inferiors. How one spoke or behaved varied according to the situation. My struggle with the complicated vocabulary of Japanese honorifics probably stemmed from the fact that I thought like an egalitarian American. Heck, even the President was "Mister" in our country.

Back home, I would not have considered myself to be overly independent, outspoken, opinionated, or feminist, but compared to the Japanese women I met, I felt like Susan B. Anthony. I had thought that in Hawai'i we tried to avoid direct conflicts, but in Japan, that was a way of life. So much so that my boss at the English school where I taught was surprised and disbelieving when I complained that a male student had ogled my chest during our individual lesson and kept asking me the word for "breast."

"But he is the *shacho* (company president)," she said, as if that settled the matter. I also found that the most terrifying question I could ask my students was, "What do you think?" In Japan, teachers told the students what to think. I was tempted to view these incidents as proof of the superiority of American culture, but in the end I acknowledged that they were merely an illustration of the differences in Eastern and Western ways of thinking. And I had no doubt as to which side of the line I fell on.

I lived in Tokyo for three years, and eventually I mastered the language. I learned to skillfully navigate the labyrinthine train and subway system, and I adapted to the crowded, compact living conditions. But just as a scuba diver, no matter how adept he becomes at maneuvering in a new environment, can never become a fish, I could have lived in Tokyo for the rest of my life, and I would never have become Japanese. I thought of my grade school friend, the one who was pure Japanese. Like me, she had grown up eating peanut butter and jelly sandwiches, playing with Barbie dolls, and watching "Happy Days" on TV. Japanese ancestry or not, if she visited Tokyo, she'd be as foreign as I was. Similarly, I thought, if the Hawaiians of today could hop on a plane and travel from Hawai'i—now to Hawai'i—then, they would be foreigners, too. The Hawai'i of today was a hybrid of many different cultures, and that hybridization made us modern Hawaiians more American than we knew.

In a weird way, perhaps what made me feel American most keenly was the fact that I was often unrecognized by other Americans. To them, I was just another Asian face. The Japanese, being a homogenous, insular people, could spot me right away as an outsider. My skin was too dark, my gestures too foreign— a thousand subtle differences that marked me as a *gaijin*. But my fellow Americans had no idea and would stare right past me. I never got the smiles and nods of recognition that often passed from one foreigner, American or otherwise, to another on trains or in passing on the street the way my tall, blonde husband did. I felt an overwhelming urge sometimes to shout, "I'm one of you!"

When I became pregnant with our son, Matthew Kekoa, my husband and I agreed that Japan had been an adventure but that it was time to go home. To me, home had acquired a new, broader meaning. Home wasn't just Hawai'i—it was the good old U.S.A. So, Bob found a job in Seattle.

When he asked me if he should accept, I asked, "Is Seattle still in the States?" He laughed, "Yes." "Take it," I said.

We've been here two and a half months, so it's still kind of early to say, but it feels good. Matthew is nearly nine months old. He has beautiful, golden skin and dark, almond-shaped eyes. I sing to my baby in Hawaiian and Japanese, and when my husband comes home from work he takes his shoes off at the door and we eat barbecued chicken with sticky white rice. It's the best of all worlds, and in America, the *great melting pot*, I think we are as American as a family can be.

salt and black pepper

Karla Brundage

i am salt
and black pepper
i am collard greens with fat back
cooked and re-cooked
for three days
at least

i am steamed white rice
eaten every evening
with fork
not chop-sticks

i am apple pie
cinnamon and sugar
cooked in pure fruit juice
covered with flaky crust
and baked
until i'm done

i am
repeat after me
i am
proud to be who i am
mama
an' i don't care what
other kids say

said
i am from the country
i am from the country

when my mind rambles
i follow a path
over squished strawberry guavas
through bamboo forest
down the gully
to the river where we used to bathe

when i remember
i hear bob marley
singin' stir it up
but we brown people
be sittin stoned
jus' listenin'
not movin'

I see tadpoles
me walkin'
barefoot
through knee-deep mud puddles
to get to school
hoping only that
they will not dry up
before 3:00
so i can swim on my way home

i smell the fragrance of fresh
picked plumeria
pikake

puakenikeni
gardenia
all together
overshadowed by my mother's
strong perfume

I smell fried chicken
and roses
greens
and the sticky air
of rice steaming

i, yes, i
i am from the country
and i surprise myself to say it
but i am a country girl

my father catches rain water
on the roof of his house
in an old water bed frame
for us to drink and bathe in
at night there are mosquitoes

my mother catches big yellow and black
garden spiders in a glass jar
to spread in her gardens
but still there are mosquitoes

i was never proud to be this
i was never proud
but i am a daughter of
thousands of years of daughtering
now i am a mother

and i pass on to my daughter
all my traits
goodandbad
so that she can take what she needs
and improve upon my faults

i am doing the best i can
like a flower in a sidewalk crack
a bird of paradise
growing in cement
not out of choice
but because i have roots here
and since i am here now
i hope that people who pass
stop to see
the color amongst the grey
texture in the monotony
softness thriving
within hardness

THE SOPRANO'S FATHER: A LETTER

Velina Hasu Houston

The year I won the county spelling bee
I learned to part my hair on the right
and you said I didn't look eleven anymore.
I combed your tangles, fed you lemon pie,
And became your nurse as time raced—
a tall man, a small girl: one life descending.

At ten I bury you in the tulip patch,
in a silver thimble, matchstick effigy.
From her sewing room, Mother frets.
From behind scratched lenses, you accept.

At nine I catch you falling,
I will away your memories of war,
The combat, carnage, and you, preserved in drink.
Why should I be another casualty?

At eight you sing to me,
your wedding photo atop the piano, your hands steady on its
        keys.
And you are here without war for one hour.
In the kitchen, Mother joins in, second soprano.

You twinkled in my life like stars then.
In my closet, we watched my cat give birth, kittens to keep,
blackberry ice cream every Saturday, picnics on Sunday.
Then May came to claim you, early heat wave.
You disintegrated in pine and flames and regret
as I sat at the upright banging the ivories,
almost twelve and inflammable. Childhood slipped away.

If ever you stand at the end of the tunnel and look back,
Whisper not of war, but sing,
and, note for note, I shall match you
                    Until the war is over.
                    Until you sleep, eternal.

THE CONQUEST OF KNOWING

Patty Cooper

Lights come up on an Asian American woman.

When I was born, I was Oriental. I grew up Oriental in the South which was rather difficult. It was hot, sticky and all of my friends were White. I had little or no idea what being an Oriental was. For a short time, I was a Boat Person, that lasted for about a few months when many of the refugees from Cambodia and Vietnam came to live in Manassas, Virginia, most famously known for the Battle of Bull Run and the town where I grew up. My refugee status didn't last long because people began to realize that my English was a little too good to be fresh off the boat.

When I was younger, I was rarely ever conscious of being Oriental. I do remember when there were a few occasions that my sense of Orientalness was heightened. It was when my family ate at a Chinese restaurant where the owners would come over and talk to my mother and be so happy to see someone else who looked like them, when people would point at me, turn up their eyes and yell out "Hey, Ching Chong Chiny Chink!" and whenever I would go to get my hair cut. It never failed. The hairdresser would always run her fingers through my hair and look at me knowingly and say, "Oh, my Lord, you've got that Oriental hair. Don't you try to tell me any different. Hey, look ya'll—*real* Oriental hair! Wow, it's so thick. You have enough hair on your head for ten people. You know, I've always been fascinated by you Orientals. You have such good teeth, and ya'll are so smart! But you know what's a shame, and I'm not talking about you, honey, you've got such a rosy complexion, but some of them

Orientals look like they have jaundice. It worries me, it really does." Of course, I would just sit there the whole time nodding, hoping that I would get a good haircut and wondering if she was staring at the Oriental buggers in my nose.

When I went to college, I was still Oriental and became a science project for many of my friends who tried to understand the great Far East by knowing me. It didn't matter that I knew little or nothing about China or nothing about the East period. The important thing was that if I looked Oriental, it meant that I had the gene—the Recessive Asian Gene. The gene that every Asian person is born with. The gene that holds all knowledge of anything and everything that ever was, is and will be Asian for all time to come!

So for a time, I played along and laughed when I was confronted with questions on the procedures for foot binding, my personal theories on Communism and Imperialism, Mao versus Chiang Kai-Shek, the One Child Policy, Tiananmen Square, the Philippines, Thailand, Hiroshima, Vietnam, Hunan, Szechwan, Cantonese, really, I can't taste the difference.

It's in the sauce I'd say.

Pause

Hey, this isn't funny. I'm not going to play Suzy China or lotus flower anymore!

It was then that I started to understand.

I wonder when I stopped being Oriental, and when I started being Asian. Was it when I used the term with someone else who I thought was Oriental, and they politely leaned over and whispered in my ear that it wasn't correct to say Oriental anymore that we were now known as Asian? Were they saving me from ignorance, or were they just part of a secret society that had decided on a whim to plant the word Asian into the cosmos? Like the red ribbons that suddenly went from car antennas of Mothers Against Drunk Driving to lapels and sequined gowns for the fight for the cure of AIDS. Do people actually sit around and decide on these things, or did someone accidently misread a fashion statement?

So shortly after that I became aware, and people asked me what I was, as if they had the right to ask. Isn't woman enough? Human being? Spirit? Of course not! I would answer— I'm Orien- I mean Asian. Ori- Asian. OrAsian. Asian. Asian American, thank you.

But not really, it was a secret, my secret because my face said Asian, but inside, I was not quite there. I was perplexed. And stayed quite perplexed, until I heard a song that made it all clear to me. "Secret Asian Girl." OK, I know it was really "Secret Agent Man." But doesn't it sound better . . . (She sings.)

> Secret Asian Girl
> Secret Asian Girl
> She doesn't have a gun
> She's got chopsticks and dim sum.

As the Secret Asian Girl, I would go out into the world and hunt down all the evildoers against Asian women. I would go into bars and listen to men dribble and drool on and on about their passion for the Orient, the fragility, the sorrow, the simplicity of a Zen garden, and their belief that they were once a young concubine in their past life. And instead of Geisha bowing my head with a shy smile, I would laugh out loud, look them squarely in the eyes and say, "Please! My sisters and I are no Suckee suckee-Mister Eddie's Father-good time fuckee-Miss Saigon-hee, hee, hee Butterfly that you will ever conquer!'"

They were stunned, shocked and I think a little scared because this little China doll karate chopped their image of the submissive Asian woman into hundreds of independent, fierce pieces.

In the home Secret Asian Girl was very effective in deciphering the wisdom in my mother's words that had eluded me for years. Suddenly words like "noonitech" and "broken wing" became very clear to me. I would take out my Secret Asian Girl micro-code translator and magically understand phrases like . . .

You better watch yourself out there, a lot of noonitech out in the loose.

She punches the word into her micro-code translator.

Noonitech . . . of course . . . Lunatics!

Smell like someone broken wing in here.

Broken Wing . . . yes . . . breaking wind!

You will always be my little hairy monkey.

Hairy monkey . . . ah . . . hairy monkey!

Wait, let me try that again.

Hairy monkey . . . oh . . . hairy monkey is just hairy monkey.

Some things are not translatable.

While Secret Asian Girl worked, I watched her and learned. I learned not to be soft spoken, to laugh loudly when I felt like it, to stomp my feet around when I walked, and that together we would accomplish the greatest conquest of all, the conquest of knowing.

The lights slowly fade to black. The Asian American woman remains.

UNTITLED

Patty Cooper

I roll against
something warm
snoring
must be last night's catch
I stare at him
mouth slightly open
dried drool on the sides
eyes smoothed over
and fluttery
he's dreaming about
something
probably some mona lisa
he thought he had sex
with
won't he be surprised
when he wakes
to find me
naked, smiling politely,
and staring

I think about
this stranger in my bed
silently envious
because he can sleep
it amazes me
he's so peaceful—

and then I think about
kicking him

there's a scar
on his right hand
another on his knee
all so personal
and mysterious
I create stories for them
so I don't feel so foreign
laying naked
with this man
that one he got
when he was ten
he fell off his bike
because he was going
too fast
he cried while blood
streamed down his legs
his dad picked him up
and ran home with him
bouncing in his arms
but wait
that's my memory

I wonder
if he was a boy scout or
enjoys cool autumn days
the way I do
maybe he's always wanted
to be king of the mountain

in a few hours
it won't matter who he is
or what his memories are
because he'll be dressed
with all scars covered
he'll say something
about the weather
or about my flair
for decorating
I'll feel nothing
anticipating the end
of the last empty word
he'll leave and say
we'll get together soon
I'll just nod
shut the door
crumble onto my bed
and sleep
to gather all the pieces of me
back together

THE ROOM
Kimiko Hahn

For T

The goal of attachment is detachment

T. Berry Brazelton, M.D.

Murasaki knew her husband's mistress played the koto
sweeter than anyone in court
and so, in spite of repeated requests
she no longer touched hers
when he came home.
Soon she would neither tune it
nor go near its brocade cover
lest his mind wander
to the smoke rising from the salt kilns
in his exile from court, from civilization,
from her.

Would exploring jealousy become a women's penitentiary,
though I could not live without women—
men, yes.

Men, yes?
Do men exist mainly in one's fantasy
and terror
as opposed to that existential state,
without mother
or perhaps *without sister:*
the sister who followed you to the hedge

dragging her bear
as she watched you leave triumphant
for a friend's house;
or the sister who stepped over the hedge,
mother adding bleach to the laundry,
chopping vegetables or measuring miso.

Many women who fell in love with Genji
evaporated with longing
or became possessed by a rival
until they twisted dead
like an iris in a vase.

I am not them.
I would not become attached
to one who could not stay till the sun rose,
slipping out the back and trampling on the garden,
disturbing the snow or gravel,
winking at the shopkeepers opening their deli counters
or newspaper stands
I imagine.

I can smell the salt.
Perhaps the water was so salty at Suma
he broke out in a rash
wading in the surf away from the heat
Was she merely a distraction?
What does she possess that I do not—
when I have formed my life within his so completely?
so like a silk caterpillar?

Until the mother reappears the infant wails
as if he has momentarily lost a limb.

When does mother become a different symbol:
one for *the other,* for *separation,*
for *the one who is not me*
with each new word or property.
Is society conducive
to the mother who nurtures separation?
When we grow older and she dies
where is the breast then?
For the mother
who will take the infant's place?
If you give in to jealousy
can the heart cool down to its normal size and shape?
Overwhelmed, you hear his voice in another room
and decide to hurt him
without his knowing.

I wouldn't have wanted to hear Genji's voice.
He should go about his business
and leave the women alone
to heal and revive.
He should get out of my face.

The taste of pickled plum flooded her mouth.
She thought of Genji thinking of *her:*
this woman was not just another woman.
He kept her attempts at poetry
and flawed though her writing might be
she evicted the others from his mind.
Thus Murasaki was orphaned
whenever she felt Genji's attention elsewhere.
In our battle to separate from mother
what is the compensation?
father?

our own small image?
a friend or sister?
When I visit mother
I still want her
holding me in a blanket on a ship to Rome,
father reading a novel
or arguing with an art historian.
I like to think I was everything for her
at that moment: asleep and satisfied,
sea spray swooshing a lullaby.

If I could return to the moment
my mother came home from the hospital
and I held the baby on a pillow in the sunlight
could I comprehend what slices through each affection?
She is *my* sister.
It was *my* room.

THE ATLANTIC

Kimiko Hahn

for V

We survive recalling crests just off the shore
just beyond the children's bobbing games
but before the swimmer, the elderly woman
in a skirted aqua swimsuit and rubber bathing cap.
She dove over the waves and now swims
slowly in the post-storm turbulence
hand-over-hand, feet splashing evenly,
her head turning in measures of breath.
The waves roll her up. She must be around 75, the age
of my mother-in-law before years of cigarettes
destroyed her internal organs.
I imagine seeing Anne with such a casual stroke
against undertow and current. It may not have mattered
after settling the girls into solid schools
that I don't play cribbage, that I don't
swim comfortably in such depth,
that my maternal grandparents were peasants from Hiroshima.
In those early immigrant years
grandfather was lucky to find a wife
among the farm families already on Maui
while his friends flipped through pictures and astrology charts.
From a single photo I know Mitsuye was delicate
with strong eyebrows that suggested a playfulness
that would save her as she labored first
to put her brothers and sisters through professional schools
then raise eight squabbling children (squabbling still)

in a yard of chickens. She was fortunate, too,
not to be misled by rumors and photo-refinishing
to find Katsunosuke, a man under twenty-five and handsome.
I wonder if he had the energy after plantation work
to be kind to her: not merely sexual but comforting.
And I am fortunate to watch this woman swim
what would amount to laps in a pool and thank Anne
for the swimmer's blood in my daughters' skinny frames
darting in and out of the surf
competing with each other for who will swim out
with their father first
beyond the swathes of seaweed into the Atlantic.

TO THE COVE

Kimiko Guthrie-Kupers

All night she lay beside her husband, waiting, stiff like the floor beneath her, the moist tatami mat itching against her skin in the sticky heat. Before her eyes opened at dawn, the waves were already calling her, like they had yesterday and the day before. She barely remembered to wake her three sons and whisper, "Get your towels, we're going to bathe in the sea," before slipping into her zoris and setting out for the cove.

Somehow it didn't matter that her husband had forbid her to continue "frolicking like a crazy child" in the waves, where other villagers could see her naked. Lately all she could think of was water. Her thoughts were hardly ever still. This had worried her at first, and she had sat by the altar at every opportunity, hands tucked beneath her chin, concentrating on letting her thoughts distill to the quiet box from which she had lived her life until only recently. But to her confusion, she was growing accustomed to the constant motion, and the last time she had met her friends at the open market, she found herself wondering why they seemed so stagnant, as though their obis were pulled too tight around their waists, and something solid had gotten stuck inside them.

Her husband had scolded her several times in the past weeks, rolling his eyes back in his nearly hairless head, refusing to acknowledge her during meals. His purple-cheeked silence had been especially frightening last Tuesday when the village matchmaker had spotted her singing naked at the cove in broad daylight. When confronted by her outraged husband after putting her sons to bed, her only excuse had been, "I'm sorry, I don't know what overcame me; my feet were swollen and my kimono was so tight. The next thing I knew, I was in the water, and for a moment I forgot myself; it was as though I'd completely forgotten who I was supposed to be. . . ." Slapping her face, he had dropped to his knees and begged, "But you have always been such a good wife—the entire village considers you far above average in all respects! Why, why, are you switching on me now?!"

Ever since that morning, nearly a month ago now, when she had first woken to voices of the waves, rising and falling in her ears like a water-choir, something inside her had shifted, and she found herself doing things which before she never would have considered. Only last week, when her husband's co-worker and his wife were visiting, she spilled a pot of hot tea onto the beautiful array of food she had prepared over the course of three days, and rather than rushing in quiet shame to clean it up, she broke into a fit of uncontrollable laughter, and invited her husband's co-worker's drop-jawed wife to join her for a stroll by the sea. Later she tried explaining to her husband that when the waves called, she had no choice; it was as if the blood in her own body were ebbing and flowing with the tides. But he had only raised his fists and tugged at the few hairs on his head, sighing in exasperation, "Crazy, crazy woman!" as he shook his way out of the room.

This morning, the waves had been calling since before she had been awake, breathless, over and over like a tired lover. The call had been stronger than any other morning; somehow she knew she had to be at the water by sunrise. So she tiptoed past her husband to wake her three sons, and the four of them slipped silently out of the house, into the dewy morning, heading quickly down the road which led to the cove. The boys, half awake, hurried to keep up with their mother who seemed almost oblivious to their presence, her eager, stockinged legs peeking out from beneath her ballooning kimono, reaching one after the other as though racing themselves down the wide dirt road.

They inched their way along the rocky cliff, her sons making the cautious effort to remain upright, she placing her small feet and hands confidently on precarious clumps of rocks, causing mini-avalanches down to the sand. She wondered as she traveled downwards whether it was the wind or the waves that had been calling her these past mornings as she lay unmoving on her mat, while her husband, snoring beside her like a beached whale, seemed to hear nothing. She had heard of voices whispering in the wind, perhaps lingering ghosts with grudges, or spirits lost in the night, but she had never heard of water calling. Yet how distinct these voices were—clear as her own, while at the same time transparent, like echoes—women's voices, only deeper, caressing her ears, commanding ever so gently, "Come."

The first morning she had been afraid, and had tried waking her husband; perhaps she was going crazy, like other women from her village she had heard about. Or perhaps some insect or baby bird had gotten caught inside her ear. But it had been impossible to puncture his thick web of sleep. During the nine years since the conception of their last son, which unto itself had been as intimate as purchasing fertile eggs at the market, he had exercised complete lack of nightly attention toward her, never so much as turning to face her on his side, or allowing his hand to brush softly next to hers beneath the blanket. Why, she asked herself after finally tiring of shaking him by the shoulders and forcing his eyes open with both hands, why should she bother trying to wake him now?

So instead, she had kicked off the wool blanket and stood up, finding it unusual to be up so early, even before her eight-year-old son who was always the first awake, running up and down the wooden floors demanding breakfast. As she stood that morning, watching her husband pulling the blanket over his head from an invisible foe, rolling onto his back with a thump, she wondered what to do with the first free time she could remember having in years. With a tingling, nervous rush in her stomach, she decided to wash her body and hair at the outdoor well before the sun had fully risen. Quietly she gathered her comb and towel, humming to herself as she slipped into her cotton washing kimono, filling the short walk to the well with her own voice so as not to pinpoint the other ones, singing a sad simple tune behind her.

The next morning, as she had been fearing and praying against all night, she had woken to the same voices, calling her name with even more assurance and temptation than the day before. But to her surprise, her fear was no longer there; it seemed to have simply floated away like a bad odor, leaving her, for the first time in her married life, feeling absolutely content in her aloneness beside her husband, giggling out loud in the dark morning at the thought that something, somewhere, was desiring and calling for her.

She hardly recalled her anxiety from the first morning now as the four of them climbed down toward the sand, the rocks cool like marble beneath their palms. The tide was high, and the water stretched before them in never-ending streaks of blue, causing her to pause for a moment and gasp, "Ah . . . how can there be such blueness all at once?!"

She pulled her kimono to her knees and headed for the foam, slipping her feet out of their zoris, rolling off her white footings in one motion, exposing her legs to the cold salt spray. She opened her mouth wide to catch the taste of sea on her tongue—nothing had ever tasted so wet and moving.

"Come, shall we take a swim?" She called over her shoulder.

"It's too cold," said the oldest, who had heard his father's warning to use caution at high tide, especially lately, since their mother had taken to thoughtless, self-indulgent moods. There were all kinds of dangers, from sharks to hurricanes; only recently a village man had been mysteriously knocked from his fishing boat just off the coast.

"Nonsense, silly boy!" she laughed as she pulled off her obi and let her kimono drop to her feet, watching the gray fabric fill with dark pools of sand. "I'm going in—whoever wants to come had better follow!"

Only her youngest son's eyes lit up at his mother's excitement. "Wait for me!" he shouted, pulling off his kimono, kicking off his slippers to join her.

As soon as her feet touched the foam, she noticed something strange. Unlike ever before, the water was warm—almost hot, in fact, like bath water. She felt her joints loosen as she walked out further into the impossible heat until she was in up to her waist. She found herself mesmerized by the tall wave approaching her, and watched with calm curiosity as it rose above her, seeming to hover momentarily before crashing down with great force, sweeping her small frame with it out far past where she could stand.

She tried looking back to her sons, but it was difficult to see above the surface because, for some reason, all she wanted to do was sink. She attempted to form her youngest son's name in her mouth, but found her tongue as limp as the rest of her, sinking exhaustedly to the bottom of her mouth. While her mind implored her arms to struggle, she watched them wilt to her sides like petals drooping, and though she knew she should be concerned, she had to laugh at the irrationality of the waves. Didn't they know they ought to be cold? "How funny we must have looked, bracing ourselves like soldiers against the ice-cold sting!" she laughed, feeling warm water enclosing her head like a gigantic fish, swallowing her into its belly.

She hardly noticed herself dropping before she was already a full body's length beneath the surface. Before she remembered to panic, she found herself thinking how fortunate she was that the water was not only warm, but was also quite different in texture; without even trying, she was breathing. As shocked as she knew she should be by this absolute contradiction of nature, taking water in through her lungs and letting it seep back out her mouth seemed natural; she had the impression that if she had only air to breathe now, she would suffocate.

She soon realized that without moving her arms and legs, her body was gliding forward through the sea. She felt water winding around her, supporting her weight like the arms of a partner in a dance. As she traveled on, no longer caring which way was up, the distinction between her own skin and the sea faded, so that soon she was no longer thinking, "This is impossible; where am I being taken?" but rather, a voice inside her was sighing, "Ah, so this is where I am."

She began to notice prickles like tiny pins followed by quick rushes of energy at the ends of what seemed like her left hand and arm. At the same time, the thought of a left hand or left arm was growing as vague to her as the notion of a third leg, or a sixth finger. Her limbs seemed as distant from her center as her heart, while her heart seemed as widespread and reaching as her limbs' greatest span. But still the sensations were growing, electric tingles throughout what her jumbled mind was still calling her left hand and arm.

Next she felt a friendly warmth near where it seemed her right ankle should be, as though a litter of kittens were licking at her fluid skin like milk. Meanwhile, her watery fingers and toes were growing, wandering like snakes outside herself, forever trickling beyond her reach. Where her stomach had always been, she felt something sinking, falling deep inside, and at once she was filled with tremendous sorrow, as though through her blood all the world's tears were pouring.

Then the strangest thing happened. While she had been overcome with countless foreign sensations, hardly able to think or question or explain, her eyes had been pressed tightly shut; in fact they had been the only points in her body which she had still been conscious of owning or controlling. But now, without even trying, eyes still closed, she felt a new pair opening. She had no idea where these had grown from—her back, her stomach, her hands? But wherever they were, they were unlike any she had ever heard or dreamt of before.

With them she saw a raging storm, collecting to violent waves near what her mind was still calling her left finger; within her former lips she saw a peaceful cove where the sun was high in the sky; what had always been her right toes were lapping against smooth sand, and children were splashing and laughing in what used to be her right foot. Near her stomach a ship was sinking, and many people were dying; out her right fingers calm rivers and streams wove their way into bends and folds of earth. She felt the earth cradling her with great cupped hands, letting her trickle in rivulets over its solid, curving body, rising to meet her deep between what her mind still wanted to call her thighs, where a volcano was erupting underwater.

The chaos of activity throughout herself was terrifying; she felt her mind yearning to hold onto itself, twisting and pulling the rest of her with all its strength back toward everything it had always known and understood. It got to the point where she was not sure if she could stand another moment of such massive, expansive restlessness; each new sensation seemed determined to make her nauseous and dizzy. She heard dozens of languages calling for help at once near the surface of her undulating skin; other dozens she heard calling playfully along her dissolving spine. The most disconcerting part was that somehow, with absolutely no effort, she could distinctly comprehend each entity as it called out, from the smallest fish to each crew member of the sinking ship. It was as though she had eyes, ears, and consciousness in every inch of her being. Still, her mind fought against it: "I will not surrender to such chaos!" a voice suspiciously like her husband's sounded throughout her wet self.

Until finally, thoroughly exhausted, without any warning at all, her mind gave way to the rest of her. She felt it opening, rushing, like a slave set free into the brilliant, blue-green flowing water. Suddenly nothing was keeping her from fully feeling. She felt the rhythm of her entire body pulsating, like a heartbeat, steady and unrelenting, rolling in and out in all directions. She felt the earth surrounding her like a body embracing, raindrops spilling into her like food nourishing, air above her like endless sheets of clear coolness. If anyone had been there to ask who she was or where she had come from, she might have answered, "I am like your mother; I have always been here."

But no one was there to ask, in fact no one had the slightest clue as to where she could be found; how were the fishermen in their boats, or her son searching frantically through the waves, supposed to recognize the quiet mother from their own village as the entire sea?

As soon as she had plunged headfirst and mindless into the water like a child, followed eagerly by their younger brother, the breath had stopped short in her older sons' throats. They had watched her small body drift swiftly beyond the crests of the waves, floating resignedly, as though nodding off to sleep; it seemed at the very touch of the water, all strength had left her, and suddenly she had no concept of danger.

Throwing off his kimono, her oldest son ran into the waver, flinging his arms wildly though the icy water. He soon felt his brother's struggling body, and carried him on his shoulders back to shore. But as he had intuitively known from the moment he saw her entering the water, his mother was nowhere to be found. The waves had already carried her out to sea, and there was nothing he could do. His father's voice buzzed in his water-logged ears, "You call yourself a man?! How dare you show your face after standing helpless as an old woman while your own mother drowned?!" He hardly noticed his own heart pounding like an angry fist against his chest until he had covered the entire area again and again. When at last he walked numbly to shore, his brothers greeted him with startled, helpless eyes.

He did not pause before turning to the cliff, running as fast as he could, ripping rocks from the dirt under his grip as he tore up the steep path, back up the dirt road and towards the house where his father lay sleeping. As he ran he had the throbbing sense that his own life was at stake, that if he were to let one more moment slip by without his father knowing the horrible truth, everything would be blamed on him.

When finally he succeeded in slapping his father awake and telling him the dreadful news, he fell to his knees in a fit of choked sobs—he could not have said if it was more out of despair at his mother's sudden death, or absolute terror at what his father might do. But his father was far too shocked to move or speak at all. To the hysterical boy's surprise, the harsh, controlled gaze which had always dwelled in the old man's face was suddenly gone from its steady post, and now a blank gaze of bewilderment took its place. For a moment his features almost seemed soft and hanging. This same baffled, ghost-white look remained on the old man's face for several days, until years of habit remembered themselves, and the sharp glint everyone knew so well was rekindled in the opaque black eyes.

The entire village was full of regret to hear the startling news. Of late, it was true, she seemed to have lost hold of her mind—either that or demons had come to visit her in the night, which was unlikely but possible. But in general it was decided that years of what had been exemplary, graceful behavior could not be wiped out by only four weeks of folly. After all, for most of her life she had been such a perfect, lovely lady, always dressed just so, always thinking of others. The service was held in the village temple, where chanting lasted all day, and for closer friends and family, well into the night.

Not a soul was unaffected by the feeling of loss which pervaded the village during the following week. Only her youngest son spilled no tears at his mother's death, and though his brothers prohibited him from saying so, he continued telling himself and his classmates at school that his mother was not at all dead, that she had only taken an extra-long swim and would be back home to make him breakfast one morning soon, before the last memorial incense had burned from the temple altar.

But the last incense was lit and burned to ash, and still there was no evidence against her death. The village resumed its usual activities, and before long her name was rarely mentioned. Her friends continued meeting at the market without her, and after the first few months they could hardly remember the time when there had been one more of them, bargaining over the price of radish and yam. There was even, to their shame and silent acknowledgment, a slight sense of relief at her absence; as much as they all wished to remember her years of impeccable, even enviable reputation, they could not deny that lately she had been causing quite a stir. Somehow they had all begun feeling uneasy in her presence, as though at any time, at any place, the utterly unspeakable was threatening to be spoken.

Her husband continued his trading business with no drop in productivity, and, in fact, noticed himself growing happier and more fulfilled by life than ever. It was not, he assured himself, that he had not loved his wife dearly; rather, it seemed to him that his love for her was only growing stronger now that she was dead. While one might have thought her death would have interfered with their married life, to him it seemed their marriage was never so happy as now in his fond memories.

Nearly nine months went by, during which he lived contentedly with his three sons and the new servant girl he had hired soon after the dreadful day. She, who he did not find at all unattractive, was a quiet, diligent girl who slept on the floor of a closet-sized storage shed in the back of the house. The fact that he was a man far past his prime, old enough to be his own sons' grandfather, did not interfere with his harmless, nighttime fantasies.

The sun was already low in the sky when one day the servant girl stepped out the back door with a basket of wash to hang dry. At the startling site of the small figure standing before her, naked and full-bellied as a ripe peach, water spilling from the loose black hair to a puddle at the swollen, milk-white feet, the poor girl, whose knees had never stood well to shock, dropped her wash to the ground as her jaw fell to her chest to let out what would have been a blood-curdling scream. But her voice had spontaneously left her mouth—no sound at all would come—so instead she stood pointing and staring like a mute, paralyzed banshee.

Neither could have said how many minutes passed while they stood staring, the older one dripping like a running brook into her own fish-filled puddle, small hands placed simply on her pink, moon-shaped belly, the younger one shivering as she prayed for the safety of her and her ancestors' souls. All that ran through her head was the babbling lecture of her mother who had warned her before accepting the job as the widower's servant, "For your dead father's sake, do what he says, but don't get involved in anything fishy! I've never known a tradesman to be honorable; I wouldn't be surprised if someday his wife's skeleton is found under the pier, a sack of stones tied to her ankles with his own belt!"

The girl looked to the woman's feet now, searching for strap marks, wondering exactly what ghosts of murdered wives did to their husband's housegirls. But to her surprise the swollen-bellied, waterfall-like woman seemed as avenging as a swan, and dead as a budding tree; the dark eyes gazed up from the modestly lowered face, emitting an unmistakable softness and invitation to trust. The full lips spread to a smile, and the flushed cheeks lit up the round face like a rice paper lantern. The girl had never seen such peacefulness all in one face. She felt her own pointing finger and hardened brow softening, encouraged by the woman's raised eyebrows, and the crinkles of laughter at the edges of her shadowy eyes.

At last the girl's voice found itself back from wherever it had fled, and she cleared her throat. "Why have you come back?" she managed to squeak. "To haunt us? Are you a ghost or are you really yourself? I swear I have never done anything to harm your husband or your sons!"

The naked woman dropped her head back and laughed at the girl's questions, gathering handfuls of thick black hair and ringing streams of water into the puddle—now more of a pond—at her feet.

"Don't worry, sweet girl, you have nothing to fear. It is me, I am no ghost; I have never died. But now I've come back to my family, and," she added with what the girl perceived to be a slight blush, "I'm going to have a baby. Perhaps one day she'll be as strong and lovely as you! Run along now, go home to your family—my husband and boys will no longer be needing a housegirl."

Though she knew how startled she should be by this nine-month-dead woman's words, the girl was not now in the least frightened. The very tone of her voice calmed her, causing

her to close her eyes and breathe deeply, much like the cushion-
ing breeze of the sea. So with no further questions, hardly a tense
muscle in her body, the girl gathered the soiled laundry, dropped
it back in its basket, and walked leisurely down the dirt road
toward her home.

Her youngest son was the next to spot her out the back
door.

He let out a yelp of glee and ran into her seaweed-
tangled arms.

"You're back!" he cried, burying his head into her
armpit, hugging the firmly stretched skin of her belly.

"Yes, I'm home," she assured him, running her fingers
through his thick, short hair.

The reunions with her oldest son and husband were not
so sweet. The impossible sight of his dead mother walking
through the back door, naked and swollen-bellied as the city
whores he had heard stories about, flushed her oldest son's face
with unbearable shame and repulsion. Shaking his head as
though hoping to dislodge a bad dream, his eyes filled with tears
and his hands tightened to fists. He opened his mouth as if to
speak, but it was all he could do to stare at his mother's pregnant
belly and shake his head furiously back and forth.

"Don't look at me that way, it's not what it may seem—"
she tried, walking toward him.

"What are you doing here?! You'd better hide yourself
fast! Don't you see? You're dead to the village already; he'll kill
you before he lets you be seen like that!"

Without looking into her eyes, the fifteen-year-old boy
turned and ran from the house, filled with more shame and
hatred than he had ever known. It was possible, he realized with
a pang of acidic guilt as he ran aimlessly down the dirt road, that
the child in her belly was his father's; he knew it took nine
months for a woman to grow that big. But somehow he also

knew that it was not his full-blooded sibling beneath that rosy, bloated skin; and he was certain the entire village would know just as quickly. During the years since his youngest brother was born, everyone in the village had begun wondering why his still young and healthy mother was not bearing more children. When he had been told one day at school that the reason he had only two brothers was that his father could no longer produce the necessary seeds of life, the boy had no reason to question what everyone else in the village had already decided. No, there could be no explanation other than the one he had known upon one painful glimpse; his mother had been captured by pirates and ruined. Either that or—but this was too horrifying to think of for more than a moment—she had taken a lover. And now she had the gall to return home to ruin the family name for good.

Her son was right: when her husband came home from work that evening, irritable and expecting the pretty, pigtailed girl to welcome him with his dinner, the sight of his dead, pregnant wife sitting quietly in the middle of the floor set him into a fit of maniacal rage. The first thing he did was pull his late great uncle's samurai sword from its silver case on the wall, and hold it with a shaking hand to her throat. But to his frustrated bewilderment, all she did was reach up with her own calm hands and gently remove the comically large sword from his grip.

"It's been awhile , please excuse my absence; I'm sure it was difficult for you and our boys. But I have returned now, and I would appreciate your cooperation. Tomorrow I am giving birth to a baby girl."

He watched the shiny sword drop from her calm hands to the floor, silently cursing as he groped to comprehend where this overwhelming sense of passivity and weakness had come from. Perhaps the fish the housegirl had served last night had been spoiled. He found himself removing his shoes and lining them by the others at the entryway, rubbing his eyes in disbelief as he seated himself cross-legged on the mat by his dead wife's feet. Angry words and gestures squirmed through his head, helpless to the will of his body which seemed utterly uninterested in backing him. He sat obediently nodding as his dead wife attempted to explain her absence. "The waves called to me and . . . I lost track of myself," she began, searching for words, "yet I could feel everything . . . I could even feel you . . . it was wonderful. . . ."

Images of other another man's arms caressing his dead wife's naked body slithered through his thoughts as she spoke, but his tongue lay heavy in his mouth, stubborn as a tired ox in the middle of the road. For the second time in his life, the baffled, ghost-white gaze overcame his stern features, and all he could do was sit and nod dumbly, as though under some unearthly spell.

Just then a high-pitched voice called outside, followed by a pair of wide, anxious eyes peeking through the cracks of the paper screen. The village mail carrier, notorious for his mile-long ears and tongue, was waving a letter for her husband to see. But when the widower's dead wife turned to smile and wave back, the startled man dropped his bags and ran around to the front entryway. Had her husband's natural strength returned at that moment, he would have rushed to slide all the screens shut. But instead he sat motionless, watching to see what would unfold before him, trying with what little muscle power he could muster to keep from falling over onto his face.

"What!" came the eager-eyed mail carrier's shrill voice. "She's come back! She's come back!" Before she could say a word to explain herself, he was jumping up and down like a clown, holding his hat on his head and slapping his thighs. Soon he was running down the dirt road, shouting his discovery at the top of his lungs for the whole village to hear.

Within ten minutes at least thirty people were gathered at the front of the house. "Is it really her?" "Perhaps it's her ghost!" "Where could she have been?" came questions and comments with squinting eyes peeping through the windows into the small, shadow-filled room.

Her husband watched with a sunken heart as his dead wife stepped gracefully past him to meet her awaiting crowd, tightening the kimono she had slipped on before his arrival to cover her shameless, protruding middle.

"Yes, I've come home," she announced, bowing respectfully to the excited, frightened faces of her village.

Most took a step back as the dead woman revealed herself at her front door, and the lively chatter of questions hushed to tentative whispers. Only the mail carrier was brave enough to step forward, slowly, as though approaching a convincing figment of his imagination, head bowed low, eyes staring despite themselves at her covered, over-grown belly, and ask the question everyone was dying to know, but was too afraid to ask.

"Please, we would like to know, have you died and come back to haunt us, or are you truly yourself, and if so, where have you been hiding these past nine months?"

At this she laughed, reassuring the crowd, "Oh no, you may all breathe easily; of course it's me, the one you've always known. Only I have not been hiding, I simply went to sea—"

"Were you captured by pirates?" came an anxious voice from the crowd: the village grocer.

"Oh no," she began.

"Which island did they take you to?" "Were you tied up and made their slave?" came others.

"How terrible, and carrying your husband's child all the while!" "I'll bet that's why they finally released you, eh? No one wants a virgin slave with a big fat belly!" The crowd let out a wicked cackle, and at once each member was embellishing on the grocer's story; all she had to do was sit back and listen.

At their persistent beckoning, her husband finally joined them outside, a perplexed, greenish hue exuding from his cheeks.

"Isn't it wonderful, she's home!" they welcomed him in chorus. "The pirates took pity on your family and brought her home!" With a sheepish grin the grocer nudged him at the ribs. "You never even mentioned you two were expecting!" he teased good-naturedly.

What could the exhausted man do but force his lips to a distorted smile and, as he had been doing since walking straight into the spellbinding presence of his dead wife earlier this evening, nod like a puppet on strings.

"Will there be a celebration?" "Has the midwife been informed?" "You look in shock—this must be the most joyous day of your life!" Exclamations and advice came flying at him until at last no one could think of anything more to say. By this time the moon was floating high in the star-specked, blue-black sky.

"Thank you all for your warm welcome. I am so glad to be home." With this she smiled graciously, bowed low to the ground, and waited until they too had bowed and turned to leave for their own homes.

As soon as they began walking, gleeful smiles spread across their lit-up faces, many of the villagers noticed the corners of their lips falling to confused, doubtful frowns, and the unquestioning celebratory mood which had overcome them like sake at the first sight of the small, pregnant woman returning from the dead began leaking away, like a balloon deflating beneath their feet. By the time they had reached their own homes, the merry mood had completely left them, and husbands and wives found themselves glancing sideways at one another, wondering but not saying, "Isn't it odd, her returning from out of the blue, and carrying an impotent man's child at that!" Some scolded themselves for not asking more critical questions, such as exactly how she had been captured, where the pirates had taken her, and how they had managed to sneak her back to shore without anyone spotting their ship. And another thing, some dared to speculate: it had been nearly nine years since the birth of their last son. Could it be that perhaps the child in the dead woman's belly wasn't really even . . . But for some reason, this idea never made it to a fully formed thought; like water it spilled between their grasping fingers before they could catch a firm hold.

Strangely enough, the villagers, without discussing it, came to the conclusion that—while granted, the circumstances were highly unusual—after such a terrifying experience of being captured and kept as a slave-woman by pirates, the least they could do for the poor, pregnant woman whom they had all known and (except for the last weeks before her departure) respected, whose husband was among the most successful tradesmen in the village, was to welcome her home with open arms. This conclusion came so easily and naturally to all, the fact that such unquestioning compassion had never been exercised among the villagers before, and most likely never would be again, did not strike anyone as being the least bit unnatural.

Luckily, the village midwife had heard the news from passersby on their way home that night, and had taken it upon herself to arrive at the widower's house before sunrise. When he slid open the front screen and tried convincing the old, hunched-over woman that they would not be needing her help for days, something in her blood was aroused, and with a polite bow she pushed her way past the still-baffled, slack-jawed husband, chin tucked to her chest and elbows raised as though he was a bitter-cold wind she was braving. She marched straight through the dark, cold house, where the three boys sat still as frightened stones on the tatami mats, and sniffed her way out the back door toward the storage shed, following the unmistakable scent of birth her fifty-five years of midwifery would not allow her to ignore.

But when he followed her outside, grabbing her violently by the shoulders before she could open the rickety door to the shed, a deep pang of despair ran through her body, and she knew as he stared pleadingly into her eyes that she must obey whatever his orders might be.

"If it's a girl, I want you to take it to the cliffs and toss it to the sea. Do you understand?!" He pronounced his words slowly, as though she were not a native speaker of his dialect. She had never been one to question a man's right to keep his house clean of too many daughters—in fact she herself had dropped many unwanted baby girls over the cliffs at the simple request of their fathers. Still, she could not help wondering why a man with only three sons should be unwilling to permit one female child into his family; this seemed selfish and unreasonable, even to her. Especially in this case, when such a sudden, miraculous reappearance of his wife so soon before the day of birth would seem to be an unusually promising omen. However, she had never so boldly contradicted a man's orders, and was quite proud of this fact; she had no intention of changing now. So she narrowed her eyes and dropped her head in resignation, mumbling in a soft, uneven voice, "Yes sir, I understand," before pulling open the shed door to find the pale mother lying restless on her back across large sacks of rice, twisting and pulling her own hair, moaning softly in the musty, mildewed room, like an injured heron, legs spread wide like wings.

But when the baby girl fell like a ripe fruit off a tree into the old woman's arms, followed by a gushing river of blood and water, she could hardly believe her eyes; this was the easiest and cleanest birth she, in all her years, had ever witnessed. As though guided by some energy other than her own, she found herself placing the smooth-skinned baby into the mother's arms, watching as the newborn girl pressed her blood-stained head into her mother's breasts as though searching her way back home. Rather than carrying the baby girl to the cliffs as she knew she should, the old woman left the mother and child lying together on the sacks of rice, her kimono fluttering like a swarm of moths around her feet as she ran fast as though under some wonderful, ecstatic spell back to the house where the husband was waiting. Her thin voice had never been so bounding as when she announced to the blurry-eyed, trembling man that his wife had just given birth to a beautiful baby boy.

By this time he was so drained of all mental and physical energy, all he could think to do was demand that the baby be brought to him at once. He waited impatiently in the house for the midwife to return with the child, chubby fists rubbing against themselves as though debating each other how on earth to handle his outrageous predicament.

Should he as patriarch take action now and put an end to the demon-sent child before anyone in the village could see it? Should he command the midwife to toss the boy into the sea and swear her by threat of death to secrecy? Why had he been so quick to believe his wife's presumption that the child would be a girl? The faces of his village swarmed through his every thought, glaring down their noses at him with raised brows.

As of now, they believed the child was his, did they not? Or were they just playing along, stalling for time so they might plan proper punishment and humiliation for the entire family? After all, wouldn't they think it odd that a man who had not produced a child in nearly nine years would suddenly prove fruitful now? At this thought a faint, involuntary smile passed over his lips. "True, I am a rather virile-looking man—always have been," he thought to himself. "Perhaps it wouldn't appear so odd at that!" But still he could not rest easy; what if later they were to find out? What if his son turned out to have ugly, pirate-like features, and somehow remembered his own shameful conception? What if his wife had taken a lover, and someday the other man came forth to reveal himself for the whole village to see? How could he put himself and his sons at such a risk of shame?

When the terrified, possessed old woman returned with the tiny, shrieking bundle in her arms, wondering what would become of herself and the baby as soon as the father saw the truth, he could not stand to touch it. Instead he had her place it on the mat, where he and his sons, who had been holding their breath all night as they watched their blank-faced father, fearing what he might do, stared down at the newest member of the family. The midwife stood by and closed her eyes, asking herself with a hysterical half-chuckle-half-cry what in the world she had been thinking at this pitiful attempt to save the life of this child; had she truly believed that lying so the girl might live a mere ten minutes longer was worth sacrificing her more than fifty, spotless years as the village midwife? But before he had folded back the blanket to confirm that his orders had not been crossed, there was a fluttering knock at the door. The midwife let out a cry of relief as she slid open the screen to see five beaming women standing like long-stemmed flowers at the entryway, arms full with baskets of fruits and other festive foods.

"We have come to bless the new baby!" one announced as they filed in, chattering among themselves as though returning to their own homes after a long day of shopping. They placed colorful treats at the altar which stood in a corner of the room, insuring good fortune and protection for the new child.

"Ah, she's beautiful!" exclaimed one when she saw the bright-eyed infant wrapped in the wool blanket, lying on her back, surrounded like a potentially dangerous foreign object by her new father and three brothers.

"It's a boy!" the oldest son corrected as she pushed through their circle and scooped the baby up in her arms.

"Nonsense," the woman giggled, unwrapping the blanket from the miniature naked body to reveal the evidence. The father and his three sons nearly dropped to the floor in shock. "And such a pretty girl at that," she went on, rocking the red-faced bundle on her shoulder.

"Oh, she looks just like her mother!" cried one of the others. "Maybe she'll have your good sense!" said one in an attempt to flatter the dreary-faced man. "Oooh, I can see she is going to have perfect complexion already!" another exclaimed as she placed a bowl of shiny persimmons by the altar.

The midwife stood back, watching the incredible scene play out before her; she could not remember the last time she had been filled with such tremendous calm. She knew there was no way this poor husband could possibly rid his house of this child now that the altar had been blessed, and the entire village would be humming with the news of the successful birth before breakfast. The defeated man walked helplessly out the back door and to the shed where his dead wife lay on her back, still breathless. He stood just outside the doorway and stared into the dark, woman-smelling room, unable to force his feet across the threshold.

"I don't know what has happened. I don't know where the wife I once knew and loved has gone. But I consider that woman dead. I have no idea where you or your filthy child have come from. I only know you are a demon's whore, and that your daughter is the very demon herself. Whatever powers you have used to bring her here cannot last; I will never treat her as my own except to the outside, and I will see that she does not remain in this house for long."

She heard his voice like a mosquito in her ear, only vague and annoying, but she did not hear or care to understand his words. Eyes closed, she felt her heart calm, and the spasms in her lower back beginning to subside. She felt as though she were floating on a gigantic raft of rice sacks down a long, wandering river of red, warm ripples climbing up her thighs and around her hips, lapping smoothly against her rising and falling abdomen. She could hear her daughter crying from within the house. With each high-pitched wail, she felt little tugs inside her. She placed her hands on her emptied belly, stroking herself, whispering under her breath, "Shh . . . shh . . . ." Before long, the distant cries faded, until she could almost hear her daughter heaving gentle sighs of relief. "That's my girl," she sung, running her fingers through her own matted hair, feeling her moist body heavy against the cloth rice sacks beneath her.

In the house, the women were passing the quieted infant back and forth, commenting in squealing voices how well-behaved and peaceful she was for a newborn. The baby girl watched with wide, absorbing eyes as each new face appeared before her. It was as though, the women were to remark on their way home that morning, she had seen them all before, and was simply trying to recall the exact place and time she had known them. Only her youngest brother stepped forward to get a better look, searching her strange little face for signs of recognition; the other two waited by the back door, wondering where their father had gone, and why their stomachs ached with such a confused, gurgling emptiness.

"There was something unusual about that baby girl, don't you think?" asked one of the women as they walked down the dirt road toward their homes in the early morning sunlight.

"Yes, now that you mention it," answered another. "The way she looked at us like we were old friends, with those dark, wide eyes—like windows opening onto a vast night sky. . . ."

They covered their mouths and giggled at such a bold, poetic statement. Where had this giddy mood come from? It certainly felt strange, and none of them could recall the last time they had felt so youthful and light. But somehow it did not matter this morning. As they watched sunlight glittering on the water below the rocks, smelling baby cherry blossoms and the pungent scent of the sea, mixed in with the lingering smell of blood and birth on their fingers, all they could think of was how lovely that new girl had been, and how lucky that mother and father were, to have produced such a healthy child after such a scare; who would have thought it would all work out so nicely?

MOVEMENTS IN EXILE:
Kyo Maclear

I.

mapless departures

Bridging
planks of a ladder
        so monumental
greased with sweat,
tendons stretched
furtively
to snap back
with each failed step

limbs shudder
muscles taut with effort

stealing
sidelong glances at fellow travelers
discerning human form,
bodies in exile—torn asunder
clasping darkness

whisper to silence:
        can you see me?

questions
unanswered

unanswerable

(shizuka na)

silence
hanging heavy
like a net
a twinelike suspension
to entangle to bind to protect

eyes brush flesh
gestures of form
that falter and slip
with each uncharted movement

searching for clues in this journey,
mapless yet necessary

whisper to silence:
       are you with me?

words careen,
float in wisps,
lock in stalemate,
then drop like a stone.

II.
bodyscape

Blood
spatters memory,
spiraling encanthus,
charting a web of crimson

remembrance,
streaking through me
a high-pitched scream

ancestral connection
fettered
birth-blood
tainted
by an accidental meeting of flesh
       carried across continents
       extended across language
       pressed across culture
       strained into blood
stream that flows through a heart carved in two pieces

My body
a minefield
discoloured by history
checkered white and yellow
kings and pawns
locking horns in a battle
that rages through sleepless (k)nights

       but my heart . . .
       hardened arteries soften
       at the possibility of
       stoking amber warmth—hibachi style
       against dim drumrolls
       beating dong doro
            dong doro dong doro doro doro

       And my voice   *watashi no kóe* . . .
       my voice . . .

melts through   *tokásu* . . .
a tower of foreign syllables'
borrowed words,   *gaikoku*
no kotoba . . .
cold as granite,
first with a squeak,

then with the velvet cadence
of an unsung melody   *utá* . . .
bursting forth,
resonating,
carrying me   onward   onward   *zenpoo e*
                    onward   *zenpoo e*   *zenpoo e*

III.
when journeys merge

Toiling
to knit a connection
from shards of (re)memory,
splinters of history,
bottled suffering.

to grasp the many ways
our pasts have intersected
                collided
a legacy of displacement

Crashing into each other's arms
touching flesh to flesh

no struggle

no despair
no joy
is ours to own alone

Extracting hope out of tumult
to share
in need
to conspire
envision

The hooks that pierce my heart
extend from my groin
stringing our souls together
are the only connection
I have.

IV.
the essence of arrival

To give form to knowledge
huddled with fear.

To create passages
from word-trails
etched in the space
that lies between us

To emerge from
an epoch of drawn tears
an epoch of searing lies

To birth ourselves.

To birth ourselves.
To birth ourselves.

Our silences swell, break.
Our voices fly in the face of
                    absence
                    contempt
                    indifference.

FOR MY BABY DAUGHTER, WHOM I WAS ONCE AFRAID TO SEE

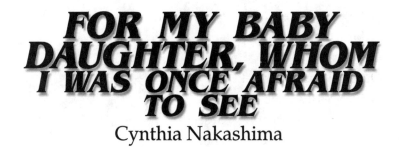

Cynthia Nakashima

For the past six months I have spent almost every waking hour looking into the most beautiful pair of blue eyes. I had not expected, nor had I hoped, that this would be the case.

When I married my high school sweetheart nearly four years ago, I did not consider him a member of another race—in fact, I am still not sure that I do. I say this because I am the daughter of a German/English American mother and a Japanese American father, and am married to a man who is socially and self-defined as "white."

There have been times when I have been somewhat reluctant to disclose the fact that my husband is white, because of my unwanted sensitivity to the attitudes and assumptions that some people of color have about those who "marry white." Examples of these assumptions are: that we have "bought in" to the white standards of attractiveness; that we are trying to raise our social status through our mates; and that we are politically and emotionally less committed to our ethnic/racial communities.

In fact, as a multiracial person who is one-half white myself, I have frequently felt that my marrying a white person is considered even "worse" than a "full-blooded" person of color marrying a white person, because it is a more extensive example of the so called process of "cultural genocide." Supposedly, through intermarriage, an ethnic group dies out by being completely absorbed, melted, and diluted into the mainstream. In the Asian American communities I have heard many times, in angry and resentful tones, how "Eurasians" always marry whites and never marry "back into" the community. Since my marriage seems to support this pseudo-theory, I have not always made the existence of my marriage and husband as well-known as I otherwise would have and should have.

Then, in the fall of 1990, I dared to do something that made it pretty much impossible for me to hide my politically incorrect marriage: I got pregnant. I have always known that having a baby would very likely make it obvious to the world (especially to the Asian American world) just "who" I had married. I knew this because I know several people who are 1/4 Asian and 3/4 European, and most of them look predominantly white. In the same way, those people who are 3/4 Asian and 1/4 European tend to look pretty much Asian. Either way, for Eurasians who have children with Asians or Europeans, there seems to be little chance of having a child who "looks mixed race."

Now don't misunderstand me—I realize that fixating on the physical appearance of people, born and unborn, and what supposedly "looks white" and "looks Asian" is nauseating and stupid, but I also know that a significant part of the mixed race experience (and the experiences of all people of color, in various ways) is indeed all about how we look racially. All of my life, on practically a daily basis, people have commented on my appearance in reference to my racial background: "Your eyes look Asian, but you have light hair and freckles," "You look right in-between," "You don't look Asian (or white) at all," or the ever popular "Mixed race people are so beautiful." These sorts of comments have contributed to the making of the person I am today, and they bind me to other mixed race people, while sometimes separating me from mono-racial Asians and whites. And admittedly, mixed race people do it to each other, too—across a room at a party, at the bank, in a classroom—we see each other and react. Whether we give each other a meaningful glance, approach each other and say, "Are you . . .?" or quickly look away and avoid one another, we react, and all on the basis of physical appearance.

So, the whole thing about how my baby would look sat at the back of my mind for the first half of my pregnancy. I knew my baby would not be just white, because, through me, she would also be exposed to the Japanese American community and issues of people of color. But still, I did not know how I would feel if my baby looked completely white. I was disturbed not only by the thought of having a physically white baby, but I was also disturbed by the fact that I was disturbed. I think that for many mixed race people who have spent their lives resisting the external pressures to "choose" just one of their races, communities, and cultures, marrying someone who happens to be one of those races feels a bit like making that final, unwilling racial choice.

I think many biracial people live, in their minds and in their hearts, on some self-created space in between their two parent groups; either consciously or subconsciously, they keep their lives and identities balanced so as not to become entrenched in just one of their "halves." Becoming seriously involved with someone who is from one of the biracial person's parent groups threatens to throw the person off-center, off-balance.

By feeling disturbed and somewhat saddened by my future daughter's possible white-ness, did that mean that I also thought outmarriage is wrong? Or that I agreed with all those who think mixed race people are inherently "less" legitimate members of a given community? Haven't I spent years arguing that physical appearance is not indicative of a person's identification and affiliation with an ethnic/racial/cultural group? And wasn't I being a totally unworthy future mother with messed-up values and neurotic fixations—I mean, isn't sadness a "bad" thing?

Then I began to remember how all the turning points in my life—leaving my parents' house, starting college, getting married, learning of my pregnancy—consisted of a combination of excitement, fear, happiness, and sadness. Change of any kind usually consists of all of these feelings.

The United States has been changing from a largely European-derived society to a more multiracial and multicultural one. The Japanese American community has also been changing, becoming more racially and socially diversified. These changes are exciting, scary, happy, and sad. People like myself, who have parents who are racially different from each other, represent a very intense turning point in the histories of our two families, and in a broader sense, our two ethnic groups. Never again will my father's family be "all Japanese," never again will my mother's family be "all white." On the one hand, this is not important. On the other hand, this is very important. In this same way, my baby's racial appearance is both not important at all and very important. The way she looks, no matter how she looks, represents changes that are exciting, scary, happy, and sad. And in this way, she looks just like I do.

Madeline Hanako was born on August 6, 1991. She has almost black hair, very pale skin, and bright blue eyes. People say she looks like Snow White or a porcelain doll. She does not look much like anyone in the family, although she looks a little like each of us. She does not look Japanese, I guess, although the shape of her forehead and way she holds her mouth when she concentrates looks very much like my father. And she is the most beautiful, the most physically perfect, the most aesthetically pleasing person I have ever seen. I do not say these things because I value white standards of beauty above all others; I say these things because I value Madeline above all others.

I like to think that Madeline represents a new generation of Americans who necessitate a change in the ways that we think about such things as ethnicity, race, community, and culture. We cannot judge a person's ethnicity by their last name or their facial features or their accent. We cannot guess a person's race by how they look or how they vote. We cannot know a person's culture by their eyes, their skin, their hair, or their favorite foods.

In the birth preparation class that my husband and I attended, every baby-to-be was racially and ethnically mixed: one 1/2 Vietnamese, 1/4 Chicano, 1/4 Anglo baby; one 1/2 Mexican national, 1/2 white baby; one 1/2 Chicano, 1/2 white baby; one 1/2 Chicano, 1/2 Jewish baby; and Madeline. Our instructor was a black woman who is married to a white man and has five kids. The reality is, we're already here, messing things up, like it or not.

I've decided that the best description of Madeline's heritage is not 3/4 white and 1/4 Japanese, but rather 1/2 white and 1/2 hapa, because who I am racially, culturally and mentally is most adequately described as hapa. Like me, Madeline is a racially mixed person. She is part of the Japanese American community because she *just is*. She is part of the European American community for the same reason. And she is part of the community of mixed race people in this country and in this world. Her particular version of the multiracial experience will be a different one from mine, but I can teach her that there is no good reason to "choose" any one group to belong to, unless that group is defined by kindness, understanding, tolerance, and generosity.

The other day I visited the house of a friend who is biracially and biculturally Japanese and European. His wife, who is Jewish European American, scooped up Madeline and said, "She looks just like my babies did!" Sure enough, pictures of their two girls as babies look very much like Madeline: the same shaped cheeks, the same shaped eyes. So all along, the fetus Madeline was planning to arrive on this earth looking just like she is supposed to look—like people who are half white and half hapa.

Perhaps years from now Madeline will see a familiar face across the room at a party, at the bank, in a classroom, and she will know that that person must be like her, and perhaps they will start a club at school or publish an anthology, and they will wonder what their kids will look like as they marry people of all ethnic/racial combinations from all over the world. I have no doubt that whatever my little Madeline Hanako partakes in, it will make this world a much more wonderful place to inhabit.

ON THE HALF WHITE EIRELAN

Carolyn Lei-lanilau

When she is carried into Chinatown,
apples, oranges and bananas wave her way.

Sniffing and wagging around for perfection
Chinese young and old calculate
her *"fresh."*

Eirelan's beach ball eyes sting imaginations.
Her fingers squeeze pear and custard.

Women and children poke from behind doors
and shopping bags
shocked by her longhaired lashings.

LIFE WITH ANA AND EIRELAN

Carolyn Lei-lanilau

We break the shells and eat unsalted peanuts
as we talk of school and fashions and think
of Japanese peanuts wrapped with puffed rice
and seaweed. Small brittle Taiwan peanuts.
Hawaiian peanuts boiled in salt water, left
drying in the sun for days on a bamboo tray
until all are eaten. We sit among islands
of our leotards, tights and broken pointe shoes
saying grand allegro. The gods
eating us as we run toward them consciously.

TO HALVE AND HALVE NOT

Donna Midori Hokumalamalama King Lance

My foremost impression of elementary school was the tidiness of my oriental classmates. They were petite and they dressed neat; they looked just as pristine at the end of the day as at the beginning; at naptime they lay quietly on their sleeping bags with their hands neatly folded.

Most inscrutable of all was their hair. Somehow, it could stay tightly braided all day. It clutched onto barrettes and never poofed up or snarled in big lumps. I was big, awkward, barefoot, and Medusa-like—an occidental outcast.

Mrs. Miyasato, my kindergarten teacher, said I was "cosmopolitan," and my five-year-old brain thought "neapolitan," but I got the idea: vanilla, chocolate and strawberry—why settle for one thing when you could have all three? Except I didn't like the strawberry. It was so pink-and-sweet, girly and neat. It didn't fit with the other two and I always left it melting in the bowl.

The disorientation I felt was compounded by comments at the end of the day when my Japanese grandma would come to pick me up and other kids would ask, "Is that your mother?" "You don't look like her!" Before I went to school, I never knew my grandmother and I were different. Education is a fine thing.

In a reductive fashion, hapa has repeatedly been interpreted as "half," but the Pukui-Elbert *Hawaiian Dictionary* gives this definition: Hapa. 1. nvs. Portion, fragment, part, fraction, installment; to be partial, less. (Eng. half.) Like many concepts undergoing indigenous-to-master dialect mutation, "hapa" loses much in the translation.

When something is made whole, or even two halves of a whole, it is reduced. Beware the denominator, calmly indicating half here, half there, calculating away our names and calcifying our parts. Hapa means to be partial, it's an infinitive, not a noun, and has infinite potential for division. Once something undergoes the initial agony of division, each half can be halved again, ad infinitum.

When I was a kid, my hapa mother, under haole hippie influence, started on a health kick. Sprouts insinuated themselves between spam and bread, bread which became progressively darker, denser, grittier. Gone forever was the soft pure white Holsum bread, floating over spam, melting like air that wasn't even there. Brown grains were sprinkled into the rice pot and our fluffy white rice turned 1/4, then 1/2, then 3/4 brown, becoming less and less mushy until it, too, was pure brown.

Although making oneself (or another) whole is diminishing, grains of a different color can be disturbing, so we fix the odd parts onto one another where we can despise and covet them. The shaky stance of partiality allows the sneaking suspicion that things are not quite as clear cut (i.e., half-and-half) as they seem; it gives rise to the fear that the world, and ourselves, may be quite fractured indeed; it hints that the "us" and "them" division may be imaginary. The kernel of fear inherent in this view may be precisely why hapas and "half breeds" are so reviled in some parts of the world. The race which is not one reflects the partiality and resultant anxiety that resides in everyone, calling up painful divisions and uncertainties.

A childhood friend migrating back to Oakland from Fiji is working on a book about his father's family, entitled *Half-Caste*. He said that although being hapa is seen as a good thing here-and-now, it was (and is), in places like Fiji and India, seen as an insufferable repulsive vile condition. And it does seem that in some parts of the world there is a feeling of dread regarding hapas, a feeling of repulsion and attraction. It is the fear of unfixedness which evokes this loathing.

After talking to Jimmy, I wondered about the loathsomeness of being half-caste in Fiji as opposed to the uncertainty but okay-ness and even privilege of being hapa in Hawai'i. Meditating on castedness, it occurred to me that:

To be cast is to be molded, petrified at the moment of becoming; there is constancy, certainty, stratification. If an object is half-cast, it is only half-hardened, it still has the potential for malleability. Being undone is a good thing because it keeps you in the state of becoming.

A cast implies a cover up, it conceals as well as molds the split it contains; fractured places heal stronger, and this strength is necessary to break the stranglehold of the mold.

And:

All the world's a stage, but if half the cast has a different script, the play is disrupted; on the other hand, the insecurity of not knowing who's going to say what has definite possibilities.

My grandma was born at Pahala sugar plantation in 1901 and migrated by boat to a coffee plantation in Captain Cook. At ninety-two, she still loves coffee with sugar, very light with lots of Half-n-Half, lukewarm and more white than brown. It was on the slopes of Captain Cook that she met my Scottish (though apparently not clannish) grandpa-to-be.

It is interesting to me that although I have a genealogy which includes many hapa ancestors, it is always the white men who are mating with and marrying women of color, the succeeding generations becoming whiter and whiter, like grandma's coffee, the opposite of our rice and our bread. Hapa offspring are often the result of an indiscretion, the combining of two previously discrete sets.

Grandpa was Captain Cook's first postmaster, a sort of proto-postmaster, and Grandma was his housemaid; the master and the maid mated in the postmaster, post-colonial plantation world and sailed off to that roaring '20s hot spot, Honolulu. In those days, the marriage of Japanese girls to haole men was quite taboo, but news had traveled to the hills of Captain Cook that *two* such events had occurred in Honolulu. So off they sailed to that safe harbor and birthed my hapa mother, a post-script.

My dad's parents are both hapa. Minnie Brown, his mother's mother, was the daughter of a Hawaiian-and-haole woman who married a white man named Brown, a jailer; her cells were white and Brown. She was a lady-in-waiting to the Queen and my dad's father's father was one of the seven supplanters who organized the deposition of the queen. When the offspring of these characters eventually met up and mated, this divisive issue lived and breathed in their marriage, and in their issue, and has been handed down to me.

And although I embrace my hapa inheritance, the fusion can be confusing. I, as well as my brother and a number of cousins, have rather mixed feelings about having money, property, power, etc.: being the oppressor *and* the oppressee is an uneasy position. But this schizophrenia has given me a clue that there may be a trace of this di-vision in all of us—this vision is the privilege of a partial perspective.

Recognizing division, acknowledging choice, can be distressing. "One" always has the option of choosing to function as one of one's parts—female, mother, hero, Japanese, haole, etc. Just as we dress one way to tend the garden and another to wait on the queen, we can outfit ourselves in a way that best suits the situation at hand. But what about the agony of indecision, the paralyzing feeling of standing in front of closets full of clothes and having nothing to wear? You never experience this particular agony if you have only one wear-it-everywhere overall, or an assigned costume. It is at once wonderfully liberating and painfully agonizing to be able to choose.

Is there ever the possibility of choosing not to choose any one part? To remain uncommitted? There is a lot of pressure to be one-or-the-other, and one of the more annoying aspects of maintaining the stance of self division is that it becomes very difficult to act. But in not acting, one can *be* . . . and others have a way of being with you that they don't if you are following your script.

And our scripts are written in invisible ink—another problem with white on white. Without a contrast we can't read anything. If one remains chaste (the Latin root of caste), one remains one and never has to look at oneself; it's only di-vision that allows this kind of reflection.

Division, cell division, is the essence of life. Why *did* our protagonist, that first one-celled protozoa, divide? And how can it be that when a cell divides, it is not into two halves, but two wholes? This is the act of love and life: to let part of yourself go and become other, and other again, eventually reuniting on another level. In one sense, all products of sexual reproduction are hapa. Hapas embody hybrid vigor because they lack double doses of recessive lethal genes. The variation inherent in sexual reproduction (if we conceive of production as play, re-production is replaying the drama with a rewritten script) is the point of the whole messy business.

Like all questions of race, the generational or cell division model has a historical perspective. In fact, you could look at the history of Homo sapiens in this same sort of cell(s)-becoming-other way: we/they began in the cradle of civilization and radiated out around the globe, evolving on the way. Now we are re-combining, meeting back up in places like Hawai'i, for example. Even though I am hapa in a number of ways, and so are my parents, I have a double recessive genetic defect called Hitchhiker's Thumb, because both my parents are descended from the same Scottish clan, the MacGregors. My genes have been hitchhiking around the world in widely variant individuals; I'm shifty, but I'm thrifty, who knows when an old trait will come in handy?

Thinking on being hapa is a choice way of di-solving the barriers of race and the cell walls, of remaining shifty rather than steadfast, half-baked rather than hard boiled; I know I'm mixing metaphors but I am, you know, mixed, and I love to mix metaphors, like the stage and the cell:

All the world's a cell and the cell wall is perfect; it cannot be broken, the willingness to live in division is the only way to "escape," the willingness to allow an other to penetrate is the only way to rejoin. This willingness is the saw in the cake. We can halve and eat our cake (with *all* kinds of ice cream) by staying half-baked.

As the fall '93 semester opens, I take out the class list, survey the cast of characters and call roll: Jodi Haunani, Lisa Michiko, Alison Kiyomi, Irvin Keli'i, Arlene Bagoyo, Scot Hideo, Keith Masaru, and it dawns on me that *nineteen of my twenty students* have haole first names and middle names of another ethnicity; and I, Donna Midori, am re-nominating and discovering just what it is that's in a name, feel that this *is* my class, the class which is 100 but not one—in English 100 we are none of us 100% English . . . we are all partial after all.

HAIR 2

Sabrena Taylor

(for Teresa Kay Williams)

Our mothers tried their best to change our image
To press our hair
To relax our hair

   as if hair was nervous
     hair would shout
       too
        L O U D

My mother's tongue I tried to cut with the knife of the tongue of
children who didn't understand my fair skin, my dark skin
Father's tongue
Moon eyes
My hair cried
The one little curl society could not press and repress
My image refused to be oppressed
That one little curl stood out, shouted

      too
       L O U D

Made waves and for that one little curl I give my deepest
appreciation
For I am alive today as I will be alive tomorrow
Making Waves

CONTRIBUTORS

Cristina Bacchilega is a professor in the English Department at the University of Hawai'i–Mānoa, where she teaches oral narratives, folklore and literature, narrative studies, feminist theory, and, most recently, South-Asian women's fiction in English. The paperback edition of her book, *Postmodern Fairy Tales: Gender and Narrative Strategies*, came out in 1999. She is Review Editor of *Marvels & Tales: Journal of Fairy-Tale Studies*. An Anglo-Indian Italian, she lives in Honolulu with her husband and her daughter, Bruna.

Kathy Dee Kaleokealoha Kaloloahilani Banggo graduated from the University of Hawai'i–Mānoa with a B.A. in English. She has won a number of writing awards, including an Intro Award from the Associated Writing Programs, and has published work in a variety of literary journals. She is Hawaiian-Filipino and was born and raised on the island of O'ahu, Hawai'i.

Mei-mei Berssenbrugge was born in Beijing in 1947 and grew up in Massachusetts. Her books include *Summits Move with the Tide, The Heat Bird, Empathy*, and *The Four Year Old Girl*. She lives in New Mexico with artist Richard Tuttle and their daughter.

Karla Brundage was born in 1967 in Berkeley, California to Kathryn Waddell and Frederick William Brundage. In 1968, the family moved to Hawai'i. Karla grew up in Ka'a'awa, which she still considers her home. She graduated from Vassar College, and recently received a master's degree in education from San Francisco State University. She currently lives in Mānoa, and is a teacher at Maryknoll High School. She has also lived in Oakland, California, and upstate New York. These places she feels, have greatly shaped her experience, as have the ancestral experiences of places she has never been, such as the segregated South, Senegal, the middle passage, Europe and pre-colonial North America.

Diana Chang's first novel, *The Frontiers of Love*, originally published by Random House, was recently reissued by the University of Washington Press. It was the first novel to have been written by a Chinese-American in this country. She is the author of five other novels published by Random House and Harper & Row, among other publishers in this country, and in England and Italy as well.

Her poems have appeared in many magazines and in over forty anthologies. The titles of her four poetry chapbooks are: *The Horizon Is Definitely Speaking*, *What Matisse Is After*, *Earth Water Light*, and *The Mind's Amazement*, just published by Live Poets Society. This most recent collection focuses on art—on poems about painting, poetry, music and dance. Diana Chang is also a painter and short story writer.

Anne Xuan Clark is a Vietnamese Irish film/videomaker living and working in Seattle, Washington. Originally from New York and California, she moved to the Northwest to attend The Evergreen State College where she majored in film/video production and Ethnic Studies. She worked at a housing and community development agency in Seattle's International District. She co-created a mixed media video installation with other mixed Asian women and exhibited at the Bumbershoot Arts Festival. Her videos have dealt with mixed-race issues, self definition/representation, community, family, incest, and sexual assault. Anne has many future projects in mind.

April Melia Coloretti was born in San Francisco, California and raised in Honolulu. She is of Filipino-Spanish-Italian extraction. Unfortunately, some people believe that this ethnic background could lead to an angry personality. April maintains that this is just not true. She graduated from Punahou in 1985 and received her undergraduate and graduate creative writing education at the University of Southern California in Los Angeles, where she was associate editor of the *Southern California Anthology*. In the early 1990s April worked as a legislative aide by day and a waitress by night. She lived in Honolulu with her husband Cleghorn, who has a Hawaiian, Chinese, Korean, Portuguese, German, English and Irish background.

Patty Cooper is a Chicago-based writer and actor. In the past she has worked with *riksha*, Asian American Notes and Images, Pintig Cultural Group, The Peach Club, and most recently The Second City of Chicago. "The Conquest of Knowing" was selected by the Chicago Dramatists Workshop's Ten Minute Series for Playwrights of Color. She currently is working on a feature-length screenplay and getting her first children's story published.

Elena Tajima Creef finished her Ph.D. in History of Consciousness at the University of California, Santa Cruz and is now an assistant professor of Women's Studies at Wellesley College. She is finishing her book *Re/Orientations: Imaging Japanese America* as well as a collaborative memoir with her mother based on "Notes of a Fragmented Daughter."

Kiana Houghtailing Davenport is hapa haole, of Native Hawaiian and Anglo-American descent. Raised in Kalihi, she attended Farrington High School and graduated from University of Hawai'i–Mānoa. Her novel, *Shark Dialogues*, has been translated into seven languages. Her new novel is *Song of the Exile*.

The 1997–98 Visiting Writer at Wesleyan University, she was also a 1992–93 Fiction Fellow at Harvard-Radcliffe's Bunting Institute. She has received a Writing Grant from the National Endowment for the Arts, and her short stories have been published worldwide. Her story "The Lipstick Tree" was selected for the *O. Henry Awards: Prize Stories, 1997*, and the *Pushcart Prize Stories, 1998*. More recently her story "Fork Used in Eating Reverend Baker" was selected for the *O. Henry Awards Prize Stories, 1999*.

Debra Kang Dean's poems have appeared or are forthcoming in several anthologies, including *Urban Nature*, *The Best American Poetry 1999*, and *The Bread Loaf Anthology of New American Poets*. *News of Home* (BOA Editions, 1998) is her first full-length collection. A graduate of the MFA program at the University of Montana and a contributing editor for *Tar River Poetry*, she lives in Lincoln, Massachusetts, with her husband and two cats.

Kara Fujita was born on July 16, 1975 in Honolulu, Hawai'i to a Japanese American father and an Irish and English American mother. After moving to Agoura Hills, a suburb of Los Angeles, at the age of nine, she decided to return to Hawai'i for college. She received a B.A. in English and a Certificate in French from the University of Hawai'i–Mānoa last year. She was also a student editor at the University of Hawai'i Press. As a recipient of the Mira Baciu Simian Scholarship, Kara is currently studying at the Sorbonne in Paris for her further education in the French language.

Lo Ri Ly Griffin: My parents met in Vietnam where my father was serving as an advisor in the United States Army in the early sixties and my mother, of Cambodian decent, was working as a waitress in a military mess hall. I have two older sisters who were born in Vietnam in 1963 and '64. I was born in Seattle, Washington in 1967. When my middle sister was born, my father consulted my maternal grandmother on possible names for her. He went through a series of sounds he knew were both in English and Cambodian and my grandmother liked both Dauri Di and Lo Ri Ly. My sister's name was Americanized to Dorri Dee and later, when I was born in Seattle, my father gave me the name my grandmother had chosen for me three years before. Like Dorri, my name was Americanized and I grew up as Lorri Lee Griffin.

After living in Taiwan for three years, I spent the remainder of my childhood in my father's hometown in Illinois. I graduated from high school in 1985 as co-valedictorian and I received my bachelor's from Illinois State University in Normal, Illinois in 1990. When I was 25 years old and pursuing my Masters of Fine Arts degree at Virginia Commonwealth University, I visited my family in Vietnam for the first time. I accompanied my mother on her first trip to her homeland since she left with my father and two sisters 26 years before. We went to Vietnam to be with my grandmother who was preparing for her emigration to the States.

What this trip opened up for me is beyond explanation. I had always felt off-center, perhaps even out of touch with the community around me. I felt as if I was never a part of the community in which I lived.

I grew up in Sheffield and Buda, Illinois (population 900 and 700 respectively). Here, I was the perpetual outsider. Going to Vietnam and standing among the people there, I felt a kinship that I had never felt in the United States. I looked as different as a grapefruit does to an orange and yet the Vietnamese people opened up to me and greeted me with joy.

What I discovered was that the people in Vietnam looked to me in the exact way the Americans did in the United States. I was different in Vietnam and everyone noticed there, too. But their words and the way they looked upon me settled within me in a much different way. Instead of feeling like an awkward outsider, I felt like an awkward member of the family.

What I discovered was that I had been walking around life on one stilt. And I was doing a darned good job walking and even running at times. But suddenly, when I stood in Vietnam, on the same ground where my mother walked as a girl and the ground where my family stands every day of their lives, I suddenly felt two stilts under me and the view was beautiful and inspiring.

I saw that it was never the American people who separated me from the community. If I had grown up as Amerasian in Vietnam, I am certain my reception would have been similar. What I learned was that it was where I was standing, my perception of myself, that dictated how I stood in the world.

Before, looking at my American family, I was only able to see how I was different from them. Now, knowing my Vietnamese family, I am able to see how I have my maternal grandmother's cheekbones and my paternal grandmother's nostrils. There is a reason I have the eyes that I do. There is a reason my toes are long and my feet narrow. Seeing has allowed me to appreciate the nuances of being both of Caucasian and Asian decent.

Kimiko Guthrie-Kupers: Kimiko is the co-founder and co-artistic director of Dancetheater, a San Francisco-based company that collides raw, emotionally driven, athletic and lyrical movement and text with theatrical scenes and gesture to explore the essence of what it is to be alive. Kimiko has been a resident choreographer for Asian American Dance Performances' Unbound Spirit Dance Co., and has danced with many other San Francisco-based companies and chore-

ographers as well. Kimiko received her B.A. in Literature/Creative
Writing from the University of California, Santa Cruz in 1993, where
she studied writing with James Houston. Kimiko lives with her
husband and creative partner Eric Guthrie-Kupers in Berkeley,
California, where she is pursuing the exploration of the endless possibilities of the human body merged with the telling of a story. She
has received several honors and awards, including a residency at the
Djerassi Resident Artists Program and a grant from the Serpent
Source Foundation for Women Artists.

Born and raised in the Philippines, **Jessica
Hagedorn** is well known as a performance
artist, poet, and playwright. Her multi-
media theater pieces have been presented at
New York's Public Theater, the Kitchen,
Dance Theater Workshop, and St. Mark's
Theater. Her books include *Dogeaters*, *Holy
Food*, *Teenytown*, and *Mango Tango*. She is
also the author of two collections of poems, prose and short fiction,
Dangerous Music and *Pet Food and Tropical Apparitions*, as well as the
editor of *Charlie Chan is Dead*. Her latest work is *Gangster of Love*,
1997. Currently she is working on documentary film projects.

Kimiko Hahn was born in Mr. Kisco, New
York on July 5, 1955, to two artists, Maude
Miyako Hamai, Japanese American from
Hawai'i, and Walter Hahn, German
American from Wisconsin.

She has published her poetry exten-
sively in such journals as *Bomb*, *Lips*, *Ikon*,
Tyuonyi, *Agni Review*, and is co-author of *We
Stand Our Ground: three women, their vision, their poetry* by *Ikon*, 1988;
two collections of poetry, *Air Pocket*, 1989 and *Earshot*, 1992 were
published by Hanging Loose Press. *The Unbearable Heart*, 1994, was
published by Kaya Press. From 1982–84 she was an editor at *Bridge:
Asian American Perspectives* and also co-edited *Without Ceremony*, an
anthology of Asian American women, published by *Ikon*, 1988, as
well as *New Asia*, a special issue of the *The Portable Lower East Side*,

1990. From 1985–1990, Hahn founded and coordinated the multicultural literature project, Word of Mouth, which focused on Asian American writers and presented programs in the Chinatown Public Library. She was on the board of directors of The Poetry Project from 1989 to 1991. She also served on the board of The Coordinating Council of Literary Magazines and Presses. She has received fellowships from the National Endowment for the Arts in 1986 and 1992 and from the New York Foundation for the Arts in 1987 and 1991.

She teaches as an assistant professor of English at Queens College (CUNY) and has two daughters, Miyako Tess and Reiko Lily.

Marie Murphy Hara: Working with so many strong women writers who happen to be of mixed race and who definitely have opinions about their identity has made me look at the role of a writer in a fuller way. Working with Nora Okja Keller over these seven years has been an unexpected, joyful gift. Writing is still my choice and my salvation. My novel *Lei* was put on the back burner for a while, but I'm cooking again. Thank you to John, Mayumi, Kasumi, and Bamboo Ridge Press.

Nanea Hoffman lives in Kirkland, Washington, a suburb of Seattle, with her husband Bob, her son Matthew Kekoa, and two very spoiled cats. At present, her primary occupation is that of full-time mother, of which she says, "The pay is low, the hours are rough, but the boss is awfully cute." This is her first published essay. Currently, she is gathering material for a novel which will chronicle the adventures of her paternal grandmother, Matsuko, the runaway picture bride.

Velina Hasu Houston: An award-win-
ning multi-genre author, Houston writes
plays for film and television, cultural criticism, poetry, and prose. Currently, she is a
Japan Foundation Fellow and a James
Zumberge Fellow. Her signature play *Tea*
has been produced internationally to popu-
lar and critical acclaim. Eight plays have
been commissioned by: The Mark Taper Forum (two), Manhattan
Theatre Club, Asia Society, Honolulu Theatre for Youth, and the Lila
Wallace-Readers Digest Foundation New Generations Play Project;
Dr. Juli Thompson Burk, the Kennedy Theatre, and the Hawai'i State
Foundation on Culture and the Arts; The Jewish Women's Theatre
Project, and Cornerstone Theatre Company. Her plays have been
produced and presented at such venues as the Old Globe Theatre,
Manhattan Theatre Club, Syracuse Stage, Smithsonian Institute,
Whole Theatre (Olympia Dukakis, producer), and many others in
the U.S. and Japan. She is an artistic associate of the Sacramento
Theatre Company; and a member of The Women's Project and
Productions (New York), the Dramatists Guild, and the Writers
Guild of America, West. For film, she has written for Columbia
Pictures, Sidney Poitier, PBS, Lancit Media and several indie produc-
ers. Currently, her play, *Kokoro*, is under option motion pictures. Her
writings are published in journals and anthologies (Temple
University Press, Vintage Books-Random House, Applause Books,
Amerasia Journal, Smith & Kraus Books, University of Massachusetts
Press, University of Illinois Press, and University of Texas Press).
Awards include the Remy Martin New Vision Screenwriting Award
from Sidney Poitier, California Arts Council fellow, Japanese
American Woman of Merit 1890–1990 by the National Japanese
American Historical Society, twice-named Rockefeller Foundation
fellow, and others. In Japan, four documentary films about her work
and family have been produced by Nippon Hoso Kai, Mainichi
Hoso, and TV Tokyo Channel 12. A Phi Beta Kappa, she is an associate professor, resident playwright, and director of the playwriting
program at the University of Southern California School of Theatre.

Cathy Kanoelani Ikeda: "Yomesan" was previously published by Bamboo Ridge Press. Since then, my father-in-law has passed away, but he always wanted to show off his "mongrel grandchildren." That's one good-looking kid eh?

Noelle M.K.Y. Kahanu: This is a photo of Noelle and baby Hattie.

Noelle existed as "Baby Girl Kahanu" for the first two months of her life, waiting for her Hawaiian great-great-grandmother to dream a dream name for her. Mumu Poepoe dreamed, finally, of five daughters who were named for their father's five favorite maile scents. Baby girl's mother chose Maile Kaluhea, the fragrant leaf maile. Since she was born three days before Christmas, Baby Girl's aunt, a French teacher, offered the feminized version of Father Christmas, Noelle. And finally, Baby Girl's Japanese grandmother Haruko chose Yayoi, which meant gentle, as a spring breeze. Thus, Noelle Maile Kaluhea Yayoi Kahanu was born, and she would spend a great portion of her future years trying to understand and keep together the divergent forces that created and shaped her.

Kyoko Katayama: I grew up in post World War II occupied Tokyo as an "ainoko," often a derogatory term referring to the children of Japanese women and American GIs. I was raised by my Japanese family until the 1960s, when I immigrated to the United States with my mother and a new step-father. Since then, both I and the terms referring to the children of mixed heritages have evolved full circle. I believe that we of many races and cultures who learn to successfully negotiate and integrate this heritage—often conflicting and sometimes complementary—

will become a model for a better world. We are "the race" of the global future because we embody the realization of wholeness out of differences. I received a master's degree in clinical social work from the University of Minnesota, and recently earned a doctorate specializing in cross-cultural and transpersonal psychology from the Union Institute in Cincinnati, Ohio. I have a psychotherapy practice in St. Paul, Minnesota, the city that has become a home for myself, my husband and three grown children.

Nora Okja Keller, author of *Comfort Woman* (Viking 1997), lives in Hawai'i with her husband and two daughters.

Originally from Hawai'i, **Jacquelyn Kim** currently resides in San Francisco, California. She has previously had her poems published in the *Hawai'i Review*.

Donna Midori Hokumalamalama King Lance is the daughter of two hapa parents and the mother of three hapa children.

Carolyn Lei-lanilau is the author of *Wode Shuofa (My Way of Speaking)* which received an American Book Award for Poetry in 1989. She has lectured on translation and criticism in the U.S. and China, particulary on *Nu Shu*, the Secret Women's Language of Hunan Province. Her second book of poetry was entitled, *The Marginalia on Gorilla/Bird*. Her essays on philosophy reflect her Hawaiian humor and Chinese compulsions. Hawaiian herself, Ms. Lei-lanilau is founder of Hale O Hawai'i Nei, an organization dedicated to promoting the culture and traditions of Hawai'i. She is also the author of *Ono Ono Girl's Hula*, 1997.

Kyo Maclear is a Toronto-based writer.

Kathleen McColley is a Ph.D. candidate at the University of Hawai'i, interested in modern American literature and criticism. She is originally from Des Moines, Washington, where she has enjoyed some of the most beautiful sunsets spilling their glory over Puget Sound from her parent's dining room windows.

Usha Lee McFarling: I have lived in many places. In some of them, like North Dakota and Maine, where people are mostly white, I stood out because of my skin color. In other places I fit in more easily: In San Antonio, most people assumed I was Hispanic. I now live in Cambridge, where because of the universities, there are people from every part of the world. I fit in more easily here, but people still don't know what I am.

The more subtle questioners say: "Where did you get that name, Usha?" Others just say, "What are you? I know you're something." Something other than white, they mean.

I am part Indian and part American. My name, Usha, is a Sanskrit word that means first ray of light. My last name is my father's. He comes from South Dakota; his ancestors came from Scotland.

Cynthia Nakashima lives in the San Francisco Bay Area with her husband, Shawn, and two daughters, Madeline and Charlotte. Madeline, for whom the essay was written many years ago, is already eight years old and the best friend a Mom could have. Her baby sister, Charlotte, was born in March of '99, with the most beautiful brown eyes ever. Cynthia is a Ph.D. student in Comparative Ethnic Studies at University of California, Berkeley, writing her dissertation entitled: "Mixed Race Women and their White Mothers: Race and Gender, Close to Home."

Susan Miho Nunes grew up in Hilo, Hawai'i. She is the author of a collection of short stories, *A Small Obligation and Other Stories of Hilo*, and several children's books, most recently *The Last Dragon*. She now lives in Berkeley, California.

Franco Salmoiraghi

Sigrid Nunez is the author of three works of fiction, *A Feather on the Breath of God*, *Naked Sleeper*, and *Mitz: the Marmoset of Bloomsbury*. She is now working on a new novel, *The Scenery of Farewell*, which will be published by Farrar, Straus & Giroux in 2001. She is currently writer-in-residence at Smith College, where she holds the title Elizabeth Drew Professor.

Marion Ettlinger

Mindy Eun Soo Pennybacker, born and raised in Honolulu, now lives in New York City with her husband Don Wallace and son Rory, deprived of family, surf, poi, Dave's Ice Cream and kim chee. She edits *The Green Guide*, an environmental newsletter published by Mothers & Others for a Livable Planet, and is co-author of *Mothers & Others Guide to Natural Baby Care* (Wiley, 1999). She writes frequently on Hawai'i politics and literature for *The Nation* magazine, and her work has also appeared in *The Atlantic Monthly*, *Fiction*, *The New York Times*, *Sierra* and elsewhere. *Surfing and Other Forms of Love* is a novel in progress.

Mira Chieko Au Shimabukuro: "Dandelions and Seaweed" was written when Mira was nineteen and in her first year of college. She now teaches composition, creative writing and literature to students in their first year of college at Highline Community College in Washington State. Her more recent work has been published in *Calyx Journal*, *The Seattle Review* and *The Raven Chronicles*. In 1997, she co-edited *Present Tense: Writing and Art by Young Women*.

Michelle Cruz Skinner lives and writes in Hawai'i. Her collection of short stories, *Balikbayan: A Filipino Homecoming* was published by Bess Press.

Cathy Song is the author of *Picture Bride* (Yale), *Frameless Windows, Squares of Light* (Norton), and *School Figures* (Pittsburgh).

Sabrena Taylor is a poet and visual artist of African American and native Japanese ancestry. She was born and raised in Galesburg, Illinois. Her poetry has been published in the following anthologies: *Watch Out! We're Talking: Speaking Out About Incest and Abuse; Skin Deep: Women Writing on Color, Culture and Identity;* and *Amerasia Journal.* She currently resides in San Francisco, California. She is a member of the San Francisco Women Artists and has exhibited in the Bay Area since 1987.

"I give reverence to all my ancestors who brought me into my existence and gave me my African American and Japanese heritage. In Galesburg there was a time in my life when the wood burning stove kept me and my seven siblings warm. There was no outhouse but a 'slop jar;' bottles of water from my grandparents' home quenched our thirst and if we were fortunate to be blessed with plenty of water our hair would be washed.

"As a mixed race child in the 1960s and 1970s in the midwest, I lived a very isolated existence from other mixed race people. Some of my siblings and I were not allowed to associate with some of the children of Japanese women who were married to Euro-Americans. The stigmatization and discrimination of coming from an African American and Japanese interracial family and having been abused as a child developed into wounds that were difficult to heal, although the passing years have somewhat changed my perspective. I am very grateful to Janice Mirikitani and Rev. Cecil Williams of Glide United Memorial Methodist Church in San Francisco who helped me to begin to heal some of my wounds. My poems have been published by the Glide Word Press and by *Fusion*, San Francisco State University Journal.

"I hope that my art will help to heal others, particularly children who often suffer in silence."

Adrienne Tien: I have recently moved from New York to California. I am living in west Los Angeles with my husband and three young sons. I am currently working on a screenplay that takes place in Beijing, China. When that is finished, I can't wait to start on an L.A.-inspired novel. My other two novels remain unpublished as well as they should, needing desperately to be rewritten.

I feel that I have a Chinese self and a non-Chinese self, or to look at it another way, a white self and a non-white self. My environment strongly affects my being and I can't help but be chameleon-like. However, I think that as I get older, I get better at knowing and, I hope, at expressing all parts of my self no matter what company I'm in.

Kathleen Tyau is the author of two novels, *Makai* (Farrar, Straus & Giroux, 1999) and *A Little Too Much Is Enough* (Farrar, Straus & Giroux, 1995). Winner of the Pacific Northwest Booksellers Award and an Oregon Book Award finalist, Tyau is the recipient of fellowships from the National Endowment for the Arts, the Oregon Arts Commission, and Literary Arts, Inc. She has worked as a handweaver, legal secretary, and writing instructor. She attended Pearl City public schools and St. Andrew's Priory and has a B.A. in